Poems of Consciousness

*Contemporary Japanese & English-language Haiku
in Cross-cultural Perspective*

Including Author Interviews, Ecocritical and Stylistic Analysis

Richard Gilbert

Poems of Consciousness:
Contemporary Japanese and English-language Haiku
in Cross-cultural Perspective

© 2008, rev. 2009, by Richard Gilbert
for Red Moon Press, all rights reserved

Published by
Red Moon Press
P. O. Box 2461
Winchester VA
22604-1661 USA
www.redmoonpress.com

ISBN 1-978-893959-72-9

Cover image, Richard Gilbert © 2008.
Yaku-sugi tree roots, Yakushima. (The *Jômon-sugi*, possibly 7,200 years old, is among the oldest living organisms on the planet.)

Photograph of the author, Keiko Gilbert © 2008.

Acknowledgement:
This research is supported by a Japan Society for the Promotion of Science (JSPS) Grant-in-Aid for Scientific Research, and the Japan Ministry of Education, Culture, Sports, Science and Technology (MEXT), Kakenhi 18520439.

Dedication

First and foremost, to you the reader. It is your interest in haiku which has enabled this work to proceed and evolve. Imagination carries us further into poetry together—this has been my inspiration and wish, to communicate a haiku research-journey to you: the excitement of new discoveries, ideas and possibilities for haiku as poetry and as community. The works contained within these pages represent meeting points of consciousness and influence, and especially of society. If I had not taken the leap to leave the United States, my native home, those who have inspired these pages would have remained unmet. It is not easy to meet new friends in one's 40s and 50s, and to share a depth of life—and so, this journey has been one of rebirth.

I would like to acknowledge Professor Masahiro Hori, for his indefatigable energy, friendship, discussions of Zen Buddhism, and for sharing his academic expertise in stylistics and literary linguistics; Professors Judy Yoneoka and Ryoji Matsuno for their many scholarly discussions and encouragement. Jim Kacian, my soul brother, has demonstrated though his poetics, cross-cultural diplomacy and publishing activities new possibilities for haiku in English, and inspired much in these pages. My critical understanding has benefitted greatly through translation via the help of poet-colleagues Itô Yûki and Takke Kanemitsu. Also my thanks to Associate Professor Philip Rowland, publisher of *Noon: Journal of the Short Poem*, and to poet-filmmaker Dimitar Anakiev for their invaluable cultural activities and inspiration. To my wife, Keiko Kinjô Gilbert and her beautiful heart, her support and belief in sharing the fruits of our life together. And finally to Japan, Kumamoto, and the Kumaso Kyûshû spirit, exemplified by Hoshinaga Fumio, who has transmitted to me through his works and personage the living flame of gendai haiku.

TABLE OF CONTENTS

Introduction *by Jim Kacian* ... 9

Author's Preface ... 11

SECTION 1: THEORETICAL CONCERNS

1. PLAUSIBLE DENIABILITY ... 27
   1a. Introductory remarks
   1b. Plausible Deniability: Nature as Hypothesis in English-language Haiku

2. HASEGAWA KAI ... 67
   2a. Introductory remarks
   2b. Haiku Cosmos 1: Bashô's 'Old Pond,' Realism & 'Junk Haiku'
   2c. Haiku Cosmos 2: Cutting Through Time and Space—*Kire* & *Ma*
   2d. Selected Haiku

3. UDA KIYOKO ... 85
   3a. Introductory remarks
   3b. Haiku and the Land 1: Toward the Future—A Haiku Ecology
   3c. Haiku and the Land 2: Ecology, Haiku & the Taste of Existence
   3d. Selected Haiku

4. THE DISJUNCTIVE DRAGONFLY ... 99
   4a. Introductory remarks
   4b. The Disjunctive Dragonfly: A Study of Disjunctive Method and Definitions in Contemporary English-language Haiku

SECTION 2: MULTICULTURAL ISSUES

Preface to the Section ... 149

5. TSUBOUCHI NENTEN ... 153
   5a. Introductory remarks
   5b. The Poetic Self 1: *Katakoto*—
       Fragmentary Language in Haiku
   5c. The Poetic Self 2: *Haigô*—Masaoka Shiki
       & Haiku Persona
   5d. Selected haiku

6. HOSHINAGA FUMIO ... 163
   6a. Introductory remarks
   6b. Sacred Language in Haiku 1: *Kotodama Shinkô*
   6c. Sacred Language in Haiku 2: 'Becoming Divine'
   6d. The Miraculous Power of Language:
       A Conversation with the Poet Hoshinaga Fumio
   6e. Selected haiku

7. KIGO AND SEASONAL REFERENCE ... 201
   7a. Kigo and Seasonal Reference:
       Cross-cultural Issues in Anglo-American Haiku

8. ÔNISHI YASUYO—GENDAI SENRYÛ ... 221
   8a. Introductory remarks
   8b. Gendai Senryû 1: History and Significance
   8c. Gendai Senryû 2: Parsing Gendai Senryû
       and Haiku
   8d. Selected Gendai Senryû

9. CROSS-CULTURAL PROBLEMATICS ... 235
    9a. A Cross-cultural Problematics—
    Misrepresentations of Zappai
    in English Translation

10. YAGI MIKAJO ... 249
    10a. Introductory remarks
    10b. Interview: "Tasting the Era"
    10c. Haiku, Commentaries and Anecdotes

11. STALKING THE WILD ONJI ... 267
    11a. Stalking the Wild Onji: The Search for
    Current Linguistic Terms Used in
    Japanese Poetry Circles

12. Afterword ... 297
    12a. Closing Comments
    12b. Author Information
    12c. Selected haiku

INTRODUCTION

English-language haiku is a mere century old. Its products in its inaugural days were less regular than what we quickly came to recognize as the standard for the genre, as questions concerning the exactitude of transcription of syllables, lines, and content, among other issues, were open to debate. But within twenty years of the first such poems, and despite the contrarian examples of such poets as Pound and Stevens, a normative form for the genre was attained. This standard was further reinforced through the writings of R. H. Blyth, the west's first great teacher of haiku. Besides bringing to the attention of the poet and reader thousands of outstanding examples of this poetic art, Blyth also codified the categories and vocabulary through which it was possible to discuss them. So armed, students of the genre proceeded to create thousands of such poems, which, in large part, exemplified exactly Blyth's sensibility and ethos. Haiku study, as a result and with very few exceptions, entered into a half-century of imitative decline.

Richard Gilbert is one of the handful of poets and scholars who have shaken haiku from this complacency and infused it with renewed vigor. His specific contributions include one we might consider of special importance: a new nomenclature and classification system, which has enabled us to rekindle the conversation about what haiku poets in the west are up to, without being limited to the language, sensibility and techniques employed by another culture for other purposes four centuries ago. This has been nothing short of revolutionary, and like all revolutions has had its champions and despoilers. But it is again at least possible to talk of these things, and through this dialogue to gain a traction which for so long had eluded us.

Gilbert's second great gift to us is his interest in the contemporary (*gendai*) haiku of Japan, which is at the same time a continuation with the haiku sensibility of the past and a break with its most overt tropes and techniques. By noting the way in which Japan's current poets simultaneously are writing to their present and innovatively reinterpreting their past, he has been able to suggest equal and necessary revaluation possibilities to us, their counterparts in the west.

The results are revealing: the kinds of poems one now discovers in journals and contests are far more various than at any previous time in the history of haiku. A greater number of techniques are on display than at any point in our haiku century. And the appreciation of haiku on an international level is unprecedented. It would be too much to claim that Gilbert is responsible for all this, but it is not too much to say that his work is one of a very few underpinnings which has provided the language and conceptual machinery that has made this possible.

You will find the theoretical bases for these subjects, and more, in the following pages, the product of ten years' study and thought. Gilbert is uniquely qualified to pursue these ideas: not only has he lived in Japan the past decade, but he has an abiding interest in the cross-cultural exchange of poetical ideas which has been largely lacking in haiku circles on both shores. He approaches these interests via an academic background which is multi-disciplinary (degrees in both poetics and psychology) without losing his grounding in the real world. Such a balance is necessary for such a task.

These essays and interviews are not for the faint of heart, for those who wish merely to follow the *shasei* style, or for those who have closed the door to possibility in haiku. But for any who remain open, Gilbert offers great things here, not least the language, ideas and examples by which our next century will talk of such things. This is his greatest gift—a future—offered not only to its poets, but to haiku itself.

—Jim Kacian
Winchester, Virginia

Preface

The haiku movement in English began in earnest in the 1950s, with "haiku" becoming both a familiar term and a known poetic genre in numerous countries. Composition and cultural activities have continued to increase throughout North America, Europe and Australasia. Although there has been increasing international interest in haiku, academic studies have mainly focused on the classical tradition, ending with the early-modern haiku reformation of Masaoka Shiki (1867-1902). As a result, there are few publications relating to the modern (*gendai*) Japanese haiku tradition. The research appearing in these pages is a result of cross-cultural studies of gendai haiku, including interviews with notable Japanese poets and critics. This research has been conducted in Japan, my permanent home for over a decade, in my role as Associate Professor in the Faculty of Letters, Department of British and American Language and Literature, Kumamoto University.

When I first arrived in Kumamoto in 1997, as with perhaps any international poet interested in Japanese haiku, I was acutely aware of the classical tradition, with the inclusion of some of the early-modern works of Shiki. The bulk of English translations I had read came from the single source of R. H. Blyth, whose literary talent in English, while at times peerless, can also be iconoclastic and reductively focused on Zen-Buddhist views, regarding haiku principles and aesthetics. Armed with this limited idea of haiku, it was only after a year or so, and improvement in Japanese, that I began to read in contemporary haiku. It was quite a shock, finding that this modern tradition stretched back over a century.

It now seems particularly ironic that in the early 1950s, as Kerouac, Ginsberg and Snyder were reading Blyth, whose style mainly follows that of objective realism, the postwar gendai tradition in Japan was experiencing a renaissance, utilizing complex combinations of influences synthesized from western traditions, such as cubism, dada, surrealism, abstract expressionism, and so on, along with experimental advances based on traditional elements. Digging deeper, and through discussions with notable critics such as Hasegawa Kai, Tsubouchi Nenten, Uda Kiyoko and others, I began to realize that haiku had *never* been primarily oriented as a poetics of objective description or objective realism (excepting for Shiki, who took liberties regarding his own realist-inspired dicta; the evolution of the pre-WWII Hototogisu school will be discussed further below).

In a nutshell, much of what has been communicated of the historical haiku oeuvre has been misunderstood in the west, and this communication itself represents only a small fraction of what is available in Japanese; cross-cultural gendai haiku studies are thus in an embryonic state. Gendai haiku has been misunderstood in contemporary Japan as well, partly due to the promotion from the early 20th century up through the wartime period of Shiki's *shasei* (objective realist) sensibility, an early-modern concept influenced by realism in western painting and philosophy. *Shasei* principles were reformulated into a quasi-religious philosophy intimately linked to an ultranationalist thematics of prototypical "Japaneseness" by authoritarian Hototogisu haiku leader Takahama Kyoshi. The *shasei*-inspired haiku became the defining style of Hototogisu, the most influential Japanese journal and school of haiku, in the prewar decades.[1]

Gendai haiku is not a rejection of the classical—though it is a rejection of Kyoshi's jingoist version of *kachofuei*, "a compositional style based upon the traditional sense of the beauty of nature and the use of officially sanctioned [*kigo*] season words," regarding the inculcation of ultranationalism (Itô, 2007). As can be seen in the arts of any era, socio-political context is relevant to reader understanding. The movement spawned by the New Rising poets (*shinkô haiku undô*), progenitors of gendai haiku, expressed not only aesthetic sentiment; these poets also fought for their values through heroic struggle, suffering, and blood, and are deserving of further consideration and remembrance. As Kaneko Tohta, the acclaimed leader of the postwar haiku movement wrote, in *My Postwar Haiku History* (*Waga sengo haiku-shi*, 1985), "When discussing the history of postwar haiku ... it is preferable that a discussion of postwar haiku history start from the midst of the war, or from the beginning of the 'Fifteen Years War' [1931-45]" (qtd. in Itô, *ibid*). In contradistinction to the Hototogisu school, the New Rising Haiku movement arose as a radical-experimental and socially progressive arts movement. Throughout the Japan wartime era, 46 New Rising poets were arrested and their associations were persecuted; some were tortured and sent to the war front, while others died in prison—their presses and publications banned and burned (parallels with Nazi Germany are evident).

This history too is likewise nearly unknown—even within Japan. In fact there are more than aesthetic differences between what is called "traditional" and "gendai" haiku in modern history, though as the generations advance there is a degree of rapprochement.

Surprisingly, the New Rising Haiku poets were known to Blyth, as he translated several of them—or so it would seem. Blyth remains a fascinating figure. In his translations and commentaries on literally thousands of haiku, he brought important elements of the classical tradition to light and did much to deepen reader understanding of universality and spirituality in haiku. In addition, in his later anthology, *History of Haiku, Volume 2*, he translated a number of modern poets, including Sanki and Santôka. Yet he avoided important works and contemporary topics expressing the central concerns of the modern; more problematically, his translations were done in a fixated objective-realist style, masking authorial intention. More problematically still, Blyth idealized the classical while devaluing the modern as at root selfish, small-minded, and confused. His modern-haiku selections seem biased toward the inconsequential, when considering the larger socio-political climate of the modern poets and works he translated. Blyth tended to select haiku which accorded well with realist depiction, avoiding most what was most "modern" in the contemporary; in short, his translations of the modern poets are diminutive. Blyth himself indicates the main cause:

> Haiku since Shiki has been, like the world itself, in a state of confusion. . . . The present age is . . . an age in which we are

more conscious of our confusion [ ] than ever before, and it is our duty therefore to point out the vagaries and inconsequentialities of the Welt-Geist, and as far as possible resign ourselves to posing the questions more clearly, giving up all pretense of answering them. . . . The best old haiku rise out of the *fudoki* [locality, sense of place]. The best modern haiku emerge as from a vacuum, or from the narrow hopes and fears and loving and loathing of the individual poet. . . . Bashô spoke for humanity, of humanity, and by humanity . . . The confusion of our modern times seems greater than ever before because people speak by themselves only, and not by humanity. . . . Having thus indirectly blasted all modern haiku, we are now in a position to be agreeably surprised... (pp. 333-34).

Denying the modern through translation, it is impossible in English to discern what is modern—in fact what is not Shiki-like, in Blyth's "modern" anthology. The result for haiku in the west has been ironic: modern haiku were translated, yet the modern never arrived. What will be shown in this book is how profoundly the gendai haiku tradition is intertwined with its classical ancestry—not only with regards to form but also concept.

The idea of haiku as "poems of consciousness" inscribes an overarching poetics of historical continuity and presence. Temporal continuity in haiku was first discussed by Bashô, in his concept of: *fueki ryûkô* ("eternal truth"+"trend, vogue, fashion"), which can be translated as "immutable mutability." This paradoxical concept indicates that while there may be eternal verities, one moment is not the same as another, as one era is not the same as another; there is progression. As a result, in order to properly articulate reality, the poet must necessarily inhabit the era, the contemporary zeitgeist (Hoshinaga Fumio discusses "era" in his 2004 interview, in the Chapter devoted to him). If "fashion" were not significant, one could simply curl up with Bashô and never need compose another poem. This idea seems decidedly contrary to his radical spirit. In each era there are new developments necessitating unique articulations that in turn serve to inform later generations.

Preface

In America, the postwar Beats saw a need to "grow their own souls," to break with superficial restrictions and artistic conventions represented by social beliefs (sexual repression, consciousness repression, racism, etc.). In this same era, haiku poets in Japan who had fought for their beliefs in freedom of thought and expression had reformed into postwar haiku associations. With a great lion's roar, the gendai haiku movement spanning the last 60 years was born in earnest. It is a further irony then that a number of New Rising poets had published radically modern haiku not long before Snyder and Kerouac were reading, discussing and popularizing the objective stylism they found in haiku, such as the following, by Shiki (published in 1886, translated by Blyth in 1952), below which Blyth comments: "This might be taken as the model for all haiku":[2]

nureashi de suzume no ariku rôka kana

The sparrow hops
Along the verandah,
With wet feet.

Gendai-movement progenitors had penned haiku such as these, less than 15 years earlier:[3]

kikanjû miken ni korosu hana ga saku

a machine gun
in the forehead
the killing flower blooms
              (Saitô Sanki, pub. circa 1937-38)

sennsisha ga aoki suugaku yori detari

war dead
exit out of a blue mathematics
              (Sumimura Seirinshi, pub. circa 1937-40)[4]

War is not only a theme for Bashô—here, Bashô's "warrior's dreams" are seen in a modern context; these haiku represent both a continuation and reply to him. As Kerouac and Snyder were romancing the past of classical haiku in response to its spiritual depth, their Japanese contemporaries were writing of, recovering from, and questioning a 20th century holocaust which included Imperial-fascism, genocidal actions and torture, napalm firebombing and destruction of 67 Japanese cities, massive civilian death, atomic bombings, persecution, postwar starvation, American occupation, etc. One wonders how the Beats own view of haiku, especially their binding together of the thematic images of haiku form, spirituality and nature might have been altered if Blyth (or Henderson, or Yasuda) had well-translated and commented on some of the pertinent New Rising and gendai haiku works authored by those who had defied the Imperial-fascist propaganda war machine. Through the recent research of Itô Yûki (2007) these New Rising wartime-era haiku can now be seen within an academically documented socio-political context, in English.

As discussed at further length in the first paper presented, "Plausible Deniability," it is difficult to codify haiku as a poetics of nature, if by nature is meant traditional seasonal imagery, flora and fauna, seasonal indication (*kigo* a "season-word," or *kidai* "a seasonal theme"), as seen in the context of realism or naturalism. In his research into haiku history, Hasegawa Kai, in the Chapter devoted to him, demonstrates the radicalism of Bashô. What transformed haiku (and hokku) into a high art was not a further nuance of literal perception occurring within a natural scene, but rather a technique Bashô divined of disjunctive cutting applied within the art form, emulating what Hasegawa refers to as "the arising of the world of mind" in haiku—a "haiku cosmos." While this brief description may appear somewhat obtuse without further context, the main point is that part of Bashô's great achievement, and certainly one of his most important innovations, was an irruptive cutting-through of naïve, descriptive realism. Bashô may have been the first "postmodern" poet, and as I will argue has codified a manner of literary innovation yet to be fully grasped.

Preface

As Hasegawa comments, Bashô's famed haiku, "old pond - / frog jumping-in / water's-sound" presents some intriguing questions: does the "old pond" exist? and, what are the naturalistic implications of unseen frogs? Hasegawa's interpretation leads to new avenues of haiku re-conceptualization, innovative ways of reading and composing. Following Hasegawa, one finds that this most celebrated haiku has not yet been accurately translated into English—Bashô in particular remains misinterpreted as a poet oriented toward naïve literalism regarding nature and objective-realist description (in Japan and elsewhere). Such re-conceptualizations of haiku may come as a surprise, yet the strands of contemporary postwar criticism do not deny the tradition so much as enlarge it, illuminating an art whose profundity is not located in a reductive present-tense AH! moment of poet-reader perception, so much as a multi-dimensional landscape combining themes of psyche, image, literary history, and social context.

As I began to learn more of haiku history from the perspective of contemporary poetics and criticism, I reflected on my own experience of haiku, as a poet and reader. Excellent haiku, whether classical or modern, in English or Japanese—in any language—have a remarkable power of impact; a poetic sensibility and aesthetic experience unique to the genre. Although gendai poets take themes from modern life and utilize irony, sarcasm, futuristic conception, temporal disjunction, "free rhythm" (*jyûritsu*), etc., in ways the classical poets do not, there remains a powerful sense of lineage and connection—a conversation stretching back throughout centuries.

Three main lines of questioning piqued my curiosity: social (and socio-political) context, ideas of consciousness and spirituality in haiku, and the relationship between haiku and nature—which led me to consider the question of what is meant by "nature" in haiku, from ecocritical perspectives. Reading any number of gendai haiku, I found these three themes repeatedly intertwined. Below is a brief quotation from a 2004 interview with Kumamoto poet Hoshinaga Fumio (presented in full in the "Hoshinaga Fumio" Chapter), who first opened my mind to the spirit of the gendai haiku world:

RG: Do you mean then, that you feel restricted, concerning traditional haiku?

HF: Yes. I have repellence, revulsion exactly against the formal rules and approach, *kigo*, and various formal necessities. (Reads the first poem of his first major collection, *100/67*, published in 1967):

> *ni-ju oku kônen no gishô* *omae no B-gata*
>
> twenty billion light-years of perjury   your blood type is "B"

I have a lot of misgivings, so I want to make visible these misgivings in myself. These misgivings are not directed toward typical persons, but rather towards any kind of authority. This kind of repellence or revulsion drives me to write haiku! [Laughter]

RG: So, in this first haiku, we have the word "perjury" . . .

HF: "Twenty billion light-years" is almost an infinitely long distance—I had been fooled for so long, concerning any and every fundamental thing—without knowing any fundamental thing in the first place. Blood-type B is rare in Japan; Type A is happier, but Type B carries a sense of melancholy. So, I felt my rebelliousness or revulsion could not be blood-type A—it must be blood-type B.

Here is part of the Postscript I published in *Cho-sen* [*A Butterfly-"Thousand"*; "*chosen*" also means, "challenge/revolt"; January 1968]:

> I do not believe the truth that the sea is blue. That I believe it is blue: an encompassing state of affairs that limits as blue, via the comprehension of my eyes: I believe *only* that. Though it is inconvenient, I wish to compose haiku with a free posture towards truth, that is, with reference to the encompassing situation. With this

Preface

thought, I've been writing haiku freely, selfishly, for half a year. This is the result of my selfish six months. . . . As a matter of fact, there is a vast wilderness of lyricism beyond these haiku: the wilderness I failed to capture with a dull, sleepy-faced rebelliousness. This book reminds me afresh—I must start again with a clean slate and to this end, I cast out this book with good grace.

So, this is the root-principle of my haiku. As a result, my order and usage of words, syntax, etc., will change and diverge from that of ordinary daily usage. I believe it is both such usage and rhythm that makes my haiku well-balanced—even though language is, generally speaking, overworked, fatigued. In any case, rhythm creates balance and helps readers to understand a haiku. I try to compose in very understandable rhythms. Definitely, in my haiku, rhythm is a very powerful and important element.

Hoshinaga (b. 1933) describes himself as,

a nationalistic, militaristic child in a militaristic environment. After the war, with the advent of democracy, gradually I discovered what I had not been able to see—what had somehow been hidden behind society. That's why I cannot believe *anything* I see: there must be some hidden meaning. That's the way I grew up. Even though I was [earlier] writing traditional haiku, I thought there must be something hidden behind it ("The Miraculous Power of Language: A Conversation with the Poet Hoshinaga Fumio," on the accompanying DVD-ROM, includes kanji for the poetry).

A child of war, Hoshinaga wrote the above Postscript in an era of anti-establishment revolution, the same year as student revolts ("May 1968" etc.) were occurring in many countries around the world, including Japan (and this university I write from). Yet there is a new possibility for poetry evident in Hoshinaga's writing, as he not only deconstructs social perception but also rebuilds it, refreshing language in ways that re-knit the world. In the same interview he comments, "disharmonies create harmonies." Hoshinaga's gendai aesthetic embodies a form of *ecos* (from the Greek *oikos*, "home"), representing a possibility for humanity similar to that expressed by Octavio Paz in his 1990 Nobel Lecture:

> ... Modernity is not outside but within us. It is today and the most ancient antiquity; it is tomorrow and the beginning of the world; it is a thousand years old and yet newborn. It speaks in Nahuatl, draws Chinese ideograms from the 9th century, and appears on the television screen. This intact present, recently unearthed, shakes off the dust of centuries, smiles and suddenly starts to fly, disappearing through the window. A simultaneous plurality of time and presence: modernity breaks with the immediate past only to recover an age-old past and transform a tiny fertility figure from the neolithic into our contemporary. We pursue modernity in her incessant metamorphoses yet we never manage to trap her. She always escapes: each encounter ends in flight. We embrace her and she disappears immediately: it was just a little air. It is the instant, that bird that is everywhere and nowhere. We want to trap it alive but it flaps its wings and vanishes in the form of a handful of syllables. We are left empty-handed. Then the doors of perception open slightly and the other time appears, the real one we were searching for without knowing it: the present, the presence.[5]

Paz, who experimented with the haiku form, was intensely concerned with the poetics of being and becoming throughout his lifetime—his perspectives on the modern emulate some of the main concerns of gendai haiku ("gendai" is synonymous with "modern, contemporary"). As well as being composed of but "a handful of syllables," haiku foreground absence ("and she disappears"); in this way, for the reader, haiku address the modern: "each encounter ends in flight." Paz, in his articulation of the "moment" (zeitgeist) of the modern seems to express a core quality of the gendai spirit: "the doors of perception open slightly and the other time appears, the real one we were searching for without knowing it: the present, the presence."

The powerful poetics and critical thought of Hoshinaga impressed me deeply. Within his work I sensed also a deep contact with nature, the wild and wilderness, something untamable in language and in mind—just as I had experienced some 25 years earlier, studying the haiku of Bashô as an undergraduate. Given such a brief poetic form, it would seem that haiku could not possibly contain vast universes, express truths flowering into the infinite, open one's heart directly to social conditions, the natural world, to the most intimate conditions of being. Yet with each exceptional poem, whatever limitations I harbored were proven wrong.

In contrast to western poetic forms, Japanese haiku has retained in large part its formal verity through the centuries, as it has moved from the medieval through early-modern and "post"-modern metamorphoses. My goal has been twofold: to communicate some of what I have learned regarding gendai haiku in Japan; and to present theoretical concepts, structures and nomenclature as a means of potentially innovating haiku traditions occurring within the international scene.

The papers, transcripts, and DVD-ROM of interviews and associated research materials and translations accompanying this book present the results of a funded research project begun in 2006: to comprehensively demonstrate the academic and artistic relevance and value of gendai haiku by producing a set of materials that might provide a basis for present and future scholarly and compositional study. While some of the materials, such as the first paper, "Plausible Deniability," take the form of theory oriented to an academic audience, for those particularly interested in primary source materials (translated gendai poetry and criticism), it is likely preferable to look at the relevant Chapters, as this book is not progressively linear. A "research bricolage" approach is followed, drawing on the work of Joe Kincheloe, an advocate of multi-perspectival research methods and multi-methodological inquiry. "The bricoleur['s] . . . attention is directed toward processes, relationships, and interconnections among phenomena."[6]

NOTES

[1] As discussed in Itô Yûki, *New Rising Haiku: The Evolution of Modern Japanese Haiku and the Haiku Persecution Incident* (Red Moon Press, 2007; available online at <http://tinyurl.com/yrka65>).

[2] In Kerouac's *The Dharma Bums* (1958, p. 59), quoting from Blyth, *Haiku* (1952, vol. 2, p. 517).

[3] Itô Yûki (*ibid*).

[4] Additional examples of New Rising wartime haiku, in English, can be found in *Noon: Journal of the Short Poem* 4, Tokyo: Philip Rowland, 2006.

[5] "Nobel Lecture," December 8, 1990 (trans. from Spanish), available online at <http://tinyurl.com/25vgba>.

[6] Kincheloe, J. in *Qualitative Inquiry*, (2005, vol. 11:3, p. 323); *cf.* "Bricolage," *Wikipedia*.

Poems of Consciousness

Section 1: Theoretical Concerns

1. Plausible Deniability

2. Hasegawa Kai

3. Uda Kiyoko

4. The Disjunctive Dragonfly

Section 1: Theoretical Concerns

1. Plausible Deniability

Plausible Deniability

Research note

The paper which follows represents a fruitful aspect of this research, focusing on the relationship between haiku and nature as found in gendai haiku, utilizing a multi-disciplinary approach drawn from the fields of literary linguistics and ecocriticism. This paper began as a lecture given at the 2007 annual international PALA (Poetics and Linguistics Association) conference, held at Kansai Gaidai University, Osaka (July 31-August 4). A call for proceedings impelled its completion, in British English, in mid-November. The ideas developed have been informed by some years of interviews with, and translations of, the words and works of several notable gendai poets.

This paper can also be seen as a sequel to an earlier work, "The Disjunctive Dragonfly" (revised and included later in this Section). In that earlier paper, the concept of disjunction in haiku was posited as more primary in function than juxtaposition (or "superposition"—the term used by Ezra Pound). Seventeen types of disjunctive techniques were also outlined. At that time, I saw a need to further investigate notions of disjunction in contemporary haiku in relation to the experience of nature and consciousness. By interviewing notable poets and co-translating their criticism I had hoped to further thread this particular needle.

Towards an ecocritical view of haiku

The relation of contemporary haiku to nature seems relevant to the recently expanding academic field of "literature and environment," whose main theoretical locus is known as ecocriticism. In this area of inquiry, modern Japanese haiku (gendai haiku) represents a literary and cultural advance in poetic thought. Unfortunately, research in English concerning the value of gendai haiku to ecocriticism, and the integration of ecocritical perspectives found in gendai haiku has yet to be performed, as there are no available publications. The following paper takes a cross-cultural view of contemporary haiku, analyzing haiku as they appear in English—whether authored natively or in translation. A goal has been to present a theoretical analysis of how gendai haiku (and similarities of sensibility found outside Japan) uniquely impart properties of poetic power, through the medium of English. A second goal concerns the dissemination of this cultural art, which may offer new avenues for haiku and the wider field of literature.

A major element of investigation concerns how gendai haiku writers address contemporary environmental concerns in their writing and aesthetic, and equally, how such aesthetic and philosophical formulations might be explicated from cross-cultural or multicultural perspectives. In determining an interpretive approach, the contemporary academic disciplines of stylistics and literary linguistics offer an innovative way of looking at haiku, via detailed descriptions of language features. PALA in particular is a literary association with a strong membership in Japan as well as Europe, and literary-linguistics concepts are able to operate across a wide number of socio-cultural language settings.

Ecocriticism in perspective

The term "ecocriticism" was first coined in William Rueckert's 1978 essay title, "Literature and Ecology: An Experiment in Ecocriticism." In the late 1980s, Cheryl Glotfelty, now Professor of Literature and the Environment at the University of Nevada, Reno, urged the adoption of ecocriticism as a term to refer to what had been a rather diffuse critical field formerly existing under the rubric, "the study of nature writing." In 1992 the Association for the Study of Literature and the Environment (ASLE) was founded, with the first two volumes of its journal, "Interdisciplinary Studies in Literature and Environment

(ISLE)," appearing in 1993. In 1994, the term "ecocriticism" was given definition and academic treatment in a series of position papers presented at the Western Literature Association symposium, "Defining Ecocritical Theory and Practice." At the present time, several university graduate programs in "literature and the environment" or ecocriticism exist in North America and Britain.

The ASLE now has branches throughout Europe and Asia. Japan has an ASLE organization (ASLE-J) which sponsors a variety of conferences and symposia. As mentioned, currently there are no publications in English which directly treat *gendai* haiku from ecocritical perspectives; there are however more general treatments. Pulitzer prize-winning poet and University of California (Davis) Professor Emeritus Gary Snyder has written extensively on the topic of literature, consciousness and nature. In 2004 he was awarded the Masaoka Shiki International Haiku Grand Prize from the Ehime Cultural Foundation (Matsuyama). Considering that Professor Snyder is not known to have published more than a few haiku, the award points to an interesting truth—the pervasive influence of the haiku aesthetic in North America, and elsewhere. Professor Snyder's writings in both poetry and prose reveal a profound knowledge of and influence from Japanese haiku and haiku culture. As one of the Beat writers of the 1950's-1960's, he was also largely responsible for popularizing haiku via Jack Kerouac's novel, *The Dharma Bums*, in which Snyder appears as the protagonist Japhy Ryder, discussing a haiku by Shiki. I was able to study with Gary Snyder and Allen Ginsberg (who had his own unique take on haiku), at Naropa University (Boulder, Colorado), in the 1980's. Snyder's lectures and writings represent an important resource concerning the topic of haiku and ecocriticism.

Having begun focusing on this area of research some years ago, it is electrifying to have found that contemporary Japanese haiku authors and works have much to add to ecocritical theory and practice, as the manner of evocation found in modern Japanese haiku seems unique in literature. Likewise, and in parallel, a small but growing number of poets writing in English are working out of an expanded toolbox.

PLAUSIBLE DENIABILITY:
NATURE AS HYPOTHESIS IN ENGLISH-LANGUAGE HAIKU

Publication. Paper presented, August 2007; *PALA 2007* (The Poetics and Linguistics Association); *PALA Conference Proceedings 2007*; forthcoming in *Stylistic Studies of Literature* (S. Kumamoto & M. Hori, eds.), March, 2008.

INTRODUCTION

A substitute title for this paper might be, 'Beyond the text horizon: Haiku, nature, and the hard problem of consciousness'. I was led to investigate the relationship between haiku, nature and consciousness, and in the course of research ended up in quite a different place than I had imagined. As a result, this paper has three objectives. The first concerns the problem of haiku definition in English, the second has to do with a few elementary possibilities for cognitive-poetic applications as a means of discovering notable linguistic features in haiku, and the third involves an explorative discussion of hypotheticality in haiku as a psychological 'move', validating the commonly-held notion that haiku on the whole reveal essentials of nature for the reader. In this paper, 'nature' implies both 'the wild' as discussed in Gary Snyder (1996), and 'consciousness' as defined in Chalmers (1995a and 1995b). I will present an overview of each topic, with the hope of stimulating further discussion.

1. STRUGGLE FOR DEFINITION

In a continual and periodically contentious search for the definition of a young genre, the recently re-written 2004 'Haiku Society of America (HSA) definitions' describe haiku as: 'a short poem that uses imagistic language to convey the essence of an experience of nature or the season intuitively linked to the human condition'. As the terms 'imagistic language', 'essence', and 'intuitively linked' are not further explicated, the attempt at definition remains problematic, as it lacks specificity—an informed linguistic analysis may be of some benefit. An explanatory note to the definition adds, 'Most haiku in English consist of three unrhymed lines of seventeen or fewer syllables'. This formal limitation to syllable-range reflects the prevalent 11-12-syllable mean length of haiku, with exceptions. There has been no strict rule for syllable counting in English for several decades[1]; in any case, the concept that Japanese 5-7-5-*on* ('sounds') should equate to 5-7-5 English syllables, or any exact syllable-count, is a linguistic misnomer. Metrical templates exist however in both Japanese and English haiku, and these template metrics mirror each other, providing a successful model of emulation, inclusive of a range English syllables. The great majority of haiku in English serendipitously follow this metrical template (*cf.* "Stalking the Wild Onji", also Gilbert and Yoneoka, 2000).

Max Verhart's informative 2007 analytical survey based on written responses from 29 published haijin (the term, meaning 'haiku poet', is a loan word[2]) in 19 countries, sums up some generally held views concerning form. The parenthetical numbers below accord with the number of respondents in agreement on each summarized topic:

> Having looked over all twenty-nine definitions, one can conclude by simply counting that a majority of the haiku poets polled agree that [A] haiku is a short (20) form of poetry (15) [B] concerned with insight (19). To a lesser extent they say that a haiku is [C] based on a moment (7) [D] experienced in nature/[E]seasons (12) or [F] reality in general (9). One feature, [G] the haiku moment, seems to be contradicted by three others, who stress that haiku reflects the changing nature of things.

The survey reveals a degree of generalization which might surprise the linguist, given that the genre presents a number of distinctive linguistic and formal features. To briefly comment on these findings, [A] 'a short form of poetry', fits for the majority of poems published over the past half-century or more, and it must be hard to find a poet willing to disagree that their work is [B] concerned with insight. Haijin do [G] disagree as to whether haiku is [C] based on a moment. Perhaps this is partly because it is unclear what a moment signifies, whether it be the reader's (subjective/cognitive?) moment, a naturalistic instant, image-schema moment, moment within possible worlds of the poem, etc. As seen in the examples just below, haiku do not necessarily reflect a moment as an instant of time. For instance, Gurga's use of 'forgotten for today' and Kacian's 'looking out...long after' are examples of extended or dislocated (nonlinear, indeterminate or paradoxical) temporality:

> forgotten for today by the one true god autumn mosquito
> (Gurga, 2003)

> swallow flight
> looking out the window
> long after
> (Kacian, 2006)

How long is 'today' for a god; or 'long after' for that birder—10 minutes, 10 days, 10 years?

The examples shown below likewise reveal temporal indeterminacy. Another theme in the Verhart survey [E] addresses 'season'. The great majority of traditional Japanese haiku relate to the seasons, as they contain kigo (a referentially complex word or phrase whose partial function provides seasonal indication (*cf.* Gilbert, 2006)), but many modern haiku in Japan and elsewhere present urban settings, topics such as war, dream-life, mytheme, political realties, surreal stylism, etc., and so lack a seasonal indication. As an aside, in the 17th century, Matsuo Bashô, in his selected-hokku collections maintained a non-kigo category, as did late-Meiji era reformer Masaoka Shiki (coiner of the term 'haiku'), who also penned a number of non-kigo haiku.

Even when a seasonal theme is indicated, as with 'athlete's foot' (summer) in Hoshinaga, seen below, the connotation in contemporary haiku often involves the distortion or semiotic transposition of the traditional kigo intention. Hoshinaga remarks that his kigo use is never purely realistic or naturalistic (Gilbert, 2004a). As this is true for any number of contemporary writers, the genre of contemporary haiku can therefore not be defined as a 'season literature'. This leaves [D] nature as an attribute ('experienced in nature', above)—begging the question of the definition of nature. Finally, in the above-quoted survey, haiku are concerned with [F] 'reality in general', and one wonders what this could not mean. In the following sections I hope to explore some avenues which may lead towards greater genre specificity.

1.1 ALTERNATIVITY

Elements of alternativity are frequently found in contemporary haiku. The examples below were chosen to show a variety of features denoting alternativity, and illustrate several specific features: (1) cognitive estrangement[3]; (2) paradox[4]; (3) futurism[5]; (4) time-space subversion[6], and (5) speculative mythopoesis[7]. Note also that two of the haiku are 'one-liners'. All the examples show cognitive estrangement to varying degrees:

>after the bombing
>ruins of a bridge
>linked by the fog
>
>>(Simin, 2001) (1)
>
>The sweet smell
>from an unknown tree
>repulses the metropolis
>
>>(Falkman, 2004) (1 + 2)
>
>Athlete's foot itches–
>still can't become
>Hitler
>
>>(Hoshinaga, 2003) (1 + 2)

A spring cliff—
in my cup
tears of a bird
                    (Yasui, 2003) (1+2)

spring wind—
 I   too
  am   dust
                    (Donegan, 1998) (1+4)

pain fading the days back to wilderness
                    (Kacian, 2007) (1+4)

leaves blowing into a sentence
                    (Boldman, 1999) (2+4)

From the future
a wind arrives
that blows the waterfall apart
                    (Natsuishi, 2004) (3+4)

Entering a dream
of that Great Fish of the South
wanting to cry out
                    (Natsuishi, 2004) (5)

Although a considerable amount of energy has been spent on haiku-definitional projects over the last decades, results to date lack adequate resolution. As a result, several critics have echoed Hiroaki Sato's statement, 'Today it may be possible to describe haiku but not to define it' (1999, p. 73). Examining the range of variation exhibited in the examples above, it may be that Sato is strictly correct as to definition but his silver lining is the implicit invitation to cognitive poetics in advancing avenues of linguistic description. Descriptions connoting those specific ways in which haiku utilise language in their creation of reader-effects would likely increase genre valuation and stimulate further interest in this young genre.

2. Out of the Water—Towards Linguistic Depiction

Haiku are poems of consciousness. This has been said in a variety of ways, most notably by R. H. Blyth, the British-expatriate promoter of Zen Buddhist readings of haiku, in his voluminous translations and commentaries (1949-1952, etc.), and by the celebrated Beat writer Jack Kerouac, who was strongly influenced by Blyth, in terms of haiku. Through Kerouac's portrayal of poet and ecocritical writer Gary Snyder in his novel, *The Dharma Bums* (1958), new generations worldwide probably first come into contact with haiku as literature, Kerouac's books remaining perennial bestsellers.[8] Partly as a result of these two contemporary influences, the English-language haiku tradition from the 1950s on has conflated the concept of a zenlike 'moment' (an 'AH' or 'AHA!' moment) with the notion if not raison d'etre of haiku—though this idea is being questioned of late (such a 'moment' is not a central critical concern or main aesthetic within Japanese haiku studies). Leaving aside the relevance of the perspective, it is difficult to discern what 'zenlike' might actually mean. In any case, good haiku seem to possess both magnetism and a near-universal appeal, judging by the many countries and languages in which they now appear. A notable attribute the haiku genre is its ability to overleap borders of language, region and culture.

2.1 *Lily*

One of the most celebrated haiku in English is the following, penned in 1963 by Nicholas Virgilio (1988):

> Lily:
> out of the water ...
> out of itself.

Some features commonly found in English-language haiku can be observed: a three-line tripartite meter, short-long-short line length, seasonal indication (lily), and kireji (a 'cutting word') designated by use of the colon after 'lily' (the semi-colon and especially en- or em-dash are also often used). The 'cutting word' is a subset (i.e. orthographic markup) existing within the wider concept of *kire* ('cutting')—a cutting of the poem in time and space which can occur through multiple linguistic and semantic disjunctions apart from, and in place of, kireji. Note that the examples of Simin, Falkman, Kacian, Boldman and Natsuishi, shown above, do not contain kireji but do exhibit *kire*. In 'lily' is the addition of ellipsis, a relatively unusual feature, as kireji is already found. The poem also successfully applies the technique of rhythmic substitution—the rhythmic repetition in the repeating phrase 'out of' in the last two lines (*cf.* Gilbert, 2004b). Virgilio's haiku is a good example of both the effect and effectiveness of kireji in English. If this text were to be interpreted prosaically, it might look something like:

1) [A] lily: [it comes/rises] out of the water [and/also (rises/comes) (to be)/(is connected with the idea of arising)] out of itself.

2) [(I/one can notice that the)/(There is a)] lily [(I am observing/observed)/(which is growing/has grown)] out the water [and] out of itself (too/as well/also).

As can be seen by the 'filled in' sentence-examples 1) & 2) above, haiku in general offer the reader propositions via a series of phrasal and image 'fragments'. 'Formal incompleteness' might well be included in future definitions of verity. In 'lily' there are propositions made concerning being, identity and becoming, which, along with the lily itself, become main loci. In fact, part of the delight in the haiku is the dynamic imbalance between foreground and background. Is the main locus the flower—or identity; birth and growth, or—being and non-being? Figure and ground are at any moment of reading both distinct *and* mutating. Because haiku are extremely brief, the reader not only reads but also re-reads. As re-reading occurs, further thoughts and feelings arise, interpretations build up, while some are discarded; you could say that the poem grows out of itself—thought grows out of itself, feeling grows out of itself, the image grows out of itself, imagination grows out of itself (and/or out of the poem). I term this process 'misreading as meaning', because haiku resist easy solutions as to meaning, resisting reader attempts to ferret out singular meanings or messages, scenes, worlds, or any singular, 'true' interpretation.

Acts of 'misreading as meaning' are abetted by absent syntactic elements, as can be seen in sentence-example 1) which has filled-in elements implied by punctuation and lineation in the haiku. Sentence-example 2) represents an attempt at an even more fulsome prose. This functional compositional-stylism of missing syntactic elements and semantic language-gaps in haiku form has been described as *katakoto*: 'fragmentary or "broken" language' (*lit.* 'baby talk'), coined by Tsubouchi Nenten (2007).

The two sentence-examples reveal that verbal action [growth], and verbs themselves are usually implicit rather than overt in haiku, and that syntactic and semantic compression is a common feature. The deictic 'I' is rarely stated in haiku, nor are pronouns commonly found. These schemes represent two of the ways in which haiku connote objectivity between imaged object(s) and experiencer/reader.

It is notable that neither 1) nor 2) above are able to prosaically inscribe the kireji in the haiku, represented by the colon in the poem. The colon is then an idiosyncratic genre-specific modifier, designed (in this case) to emulate the character '*ya*' in Japanese, 'a post-position particle used to express emotion, inspiration, feeling' (Hasegawa, 2007). As the kireji 'cuts the ku'—that is, breaks the haiku apart spatially, psychologically and temporally, its semantic connotation might be illustrated as:

> [there is a] lily
>> [something is] out of the water
>> [something is] out of itself

Something, but not the lily. The lily, as a realistic, deictic object, indicating place and world as *origo* is cut off from the last two lines. So, what is it that is 'out of the water'? Lily-ness, perhaps. The quality of what it is to be a lily. Use of kireji indicates it cannot be 'the lily out of the water'— as realism or literalism. If this were the case, there would be no colon and likely no lineation between first and second lines. Something else is meant. As Heidegger stated, we may liken it to the 'thingness' of things[9]. So, primary disjunction in haiku is often brought by kireji (colon). This linguistic role seems unique to haiku, among poetic genres.

Certainly, *kire* (cutting) is fundamental to haiku. It is the semantic act of cutting which paradoxically forges the sense of non-duality, that is, a reader-sense of coherence arising from the fragmentary aspects (*katakoto*) of haiku. If coherence did not occur, we would not have a poem, but merely a grouping of linguistic fragments. Why and how does coherence in haiku occur? While this experience cannot easily be defined, the celebrated 'lily' haiku is acknowledged as an exemplar. There is an aspect of what I term hypotheticality occurring between the first and second lines, as 'lily' becomes something like (the lily quality of) which it is to be 'out of the water'. But what of the third line? Here, impossibility or paradox arises, revealing a high degree of unusuality and alternativity, spawning metaphoric identity: what it is to be the quality of something of itself coming out of the origin of its selfness.

And, what, or how, might this 'image'? How does the haiku cohere? The final 'outcome' or ending is hypothetical—an imaging (process) incomplete as to meaning—as the poem and its languaged paradox trail off into space—and then return to 'lily' at the beginning again, in an uroboros-like circulation of re-reading.

2.2 Out of itself...

The haiku apparently centres on 'lily', remaining sensual and somewhat deictic ('lily' is with you right to the end), yet is *also* paradoxical as to action, and *also* metaphorical, due to the irruption of realism (the lily does not literally come out of itself). We can say as a result that the deictic recedes to a contextual resonance rather than figurative ground. At the same time, there exists another figuration: a pond (indicative of Bashô's celebrated 'old pond' haiku), as background—but this image remains halfway-seen, as the body of water remains unstated. The lily could as well be a product of hydroponics. This tableau contains then both realism and surrealism in a near-symbolism, existing in a psychological space between realism, fantasy and dream; a realm which psychologist James Hillman discusses as daimonic (*cf.* 'On Psychological Creativity,' 1998), an aspect of soul which 'deepens events into experiences' (2004, p. 26). I speculate that haiku often begin with 'objective' facts: things, objects, events, and psychological deepening proceeds; that is, following Hillman, objective 'events' become experiences via a process of deepening (are ensouled, in the terminology of archetypal psychology).

The haiku ends with a multi-layered experience of realistic image (e.g. lily, lily pond), imagined sensation/perceptions of qualities (lily-ness-coming out-of-water-ness), and impossible tautological truths (how can what it is come out of what it is?). In actuality, there is no 'come' or 'become' in the haiku, only the repetition of the phrasal 'out of'. The semantic idea of coming or going or any evolving of image-schema remains reader-interpretive—perceived movements or actions between planes of reality rely on absences or lacunae between language parts. As a result, there impends a 'languaging' which extends beyond the given text-language and image-schema—this languaging aspect necessarily arises in searching out coherence.

In a sense, haiku evoke islands of cognitive coherence (those language parts and image-constellations which follow familiar lexical and syntactic rules), while by contrast cognitive disjunction (dissonance, alternativity) is evoked via lacunae, *kire*, and 'misreadings as meaning' evolving in reader-consciousness. In discussing the *via negativa* of haiku, Tsubouchi Nenten applies the term *katakoto*; Hasegawa Kai uses *ma* (especially psychological *ma*, connoting a 'psycho-poetic interval of betweenness'[10]); Natsuishi comments that, 'the nothing (*nihil*) can connect with everything, or turn into a more positive philosophy. Through negative stages, it is possible to reach some positive dimension' (2004, p. 68); and American haiku author and critic Jim Kacian writes in his prose poem, 'Presence', 'In this way haiku can be poised between language and silence / In this way it can suggest the centrality of silence' (2006, p. 13). Excellent haiku evoke coherence beyond the text horizon.

2.3 *LIKE A LILY* — '*KIRE*' *AND THE HARD PROBLEM OF CONSCIOUSNESS*

It is *kire* which most strongly separates haiku from epithet, and this key semantic feature is applied via a variety of linguistic techniques (*cf.* Gilbert, 2004b). The haiku form necessitates extreme concision, minimalism, and attributes of 'image'—but without *kire*, we do not have have haiku. *Kire* can be taken as 'cuttings' or 'irruptions', or strong, abrupt 'distortions' of space/time/worlds in reader consciousness.

Having a sense of disjunction, and the separation of realistic object and deixis from its ending fruition, in 'lily' the last line applies the reflexive pronoun 'itself' to create a paradoxical image, neither realist nor surrealist. What is the thing that is a 'self' of 'it'? Of course, it is a lily, only the lily, but it is also what it is to be like a lily in its thingly character. A further exegesis of this haiku approaches the centre of a fundamental debate in cognitive science and the philosophy of consciousness: what it is like to be something that experiences the feeling of experience. A well-known paper by Nagel (1974) asked the question, 'What is it like to be a bat?'; and David Chandler developed this problem for cognitive science, coining the sobriquet 'the hard problem of consciousness':

> The really hard problem of consciousness is the problem of *experience*. When we think and perceive, there is a whir of information-processing, but there is also a subjective aspect. As Nagel (1974) has put it, there is *something it is like* to be a conscious organism. This subjective aspect is experience. When we see, for example, we experience visual sensations: the felt quality of redness, the experience of dark and light, the quality of depth in a visual field. Other experiences go along with perception in different modalities: the sound of a clarinet, the smell of mothballs. Then there are bodily sensations, from pains to orgasms; mental images that are conjured up internally; the felt quality of emotion, and the experience of a stream of conscious thought. What unites all of these states is that there is something it is like to be in them. All of them are states of experience. It is undeniable that some organisms are subjects of experience. But the question of how it is that these systems are subjects of experience is perplexing. Why is it that when our cognitive systems engage in visual and auditory information-processing, we have visual or auditory experience: the quality of deep blue, the sensation of middle C? How can we explain why there is something it is like to entertain a mental image, or to experience an emotion? (1995a).

The problem is 'hard' because *experience* cannot yet be explained or defined by cognitive science. Generally speaking, haiku formally address the hypothetical question posed by the hard problem of consciousness: of how it is to know the feeling of how consciousness is[11], apart from the 'easy problems' (see the Addendum for these), via the creation of paradox, ambiguity and hypotheticality, so that image foregrounding, linguistic seriality, image-schemas, become weak, non-existent, or ambivalent. In consequence, a *via negativa* arises. That is, a haiku acts as a finger or peninsula of language, jutting out into languageless potentialities in which something inexplicable to cognitive science (indefinite, non-definable) is occurring. One may say that the haiku text points beyond itself. Not every haiku achieves this locus in a strong manner, yet those that do so may represent a limit for cognitive poetics, an idea I would like to explore in the remainder of this paper.

3. Putting the period deeply: Hypotheticality and the hard problem

To the extent there is reader/poem-coherence experienced in haiku which present with disjunctive, fragmentary language and *kire*, haiku propositions evoke Chandler's hard problem—how it is to know the feeling of how consciousness is—and are intriguingly separated from the more 'easy' problems of consciousness. I would like specifically to show how a dualistic cognitive fundament, the 'discrimination of figure and ground' (and those modes of attention which create this orientation), can be subverted within the haiku landscape,[12] by discussing an example presenting an abundance of hypotheticality. Easy aspects of consciousness are not negated in the evocation of hypotheticality in haiku, but rather relegated to the background, much like the landscape in the rear view of a car mirror. We know what got us to where we are, but coherence in the poem does not seem to lie in returning to those previous cognitive stages.

While it is impossible to address the hard problem directly, an example demonstrating how haiku bring the reader toward the phenomenology of the hard problem via adumbrations of the paradoxical and hypothetical can be found in this haiku by Natsuishi Ban'ya:

Shin-tairiku no chûshin no sabaku ni fukaku kuten o ute
(24-*on*) (2004, p. 24)[13]

Put a period deeply
into the desert
at the center of the new world

'Put a period' begins with what seems a trivial action: put a period somewhere. Usually we put them on paper; yet the second line represents a left turn with 'into the desert', reversing semantic expectation. Putting a period 'into the desert' evokes a different line of image, action and form from what might conceivably be done with a literal, textual 'period'. And so, realism is subverted. The sense of paradox is heightened by the imperative grammatical tone.

The aspect of explaining, in fact, the 'explainer' of intellect rides behind the propulsive process of reading/misreading.

3.1 Figure and ground as Möbius

Hypothetical speculations: the period implies 'end of an era,' death, finality, a flag (of some sort), a statement; the desert is real and inhabits the new world, or a speculative new world; is an actual place (e.g. Death Valley, the high desert of Nasca); the haiku is political, 'center of the desert' represents America's current government and its war in Iraq; the period is a wounding; the haiku is historical, relating to Columbus' 'discovery' and eurocentrism; so, the haiku is revisionist and ironic, accessing 'new world' in a postcolonial manner; the haiku landscape is that of another planet awaiting discovery; an alternative universe where putting a period exactly thus makes good sense; the haiku is a surreal remembrance, a novel myth.

Alternativity spawns alternativities. The period is wherever my attention is.

There are a number of linguistic features which act as semantic attractors here—as much as the poem resists rational sense, it also resists non-sense. Some of these cognitive attributes are that,

1) Something is being done (i.e. use of 'put', 'into', 'of' in prepositional phrases).
2) There is a desert (geography).
3) There is a period (a common noun).
4) 'New world' is a familiar term (compound noun) for a place and/or idea of region.

Due to the use and arrangement of the above four elements (representing actions, things, biome, and region), the haiku stubbornly resists being taken as nonsense, as it applies familiar notions and deixis. Nonetheless, the haiku grazes the nonsensical—one thing this poem is not doing is putting a period anywhere —but then again . . . This flashing back and forth, between sense and the *nons-* of sense; between meaning and its irruption; between Newtonian time, space and form, and its quotidian counterpoints is emblematic of *gendai* (modern) haiku in Japan and a growing number of '21st-century modern' haiku in English.[14]

The text has an uroborous-like quality, turning round on itself like a Möbius strip. An uroborous is a pattern of infinite progression and return—a Möbius has the additional property of collapsing dimension (two surfaces become apparently one). In that attention itself becomes the primary focal point of the haiku lens, the familiar scenario of figure/ ground polarity collapses into the 'zero dimension' of attention itself.[15] The uroborous and Möbius are paradoxical, yet strong paradoxicality can impend in a form of 14 words within a pattern of 7-5-8 syllables.

3.2 MUMS: MODES OF PROVOCATIONAL FORGETTING

How does the reader organize cognitive landscapes, in reading this haiku? Are you sussing out how the poem is organized? Rescanning the poem? Has the sense of figure, ground, and meaning been shifting and shuffling with re-reading? Have a variety of propositions and possible worlds been formulated, with certain image-schemas discarded—some of which are revisited? I think of this process as 'misreading as meaning'.

To the extent such a cognitive process becomes potent as a foreground, an interesting dance develops between multiple hypothetical strands of feeling, image-schemae and logics—a dance of MUMS: 'Modes of provocational forgetting under the influence of creative misreading(s)'.

3.2.1 *Defamiliarization*

At least three cognitive aspects seem involved in provocational forgetting. The first involves iterative experiences of *defamiliarization*, as the journey of 'misreading as meaning' continues. This is the provocational aspect of a MUM. Defamiliarization occurs in terms of semantics, syntax, schema, and deixis. As possible worlds rise, are discarded, mutate, and are re-run, the reader swims on through various novel landscapes, and so, normative grammatical and semiotic structures are usurped ('forgotten' or left behind, so to say) as novel cognitive structures and orientations arise and evolve. Development, in this sense, involves 'dishabituation' (a variety of forgetting; loss of prevailing pattern).

3.2.2 *Forgetting to learn*

A second aspect of 'forgetting' was advanced some decades ago by the noted neurologist Julian Jaynes (1976), who outlined stages of cognitive learning in his speculative work on the evolution of subjective consciousness. In Chapter 1, 'The Consciousness of Consciousness' (pp. 21-47) Jaynes explains that as elementary steps of a learned process become unconscious (lost to or 'forgotten' by consciousness), this developing unconsciousness allows for an increase in expertise (i.e., without increasing unconsciousness expertise could not develop). In his example, if an accomplished pianist were to suddenly have to consciously experience the beginner-level of playing—where to place each finger on each key—there would be a return to a novice level of performance. Mastery relies on a great deal of information, at one time conscious, having become unconscious. This idea seems a common-sense truth for craft in general. Corollary to this is the concept of reader-expertise in haiku reading—there is a developmental curve involving iterations of provocational forgetting in the evolution of reader engagement.

3.2.3 *Foraging anamnesis*

Another aspect of forgetting, indicative of psychic potency, can be illustrated via the perspective of depth psychology. In a primary mythos of the underworld journey, taken from classical Greece, there exist two great underworld rivers/goddesses: Lethe and Mnemosyne. It was said that departed souls must first drink the waters of Lethe (forgetting, amnesia), before travelling through her lands to finally drink the waters of Mnemosyne (anamnesis) (*cf.* Hesiod, *Theogony*).[16] To briefly summarize the concept, via the 'forgetting' of certain cognitive patterns and structures (cognitive amnesia)—a variety of psychological death (underworld rivers convey *thanatos*)—*divergent orders of recollection* (re-memberings consequent to one's descent) are inspired; the goddess Mnemosyne is mother to the Muses.

Altogether, taking this view of the forgetting/re-membering process, finding or resolving coherence first seems to involve an iterative process of defamiliarization and forgetting(s), antecedent to re-memberings, anamnesis. Unfortunately, a continuation of this topic is beyond the scope of this paper.[17]

3.2.4 *(Re)birthing coherence*

Perhaps haiku resist strict definition in that the main locus of *poesis*—experiences of coherence—cannot be adequately described in language. Cognitive-poetic aspects such as MUMS can however offer a process-description of possible reader-phenomenology. There seem useful hints to the phenomenology of consciousness within haiku coherence, as experiences birthing novel modalities (anamnesis) of experience/remembrance. This may be an unsurprising statement for art in general; however, it is really about how the MUMS get you there. That is, it is the unique, sensate taste of poetic *experience* within the haiku cosmos that matters, pragmatically.

3.3 *Cognitive reflexivity — Metaxic ambiguity*

Peter Stockwell in his 'Surreal Figures' (2003, p. 15) outlines five psychological aspects involved in *selective attention* (an 'easy' problem of consciousness) based on classical Gestalt psychology. Here, each of these is summed up, with examples given from 'Put a period':

1) Elements positioned close to each other will be treated as having a unified relationship. Ex. (put/period), (deeply/desert), (centre/world)

2) Elements that appear similar will be assumed to be related. Ex. The nouns: (period/desert/new world)

3) Figures with a perceived closed boundary will be seen as unified. Ex. (Into the desert/at the centre)

4) Elements with few interruptions between them will be seen as connected. As the haiku form is extremely brief, *all* elements have few interruptions between them.

5) Elements which seem to share a function are treated together. Ex. (Put/deeply/into/at), (a period/a desert/a centre/the new)

Even with these gestalt-semantic cues, 'Put a period deeply' has no solution, and does not resolve as to figure and ground, as it contains several layers and types of abrupt paradox (and any given paradox may be paradoxical to the others)—and yet—cohesion. The phrasal fragments contain commonplace semantic, syntactic, and logical elements, as well as simple, realistic images (period, desert, new world). There is also a high degree of *cognitive reflexivity*, which I ascribe as the evolving awareness in reader experience of 'imagining as imagining, reading as reading, knowing as knowing' (the 'out of the water / out of itself' effect).

There is another layer to this reader experience, the psychological space that opens up within the disjunctive paradoxicality of real semantic notions exhibiting incompleteness—a space wherein the known, and the knower of *what* is known, have become unblended or unbonded. Hillman refers to this as *metaxic*. 'Metaxy denotes the intermediate realm between two opposites' (1966, pp. 379-80). To enter this psychological realm of 'between' is more or less equivalent to Hasegawa Kai's depiction of 'psychological *ma*' in haiku, mentioned earlier. As metaxic ambiguity occupies consciousness, a variety of psychological space opens, which Karl Kerenyi denotes as *'das Moment des Unerklärlichen*: the moment of the inexplicable.[18] This interval of the space of 'betweenness', *psychological inexplicability as poesis*, represents a journey between haiku and reader.

Cognitive reflexivity is a heightening of cognitive self-awareness, yet there is incompleteness and paradox which likewise evolves, due to disjunctive paradoxicality. At this point we have come to a psychological 'moment' (*das Moment des Unerklärlichen*), but it is not an AHA! (which implies that you 'get' something). Or, if so, the getting is all about the losing; that is, getting lost. A 'moment of the inexplicable' is a bit deceptive—the plural form, 'moments of', and alternatively, 'field of', or 'landscape of', could be substituted. The approach here, utilizing cognitive poetics and western depth-psychological notions, hopefully retains a sense of the complexity of haiku-poetic experience. In Japanese, the term *kire*, 'cutting', described (in brief) as a cutting through time and space, is an elegantly concise description for a complex, indeterminate, cognitive process. For Bashô, *kire* was at the heart of his haiku aesthetic.[19] That this term and its implications remain undiscussed in English is indicative of a knowledge gap that exists in Anglo-American haiku studies concerning fundamental haiku principles.

A central feature of haiku exhibiting strong hypotheticality is that they ride the horizon-line of inexplicability while also diving in. Yet if inexplicability alone were itself the outcome, confusion would result rather than coherence. This issue of confusion versus coherence leads to a final topic, the relationship between haiku and nature. It may be that the haiku journey here encounters something wild, unbounded, and unconfined by normative structures.

4. The Grain of Things: Nature and Haiku

Plausible deniability in haiku has to do with how haiku articulate multiple possible worlds, each one hypothetical, plausible, and at the same time also deniable as to its existence or viability, in relation to the text. What does all this have to do with nature? Gary Snyder writes,

> So I will argue that consciousness, mind, imagination, and language are fundamentally wild. "Wild" as in wild ecosystems—richly interconnected, interdependent, and incredibly complex. Diverse, ancient, and full of information. At root the real question is how we understand the concepts of order, freedom, and chaos. Is art an imposition of order on chaotic nature, or is art (also read "language") a matter of discovering the grain of things, of uncovering the measured chaos that

structures the natural world? Observation, reflection, and practice show artistic process to be the latter (1996, p. 168).

That we are fundamentally wild: language and consciousness are fundamentally wild. Snyder's depiction of the wild differs from the idea of chaos as an inchoate order of being. Echoing classical Greek ideas of beauty as 'pattern', Snyder writes of 'a measured chaos that structures the natural world'; that there arises in consequence, 'the grain of things . . . uncovering the measured chaos that structures' the pattern, forms, and (emergent) structures evident in what is wild in universe. Heidegger likewise indicates an aspect of wildness in that things in their fundamental nature (things in their thingness; lily in its lilyness; to 'put a period deeply'), resist and evade thought, being 'seldom expressible':

> This exertion of thought seems to meet with its greatest resistance in defining the thingness of the thing. . . . The unpretentious thing evades thought most stubbornly. Or can it be that this self-refusal of the mere thing, this self-contained independence, belongs precisely to the nature of the thing. . . That the thingness of the thing is particularly difficult to express and only seldom expressible is infallibly documented. . . . The world is not the mere collection of the countable or uncountable, familiar and unfamiliar things that are just there. But neither is it a merely imagined framework added by our representation to the sum of given things. *The world worlds*, and is more fully in being than the tangible and perceptible realm in which we believe ourselves to be at home. World is never an object that stands before us and can be seen. World is the ever-nonobjective to which we are subject . . . (2001, pp. 31, 43).

The '*world worlds*', as a verb: 'World is never an object that stands before us' because it is 'ever-nonobjective' and we ourselves are subject to this nonobjectivity; 'world' ('being', as Chalmer's *experience*) can, then, be neither imagined schema nor the representations of given things—Heidegger's idea seems similar to Snyder's 'measured chaos' presenting 'the grain of things'. Both seek a non-dual, integral continuum for nature and consciousness—a continuum which evades, resists or otherwise challenges its easy problems. Snyder's 'nature' and Heidegger's 'world' indicate epistemological spaces in which the wild is fundamentally extra-human, extra-rational/objective, and primary rather than primitive.

The issues raised are relevant to a description of haiku and nature, in that they approach the difficulty of inscribing nature and consciousness within a single phenomenological field. Perhaps it is only via forms of psychological inexplicability as *poesis* that the reader is able to be led through a labyrinth of creative, hypothetical image-schema, away from the easy problems of consciousness toward the intimate wilderness of 'what it is like to be something', apart from the functional utility of 'modes of attention' ('the object that stands before us . . . tangible and perceptible'). Looking at Snyder's definition of 'wild ecosystems' there are strong parallels with the cognitive-poetic haiku landscape: richly interconnected, multifarious, interdependent.

Snyder also discusses an historic Anglo-European bias which has opposed civilization to nature; civilization as a garden which keeps nature at bay, and out. From Snyder's same essay:

> Many figures in the literary field, the critical establishment, and the academy are not enthralled with the natural world, and indeed some positively doubt its worth when compared to human achievement. Take this quote from Howard Nemerov, a good poet and a decent man:

> *Civilization, mirrored in language, is the garden where relations grow; outside the garden is the wild abyss.*

The unexamined assumptions here are fascinating. They are, at worst, crystallizations of the erroneous views that enable the developed world to displace Third and Fourth World peoples and overexploit nature globally. Nemerov here proposes that language is somehow implicitly civilized or civilizing, that civilization is orderly, that intrahuman relations are the pinnacle of experience (as though all of us, and all life on the planet, were not interrelated), and that "wild" means "abyssal," disorderly, and chaotic (p. 166).

In contemporary haiku a shape-shifting landscape develops, partly form and image, partly uncertainty, partly remembrance, partly those ideas and feelings which recede, as palimpsest—impelling the inexplicable, through cutting (*kire*). When haiku are described as poems evoking nature, this sensibility may at root be related not so much to evocations of season or naturalism, as an evolving process of indeterminacy in reader-experience, evoking a sense of interdependent systems, 'ecological' landscapes, and non-duality inhabited via metaxy. As such, the move toward alienation exhibited by textual language (described in Abram, 2005; Manes, 1992) becomes a primary poetic subject and subversive mode of exploration in modern haiku, which use language with the intention to recast the ground of the natural in both literature and the reader. This intention locates haiku in English uniquely within the purview of ecopoetics and the academic field of literature and the environment.

Conclusion

In this paper, some possibilities have been offered which may lead to more specific definitions of the haiku genre (e.g. formal incompleteness, *kire* stylism, *katakoto,* modes of plausibly-deniable hypotheticality, MUMS, metaxic ambiguity). Also, several unique features of contemporary haiku such as time dilation, futurism, mythopoetic realities spontaneously generating alternate universes, and the positing of unique physical laws and behaviours have been examined, as they occur in the course of generating plausibly deniable disjunct paradoxicality.

Haiku which utilise *kire* effectively have the potential to evoke reader-experiences of coherence, arising as *ecos*, and anamnesis. Haiku are radical in the way they use language to recast relations between consciousness and nature. There seems no more sufficient rationale to explain the survival of this extremely brief genre as a high art for over four centuries, and its recent internationalization.

Although who we are and what we become within points of poetic coherence arising out of disjunctive hypotheticality cannot yet be described by cognitive poetics, modes and stages of reader phenomena in haiku may be outlined and the genre more specifically defined. I would like to end with a remark by C. G. Jung (1969, p. 420) in relation to the hard problem of consciousness, which seems relevant to evocations of the wild in haiku: 'The psyche and its contents are the only reality which is given to us *without a medium*'.

Endnotes

[1] In America, the growing pains of the new genre are hinted at by Anita Virgil, one of the early leaders of the HSA, in a recent interview discussing her experiences, circa 1971 (Wilson, 2005):

> Hard as it was for many to take, and hard as it was to convince many practitioners of this simplistic adaptative [*sic*] 'solution' to writing haiku in another language (and, unfortunately, to this day in the American educational system it persists!), it meant moving away from the dictum of 17 English-language—and later foreign-language—'syllables'! Throughout the book *The Japanese Haiku* by Kenneth Yasuda, the top of every page all the way across reads: 57557557557557557557. And at the back of the book where he had his own haiku in English, he wrote them in 17 English syllables. How is a beginner to ever shake this off? Talk about subliminal messages! Yes, to the Japanese it had relevance, but to some of us outlanders, it was not the whole story. It was rarely applicable when writing in English.
>
> In critiquing the poems of that era, it was not too difficult to see where the writers in English added words SIMPLY FOR THE SAKE OF MAKING THAT 17-SYLLABLE COUNT. It was referred to as "padding." In most every instance, these 'extra' words were no more than redundancies. They did not add to the poem. To the contrary, they weakened the impact by dragging it out, repeating the same idea. Since the greatest beauty of the haiku for me is their power of concision with which one can open up worlds of implication, suggestion—if one selects only the essence of the moving experience that gave rise to the poem, this verbosity was a real handicap. In the main line poetry circles of those days (and still today somewhat) American haiku was totally disdained. Ignored. Not published. Dismissed.

[2] The term 'haijin' is not italicized as it has become a loan word within haiku studies. Other terms, such as *kire* ('cutting') have not yet taken hold, so they remain in italics.

3. 'Cognitive estrangement' is a term coined by Darko Suvin (b. 1930, Professor Emeritus, McGill University), primarily in relation to science fiction and fantasy genre-studies, which implies an awareness on the part of the reader that the text does not present a world as familiarly known, but rather a cosmos whose alternative phenomena, through the displacement of empirical and materialist views, impels a reconsideration of habitual, scientifically-based perspectives.

4. 'Paradox' here indicates causal or ontological impossibility; e.g. a tree smell cannot repulse a metropolis (in Boldman), nor can one (still can't) 'become Hitler' (in Hoshinaga), or 'fading the days' in Kacian, etc.

5. 'Futurism' in this context indicates a time set in the future which is imbued with poetic, if not visionary (or at minimum speculative) possibility.

6. 'Time-space subversion' indicates the upsetting, overthrow or even destruction of a space-time continuum via the images presented in a given haiku. For instance, in Donegan, 'spring wind' exists in a time-space framework in which a cogent author writes a haiku—thus, 'I . . . am dust' subverts the time-space of both spring as season, and the author's lifetime as a cogent being (there is in addition the paradox of wind as dust); in Kacian, 'pain' is experienced by a cogent author, thus it embodies a specific deixis, which is subverted by a possible world in which pain, or its causal result is 'fading the days' back to wilderness—which, whatever this outcome may be, is no longer framed by the time or space of the antecedent deixis.

7. 'Speculative mythopoesis' involves novel, hypothetical mythic creation.

8. Two different editions of Kerouac's *On The Road* are currently ranked within the top 1500 best-selling books, and *The Dharma Bums* is ranked just over 6000, at amazon.com [Accessed 12 November 2007].

9. In 'The Origin of the Work of Art', Heidegger (2001) describes the 'thingly character' of things (an evolution of the Kantian 'thing-as-such') as a phenomenological arising apart from any particular set of sense-data given by that thing, thus implying that 'the sense of what it is like to be something' (which David Chandler discusses as the hard problem of consciousness), is intimately fused with the most basic apperception of image. See Section 4 of this paper for a further quotation of Heidegger.

10. This is my interpretive translation; Hasegawa's appellation of *ma* presents a conundrum for the translator.

11. The leading explicator of the hard problem of consciousness, David Chalmers (Professor of Philosophy; Director, Centre for Consciousness Studies, Australia National University), defines the hard problem of consciousness as, 'explaining why we have qualitative phenomenal experiences. This is contrasted with the "easy problems" of explaining the ability to discriminate, integrate information, report mental states, focus attention, etc'. Easy problems are easy because all that is required for their solution is to specify a physical mechanism that can perform the function. Hard problems are distinct from this set, 'because they persist even when the performance of all the relevant functions is explained' (*Cf.* David Chalmers, 1995a and 1995b. For additional information visit: http://consc.net/Chalmers, and Wikipedia: http://tinyurl.com/2ws2zq [Accessed 12 November 2007].)

12. Please see the Addendum for a further explanation of differences between the hard and easy problems of consciousness, as well as Chalmers, 1995a, 1995b, 2008.

13. This haiku is published in English translation from the Japanese. Ban'ya was a co-translator, and had final approval of the translation. The romaji was included in the published English-language text.

14. I have borrowed Marjorie Perloff's coinage, from her overview of contemporary poetry, *21st Century Modernism* (2002). In the

Introduction, Perloff addresses the 'unambitious attitude' found in much contemporary poetry:

> [O]ne need no longer pay lip service to the tired dichotomy that has governed our discussion of twentieth-century poetics for much too long—that between modernism and post-modernism. . . . Far from being irrelevant and obsolete, the aesthetic of early modernism has provided the seeds of the materialist poetic which is increasingly our own. . . . what interests me is the unfulfilled promise of the modernist (as of the classical) poetic impulse in so much of what passes for poetry today—a poetry singularly unambitious in its attitude to the materiality of the text, to what Khlebnikov described as the recognition that "the roots of words are only phantoms behind which stand the strings of the alphabet." It is this particular legacy of early modernism that the new poetics has sought to recover. '"To imagine a language," said Wittgenstein, "is to imagine a form of life"' (pp. 1-5).

[15.] Paradoxes abound in science and have some resonance with the contemporary haiku cosmos: Klein bottles, paradromic rings, black hole singularities, the nature of 'universe' prior to the big bang, dark matter, dark energy, the double-slit experiment, etc.

[16.] 'Here [at the Chthonian Oracle of Trophonios in Boiotia] he [the supplicant] must drink water called the water of Lethe (Forgetfulness), that he may forget all that he has been thinking of hitherto, and afterwards he drinks of another water, the water of Mnemosyne (Memory), which causes him to remember what he sees after his descent (Pausanias, circa 200 CE, *Guide to Greece*, Book 9, sec. 39:3); a mimetic ritual of the underworld experience. Available from: http://tinyurl.com/3alt6y [Accessed 12 November 2007].

[17.] The connection between haiku and remembrance is conceptually fertile—the following stanzas of Heidegger (2001, p. 10) seem relevant, if as calling cards:

The oldest of the old follows behind
us in our thinking, and yet it
comes to meet us.

That is why thinking holds to the
coming of what has been, and
is remembrance.

[18] The translation is found in a Ph.D. thesis by Johnston, 2006 (Chapter III, 'The soul's sphere of infinite images', para. 40). Available from: http://tinyurl.com/3bo6me [Accessed 12 November 2007].

[19] The following is a draft translation from the *Kyoraishô*. Kyorai was one of Bashô's main disciples, and this text is considered among the most important of those illustrating Bashô's teachings:

> Placing kireji in hokku [haiku] is for those beginners who do not understand the nature of cutting and uncutting very well. . . . [However,] there are hokku which are well-cut without kireji. Because of their subtle qualities, [for beginners] more common theories have been founded, and taught. . . . Once, the master, Bashô, said, as an answer to the question of Jôsô [one of Bashô's ten principal disciples. b.1662?–1704]: 'In waka, after 31- *on*, there is *kire*. In hokku, after 17-*on*, there is *kire*.' Jôsô was immediately enlightened. Then, another disciple asked [on the same topic], and the master, Bashô, answered, 'When you use words as kireji, every word becomes kireji. When you do not use words as kireji, there are no words which are kireji.' And the master said, 'From this point, grasp the very depth of the nature of kireji on your own.' All that I have described here is what the master revealed, until the very threshold of its true secret [oral tradition], the thickness of one leaf of shoji-paper (Kyorai, 2001, pp. 497-99).

Acknowledgements

This research is supported by a Japan Society for the Promotion of Science (JSPS) Grant-in-Aid for Scientific Research, and the Japan Ministry of Education, Culture, Sports, Science and Technology (MEXT), *Kakenhi* 18520439.

Addendum

David Chalmers briefly defines the hard problem of consciousness, and the difference between the easy problems of consciousness and the 'hard problem' (1995a, excerpted from pp. 200-202):

> There is not just one problem of consciousness. "Consciousness" is an ambiguous term, referring to many different phenomena. Each of these phenomena needs to be explained, but some are easier to explain than others. At the start, it is useful to divide the associated problems of consciousness into 'hard' and 'easy' problems. The easy problems of consciousness are those that seem directly susceptible to the standard methods of cognitive science, whereby a phenomenon is explained in terms of computational or neural mechanisms. The hard problems are those that seem to resist those methods.
>
> The easy problems of consciousness include those of explaining the following phenomena:
>
> - the ability to discriminate, categorise, and react to environmental stimuli;
> - the integration of information by a cognitive system;
> - the reportability of mental states;
> - the ability of a system to access its own internal states;
> - the focus of attention;
> - the deliberate control of behaviour;
> - the difference between wakefulness and sleep.
>
> All of these phenomena are associated with the notion of consciousness. For example, one sometimes says that a mental state is conscious when it is verbally reportable, or when it is internally accessible. Sometimes a system is said to be conscious of some information when it has the ability to react on the basis of that information, or, more strongly,

when it attends to that information, or when it can integrate that information and exploit it in the sophisticated control of behaviour. We sometimes say that an action is conscious precisely when it is deliberate. Often, we say that an organism is conscious as another way of saying that it is awake.

There is no real issue about whether *these* phenomena can be explained scientifically. All of them are straightforwardly vulnerable to explanation in terms of computational or neural mechanisms. . . . In each case, an appropriate cognitive or neurophysiological model can clearly do the explanatory work. . . .

The really hard problem of consciousness is the problem of *experience*. When we think and perceive, there is a whir of information-processing, but there is also a subjective aspect. As Nagel (1974) has put it, there is *something it is like* to be a conscious organism. This subjective aspect is experience.

REFERENCES

Abram, D. (2005). 'On the Ecological Consequences of Alphabet Literacy: Reflections in the Shadow of Plato's Phaedrus', *Aisling Magazine 32*. Available from: http://tinyurl.com/39ems4 [Accessed 12 November 2007].

Blyth, R. H. (1949-1952*). Haiku* (4 vols). Tokyo: Hokuseido.

Boldman, B. (1999). 'leaves blowing' in Cor van den Heuvel (ed) *The Haiku Anthology, 3rd ed.* New York: Norton.

Chalmers, D. (March 2008, forthcoming). *The Character of Consciousness*. Oxford: Oxford University Press.

———. (1995a). 'Facing Up to the Problem of Consciousness', *Journal of Consciousness Studies* 2(3): 200-219. Available from: http://imprint.co.uk/chalmers.html [Accessed 12 November 2007].

———. (1995b). *The Conscious Mind: In Search of a Fundamental Theory*. Oxford University Press.

Donegan, P. (1998). 'spring wind', First Prize Recipient, Yomiuri Shimbun 1998 Annual International Haiku Competition, Tokyo, Japan.

Falkman, K. (2004). 'The sweet smell' in *Ginyu 21*. Tokyo: Ginyu Press.

Gavins, J. (2007). *Text World Theory: An Introduction*. Edinburgh University Press.

Gilbert, R. (2007). *The Gendai Haiku Website*. Available from: http://gendaihaiku.com [Accessed 12 November 2007].

———. (2006). 'Kigo and Seasonal Reference: Cross-cultural Issues in Anglo-American Haiku', *Kumamoto Studies in English Language and Literature 49*: 29-49. Available from: http://tinyurl.com/2u37xf [Accessed 12 November 2007].

———. (2004a). 'The Miraculous Power of Language: A Conversation with the Poet Hoshinaga Fumio', *Modern Haiku* 35(3). Available from: http://tinyurl.com/2acz48 [Accessed 12 November 2007].

———. (2004b, revised 2008). 'The Disjunctive Dragonfly: A Study of Disjunctive Method and Definitions in Contemporary English-language Haiku', *Kumamoto Studies in English Language and Literature 47*: 27-66. Available from: http://tinyurl.com/36rgw5 [Accessed 12 November 2007].

Gilbert, R. and Yoneoka, J. (2000). 'From 5-7-5 to 8-8-8: Haiku Metrics and Issues of Emulation—New Paradigms for Japanese and English Haiku Form', Language Issues: Journal of the Foreign Language Education Center *1*. Kumamoto, Japan: Prefectural University of Kumamoto. Available from: http://tinyurl.com/3e4705 [Accessed 12 November 2007].

Gurga, L. (2003). 'forgotten for today', in *ant ant ant ant ant: issue six*. Portland, OR: Chris Gordon.

Haiku Society of America. (2004) 'Official Definitions of Haiku and Related Forms', *HSA Website*. Available from: http://tinyurl.com/354482 [Accessed 12 November 2007].

Hasegawa, K. (2007) 'Cross-cultural Studies in Gendai Haiku: Hasegawa Kai: Interview Excerpt 2', R. Gilbert (ed., trans.) *Gendai Haiku Online Archive*. Available from: http://gendaihaiku.com/hasegawa [Accessed 12 November 2007].

Heidegger, M. (2001). 'The Origin of the Work of Art', in *Poetry, Language, Thought* (Albert Hofstadter, trans), pp. 15-86. New York: Harper & Row.

Hillman, J. (2004). *Archetypal Psychology*. Dallas, TX: Spring Publications. (See particularly the sections on soul and soul-making, pp. 24-39.)

———. (1998). 'On Psychological Creativity', in *The Myth of Analysis: Three Essays in Archetypal Psychology*, pp. 11-116. Evanston, IL: Northwestern University Press.
———. (1966). 'On Psychological Creativity', *Eranos Jahrbuch 35*: 349-409.
Hoshinaga, F. (2003) *Kumaso-Ha*. Tokyo: Honami Shoten.
Jaynes, J. (1976). *Origin of Consciousness in the Breakdown of the Bicameral Mind*. New York: Houghton Mifflin.
Johnston, A. (2006). 'Narcissism and D. G. Rossett's "The House of Life"', Ph.D. thesis. *Leopold Szondi Forum (szondiforum.org)*. Available from: http://tinyurl.com/3b06me [Accessed 12 November 2007].
Jung, C. G. (1969). 'On the Nature of the Psyche', in *Collected Works Volume 8: The Structure and Dynamics of the Psyche*. R.F.C. Hull (trans.), pp. 159-236. Bollingen Series XX. Princeton, NJ: Princeton University Press.
Kacian, J. (2007). *Orbis Tertius*. Winchester, VA: Red Moon Press.
———. (2006) *Presents of Mind: Bilingual Edition* (Japanese trans., Gilbert et al). Winchester, VA: Red Moon Press.
Kerouac, J. (1958). *The Dharma Bums*. New York: New American Library.
Kyorai. (2001) 'Kyoraishô', in Isao Okuda (ed) *Shinpen nihon bungaku zenshu vol 88: Renga-ron-shu, nogaku-ron-shu, hai-ron-shu* [The new edition of the complete works of Japanese classic literature vol 88: Theories on renga, noh, and haiku], Y. Itô and R. Gilbert, trans., pp. 497-99. Tokyo: Shogakukan.
Manes, C. (1992). 'Nature and Silence', *Environmental Ethics 14*: 339-50; reprinted in Glotfelty and Fromm (eds.) *The Ecocriticism Reader* (1996). Athens, GA: University of Georgia Press.
Nagel, T. (1974). 'What is it like to be a bat?', *The Philosophical Review LXXXIII(4)*: 435-50. Available from: http://tinyurl.com/2y2ap [Accessed 12 November 2007].
Natsuishi, B. (2004). *A Future Waterfall: 100 Haiku from the Japanese*. Winchester, VA: Red Moon Press.
Perloff, M. (2002). *21st-Century Modernism: The 'New Poetics.'* New York: Blackwell.
Rush, F. (2001). 'The Availability of Heidegger's Later Thought', *Inquiry 44(2)*: 201-222.

Sato, H. (1999). 'HSA Definitions Reconsidered', *Frogpond: Journal of the Haiku Society of America 22(3)*: 71-73.
Simin, N. (2001). 'after the bombing', in Anakiev, D. and J. Kacian (eds.) *Knots: The Anthology of Southeastern European Haiku Poetry*. New York: Weatherhill.
Stockwell, P. (2003). 'Surreal Figures', in Gavins and Steen (eds.) *Cognitive Poetics in Practice*, pp. 13-26. London: Routledge.
Stockwell, P. (2002). *Cognitive Poetics: An Introduction*. London: Routledge.
Snyder, G. (1996). 'Unnatural Writing', in *A Place in Space: Ethics, Aesthetics, and Watersheds*, pp. 163-72. Berkeley, CA: Counterpoint LLC.
Trumbull, C. (2004). 'Analysis of Haiku in 12-dimensional Space', *Simply Haiku Online Journal 2(5)*. Available from: http://tinyurl.com/3cseej [Accessed 12 November 2007].
Tsubouchi, N. (2007). 'Cross-cultural Studies in Gendai Haiku: Tsubouchi Nenten: Interview Excerpt 1', in R. Gilbert (ed., trans.) *Gendai Haiku Online Archive*. Available from: http://gendaihaiku.com/tsubouchi [Accessed 12 November 2007].
Tsur, R. (2003). *On the Shore of Nothingness: A Study in Cognitive Poetics*. Exeter, UK: Imprint Academic.
Virgilio, N. (1988). 'Lily', in *Selected Haiku* (original 1963 journal publication in *American Haiku, Issue 2*). Windsor, Ont.: Black Moss Press.
Verhart, M. (2007). 'The Essence of Haiku as Perceived by Western Haijin', *Modern Haiku Journal 38(2)* (trans. from German). Available from: http://tinyurl.com/267tdy [Accessed 12 November 2007].
Wilson, R. (2005). 'Interview with Anita Virgil', *Simply Haiku 3(1)*. Available from: http://tinyurl.com/y4tya7 [Accessed 12 November 2007].
Yasui, K. (2003). *Kuhen* [Haiku Psalms]. B. Natsuishi and E. Selland, trans. Tokyo: Chûsekisha.

Section 1: Theoretical Concerns

2. Hasegawa Kai

Hasegawa Kai

INTRODUCTORY REMARKS

Japanese haiku and Japanese culture have had a profound influence on Anglo-American letters. It may be that the first truly modernist poem was a haiku or pseudo haiku penned by Ezra Pound, "In a Station of the Metro," published in 1913. This western discovery and radical advance was significantly based upon the scent of an aesthetic now some 400 years old in Japan. The great innovator Matsuo Bashô introduced a *hokku* style (haiku is the modern term) which introduced radically disjunctive acts of 'cutting through' realism in order to express consciousness. Due to a historical overemphasis upon Zen Buddhism and the Image as a *sine qua non* of Japanese haiku on the part of western interpreters, several literary and cultural elements of haiku which Bashô instituted are just now coming to light.

In the first interview segment, "Haiku Cosmos 1: Bashô's 'Old Pond,' Realism & 'Junk Haiku,'" Bashô's celebrated "old pond" haiku is examined in detail by Hasegawa Kai. This segment is a condensed summation of his main thesis presented in, *Did The Frog Jump Into the Old Pond?* ([*Furuike ni kaeru wa tobikonda ka*], Tokyo: Kashinsha, 2005), which offers a wealth of further evidence and analysis of Bashô, the history of haiku, haiku composition and conception.

This first interview segment is followed by, "Haiku Cosmos 2: Cutting Through Time and Space—*Kire & Ma*," two central concepts of the Japanese haiku aesthetic which have not yet been presented in English-language haiku studies. The term *kire* means "to cut." Bashô discussed this concept as a central tenet (please see the *Kyoraishô* translation, "Endnote 19" in the "Plausible Deniability" paper for this). The term *ma* resists easy translation when applied to aspects of nuance within the haiku aesthetic. Hasegawa here illustrates the use of *ma* by explicating a haiku by Bonchô (a disciple of Bashô). We have translated *ma* variously as: "psycho-poetic interval of betweeness," "psychological interval (of time/space)," "psychological interval of betweenenss, "between dimensions," and "the arising of psychological space"—the term resists a singular, brief translation.

Please note that parenthetical information in the transcripts indicates clarification by the translators. Example haiku with original kanji and additional commentaries can also be viewed on the accompanying DVD-ROM, and at the Gendai Haiku Website.

Hasegawa Kai—Life and Works, in brief

Personal History
Hasegawa Kai (1954–, Kumamoto Prefecture). Graduated from Tokyo University with a Degree in Law, 1976; became a reporter for the Yomiuri Newspaper and in 1993 founded his own haiku circle and journal, *Koshi*. Currently also holds a Professorship at Tokai University, and is a judge of the "Asahi Newspaper Haiku Corner." Hasegawa is a member of the Haiku Poets Association. Professor Hasegawa Kai is the author of over 20 books of haiku criticism, and is an award-winning poet. He currently holds a post at the Yomiuri Newspaper as a reviewer of haiku and other literary and cultural works, frequently serving as a judge of national haiku contests.

Publications
Haiku: *Koshi* [Old Will], 1985; *Kokû* [Empty Space], 2002; *Hatsukari* [The First Wild Goose], 2006, and others.
Literary criticism: *Haiku no uchû* [Haiku Universe], 1989; *Furuike ni kaeru wa tobikonda ka* [Did the Frog Jump in the Old Pond?], 2005; some two dozen additional critical works.

Haiku Cosmos 1:
Bashô's "Old Pond," Realism & "Junk Haiku"

Hasegawa Kai (interview), December 9, 2006
Kanagawa Prefectural Museum of Early-Modern Literature
(*Kanagawa Kenritsu Kindai Bungakukan*), Yokohama, Japan

To begin, I would like to read from my notes; and would like to talk about the *furuike* ('old pond') *ku* (an epithet for hokku or haiku) of Bashô. One reason for interpreting this classic haiku is that it offers us several relevant contemporary topics. The reason for its contemporary nature is that we are composing haiku today, and the interpretation of this haiku directly concerns our notions of composition. In other words, this haiku can function as a guide for how to compose haiku. Another reason concerns Japanese culture and social problems in Japan, and elsewhere as well—I think this haiku can offer us some suggestions.

First of all, I said this ku contains a clue to such problems; that is, how to compose haiku. In a nutshell, modern haiku after Masaoka Shiki (circa 1900) has been influenced by Western realism, and as a result haiku has become an art of realism. And the outcome of haiku compositions based only upon those things you have directly seen has been – can I coin the term, "junk haiku" (*garakuta haiku*). Haiku that contain only objective material have created a nearly stagnant situation. So, the question is, how shall we overcome realism? Bashô's haiku offers us some important clues.

Bashô's '*furuike ya kawazu tobikomu mizu no oto*' (lit. 'old pond/ frog(s) jump-in water's sound') haiku is his most popular work. And Bashô is himself the most popular haiku poet. In various countries around the world, many may not know the name of the Prime Minister of Japan, but know of Bashô. I think he is perhaps the most renowned Japanese personage, and this haiku is the most celebrated—being such a renowned work, when one says "haiku" this *furuike* ku often comes first to mind. Additionally, it has been said that it was through this *furuike* ku that Bashô found his style, known as "Shôfû." This ku has been called the 'enlightenment of shôfû,'—this sort of thinking has been in evidence for some time.

So then, Bashô's haiku has been said to be both celebrated and valuable, but on the other hand, it has also been thought of as a mysterious haiku. The reason for this is that if you interpret, "A frog jumped into (an old pond) and a-water-splashing sound occurred," the haiku becomes overt, simplistic; and we cannot discern what could be so valuable about it. People say, "ah, a good ku," sympathetically, based upon the reputation of this haiku as the "enlightenment ku" of the shôfû style, vaguely thinking of it as a good ku. Yet at the same time, no one seems to know precisely where in this ku "Shôfû enlightenment" resides.

If we consider this ku as an enlightenment of Shôfû, it must be that Bashô discovered a new cosmos via this haiku. A further point is that many of Bashô's haiku following this one were influenced by it. To sum up, it seems essential to learn how the *furuike* ku influenced his later works, although the reasons do not seem to have been well understood.

To continue, some time ago I read, *The Pine Field of Kuzu* [*Kuzu no matsubara*] a book by Kagami Shikô (1665-1731), Bashô's disciple, and found a partial record the birth of this *furuike* ku. I'll quote a little bit to you, which is written in Edo-period Japanese:

> It was the traditional time of regret for the ending of spring. There were sounds of frogs jumping into the water at intervals. From this rather inarticulate atmosphere Bashô hit on the idea of the 7-5-*on* "*kawazu tobikomu mizu no oto*" Then, *Kikaku* [a celebrated disciple] offered his suggestion of '*yamabuki ya*' [*yamabuki* is *Kerria Japonica*, the Japanese yellow globeflower] for the capping [first line] metric of 5-*on*. However, Bashô rejected this suggestion, finally deciding on "*furuike*."

This is how it was written. (In contemporary nomenclature,) "the traditional time of regret for the ending of spring" is March in the lunar calendar; late April in the modern calendar. At that time, "There were sounds of frogs jumping into the water at intervals." "At intervals" here does not mean (the frogs were jumping) 'every so often.' "At intervals" actually means that every so often Bashô *heard* jumping sounds in the distance. So, he composed, *kawazu tobikomu mizu no oto* (lit., "frog(s) jump-in water's sound"). Then Bashô contemplated what should be the capping element. Shinshi [one of Kikaku's various epithets], suggests "yamabuki" as a good cap—in other words he proposed, "*yamabuki ya kawazu tobikomu mizu no oto*" ("yellow globeflower—frog(s) jump-in water's sound"). However Bashô did not accept this, and in the end he placed on top, *furuike ya* (old pond).

The problem is, shall we trust this document? The author of this book, Shikô, is a disciple of Bashô's late period; as he did not become a disciple until after 1686, the year this ku was composed, we know he was not present at the time. However, the book's title, *The Pine Field of Kuzu*, was given to him by Bashô. This means that Bashô has in a very real sense vouched for the contents of the book. Thus, I think the record of this episode, the birth of the "*furuike*' ku, has been approved by Bashô, and that we can rely upon this evidence.

And now, the next question is, what kind of information was it that was written here? First it was written that Bashô and his disciples heard frog-jumping sounds; in other words, if Bashô had seen frogs jumping into the water he would have written what he had seen (not heard). Instead, he wrote of the sounds that met his ear. This means that Bashô hadn't seen frogs jumping into water. We can imagine Bashô in his hermitage *Bashô-an* (in Fukagawa, Edo), listening to the sound of frogs jumping into water, heard outside. Another important fact is that when we read, *furuike ya kawazu tobikomu mizu no oto* (old pond/frog(s)-jumping/sound of water), we image the ku happening in the order in which it is read; but in fact, it was first written just as: *kawazu tobikomu mizu no oto* (frog(s)-jumping-in sound of water). Moreover, sometime after, the phrase, *furuike ya* was 'capped' to complete the composition of this ku. So, this ku is not in reality consecutive. It is not: "there is an old pond and a frog jumps in and the sound of a splash," because *kawazu tobikomu mizu no oto* was written first, and *furuike ya* was only added later.

Therefore, we can say that this ku is not consecutive, and on the contrary has a break within it—there are two different levels, two different elements, intermixed. So, Bashô neither saw an old pond nor a frog. And also, there is a break between *furuike ya* and *kawazu tobikomu mizu no oto*. Examining these two ideas leads to the conclusion that Bashô was listening to the frogs-jumping-into-water-sound, and then he imaged an old pond. This means he was listening to sounds of frogs jumping into water, and a vision of an old pond arose in his mind.

The important thing is, as I mentioned earlier, if we have: "There is an old pond and the frog jumped into it and then water splashing sound"—such a consecutive ku is known as *ichibutsujitate* (the opposite of image juxtaposition: kireji (a cutting word) exists *and* the two parts of the ku logically connect; unitary image). But this ku cannot be *ichibutsujitate*; this ku juxtaposes two different material dimensions (*toriawase*): the first dimension, which is objective: "frogs-jumping-in sound," and a second, completely different dimension: "old pond."

Thus, "old pond" (*furuike*) exists in the world of mind. At the same time, "frogs jumping-in water-sound" (*kawazu tobikomu mizu no oto*)—real sounds existing in the real world—are a trigger (catalyst) for "old pond" (*furuike*). Summing up, a proper interpretation of this ku might be: on a late spring day (in the lunar calendar) Bashô was in his hermitage listening to the sounds of frogs jumping into water, and he envisioned an old pond, in mind.

In terms of interpretation, for example, interpreting the ku as: "there is an old pond and a frog jumped into it and then splashed the sound of water"—this interpretation would be of only actual things; but we can rather consider that (as explained in greater detail in Hasegawa's, *Did The Frog Jump Into the Old Pond?*), while "a frog jumped into the water" is a real fact, an "old pond" arises out of Bashô's world of mind—there is thus a juxtaposition of two alternate dimensions of being. Read this way, this haiku is not a scene composed of the viewing an object, but rather of listening to sounds, and furthermore, Bashô composed this ku via active imagination (the haiku is not *shasei*, an objective sketch).

The reality is that we have interpreted this haiku in a superficial way, without giving it deep reflection, perhaps thoughtlessly viewing the haiku image as, "a frog jumped into an old pond and then the sound of water"—this interpretation represents a misunderstanding. This haiku was written 300 years ago and it has been misunderstood for 300 years.

Haiku Cosmos 2:
Cutting Through Time and Space—*Kire* & *Ma*

Hasegawa Kai (interview), December 9, 2006
Kanagawa Prefectural Museum of Early-Modern Literature
(*Kanagawa Kenritsu Kindai Bungakukan*), Yokohama, Japan

So at this point, we have discussed the reasonable appreciation of Bashô's haiku of "old pond," the enlightened innovation of his haiku style, and how this haiku has affected or influenced the poet's style. Now, I'd like to examine the haiku's significance from the viewpoint of *kire* (cutting). As discussed,

> "noticing the sound of water that a frog jumped in, the image of an old pond arises in mind"

is a reasonable interpretation of this haiku. And on the other hand, there is the prevalent misinterpretation which has existed for quite a long time:

> "a frog jumped in an old pond and made a water sound"

What is the cause of the difference between the two interpretations? One cause has to do with the interpretation of the *kireji* (the cutting word) of "*ya*" in this haiku. To explain further, I should first discuss what a *kireji* is, and what *kire* (to cut/cutting) represents in haiku. Please look at the example (seen just below) as I have illustrated. This haiku has three 'cuts' (represented by the slash symbols):

> / *furuike ya* / *kawazu tobikomu mizu no oto* /

> / old pond / frog(s) jump-in sound of water /

(The slash marks indicate a place/action of *kire*)

So you can see, this haiku has *kire* both before and after the phrase "*furuike ya*," and also after "*mizu no oto.*" It is easy to see that there is *kire* after "furuike ya," (due to the presence of the *kireji* "*ya*.") However, "*zengo no kire* ('before' and 'after') *kire*," represented by the first and last slash marks) is harder to understand. The *kire* that is created by a *kireji* (an actual word, and orthography) is called "*ku chu no kire*" (*kire* within the main body of a haiku). So, what is the means for creating *zengo no kire*, and what kind of *kire* is it? *Zengo no kire* is the cutting which cuts a haiku from this reality within which we live—from the literal place/environment/atmosphere ("*ba*") of literal existence. In fact, this type of cutting, this type of *kire*, is quite important—but it usually goes unnoticed. However, if we do not pay attention to this type of *kire*, we cannot understand the essential nature of *kire* in haiku; and thus, what haiku is. In short, haiku is "cut out" or "cut from" this world, via this type of *kire*.

When we read a haiku which is based on some obvious context, as with *Oku no hoso michi* (Narrow Road to the Deep North, by Bashô), *zengo no kire* is easy to understand. I mean, for example, when a haiku is first introduced by a prose description (followed by the haiku), as is the case with:

natsukusa ya tsuwamono tachi ga yume no ato

summer grass—
all that remains
of warriors' dreams

Here, it is easy to understand that there are cuttings before and after this haiku (as Bashô discusses the ancient battlefield of Hiraizumi, etc., both preceding and following this haiku). On the other hand, a haiku such as *furuike ya* exists independently. As a result, the *zengo no kire* before and after this (*furuike*) haiku may be neglected (not be acknowledged or perceived).

Now, given that we find *zengo no kire*, next let us examine the *kire* occurring right after "*furuike ya*," (created by the *kireji "ya"*). Words such as *"ya"* are known as *kireji*. There are other *kireji*: *kana*, *keri*, and so on. But what effect does the *kire* or *kireji* create? The *kireji* is literally a word which cuts: cutting language. The aim of cutting is to create *"ma"* (space—'betweeness,' alternate dimension or time, a psycho-poetic interval of betweenness—non-literal reality arising as resonance, between and through words, and beyond them). *"Ma"* is the crucial effect of *kire*, and the specialized words for creating this effect are *kireji*. Due to cutting, a variety of (types of) *"ma"* arise in haiku.

So, the *kire* before the haiku (e.g. before *furuike*) creates *"ma"* between reality and the haiku. And as well, the *kire* after *"furuike ya"* creates *ma* between the old pond and the water-sound a frog jumped in. Last, the ending kire after *"oto"* creates *ma* between reality the haiku once again.

So, why do haiku exhibit *kire*, which create *"ma"* (betweenness)? In prose and some longer poetic forms, we can express many worlds using many words—but in haiku, length is limited to around 17-*on* (sounds). To express worlds equivalent to prose and beyond it, we require an inventive method, but what kind of method? We find that the technique of utilizing *kire* ('cutting') has been born, in order to fulfill such needs.

So we can see that *kire* creates *ma*. *Ma* can convey notions and qualities of depth, beyond language. Please think of Japanese plays, in this regard. In the plays, an actor speaks, and creates silence—and then speaks again. Such a method of creating *ma*—in the silence and pause—is crucial to expressing a character's grief, laughter, joy—in dimensions beyond language.

In this sense, we can consider such a method of *ma* as *a method of silence*. The same effect (as found in Japanese plays) exists in the *ma* which is created by *kire* (cutting) in haiku.

Now, let us go further into this discussion. As I explained, *ma* can express realities beyond language. Here, a question arises: what is the nature of *ma*? From the aspect of vocabulary usage, the word *ma* is used in various ways. The first meaning is related to: 'an empty place.' This sort of spatial *ma* is what Japanese people may first imagine. For example, when we go to Ise Shrine (the most important shrine of Shintoism, founded before the introduction of Buddhism in Japan), we will see the various buildings; and in the heart of the shrine, meet its empty place.

These empty places, so central to the shrine; this type of *ma* is what Japanese people may first imagine, I think. *Ma* then can thus be likened to the wellspring of a spiritual pilgrimage.

In addition, in contemporary Japan the spatial *ma* is also used in daily life. For instance, *ma-dori*: (the layout) of a room; the *ma* between supporting pillars, is such a usage. But there is another usage of *ma*, found in phrases such as: "To speak with '*ma*'" or "Please come with '*ma*.'" These usages of *ma* show the use of *ma* for time (a silent interval). So—there are *ma* of time and *ma* of space.

Furthermore, as Gilbert-sensei said, there is "psychological *ma*." This type has complex effects. For example, regarding psychological *ma*, there are sayings like: "His *ma* is bad with me, he is such a person." This saying, "*ma-ga-warui*" means literally that *ma* is (*ga*) bad (*warui*)—a very difficult Japanese idiom to explain! This "*ma*" is neither in space nor time. It means: "He and I are in different rhythm, not in accord, there is no sense of chemistry between us, etc."

Such a subtle psychological gap is expressed through the Japanese idiom *ma* (as in *ma-ga-warui*, just mentioned) implies negative capacity. As shown by this next example, there is likewise "psychological *ma*" utilized in haiku. This is the type of *ma* within a haiku (*kuchu no kire*) which is created by *kireji*: '*ya*,' '*kana*,' '*keri*,' and so on.

In truth, "*ya*," "*kana*," "*keri*" are called *kireji*, but originally they were all auxiliary verbs (and post-position particles) used to express emotion or psychological sense. Indeed, "*ya*" is a post-position particle used to express emotion, inspiration, feeling; to call to someone/something, and, the feeling of: "isn't it?"

"*Kana*" is a post-position particle which expressed admiration; and the feeling of: "ah... yes, it is."

"*Keri* " is an auxiliary verb which carried the feeling of: "inadvertently noticed, it has been."

In a like manner, we use the auxiliary verbs and post-position particles to convey these subtle psychological senses, as *kireji*.

Next, the haiku which I will show you was written by Bonchô (a disciple of Basho. (?–1714)):

akuoke no shizuku yamikeri kirigirisu

the dyeing tub
dripping ceased—
tree cricket

This haiku can be described, in contemporary interpretation, in this way: an "akuoke" is a tub for washing and dyeing clothes with an alkaline liquid dye made from ash dissolved in water. The tub has a spout, like a faucet, at its base. As a result, the contemporary interpretation of this haiku has been given as,

"Because the dripping sound has stopped, the cricket song is heard."

However, in the era of Bonchô and Basho, both the interpretation and sense of the author's intention were rather different. So, what was the original meaning? The key here is the effect of the *kireji* '*keri*' (found) in (the word) "ya*keri*."

What is the effect of '*keri*'? '*Keri*' means "inadvertently noticed, it has been ..." Therefore, in this haiku, the poet "inadvertently noticed that the dripping sound of a dyeing tub had stopped." That is, the song of a cricket was heard first; then, listening to its song attentively, the song became much clearer than a moment before. Suddenly, the poet notices the dripping sound of the dyeing tub had stopped; he had been hearing it just a moment before; he suddenly notices the absence of the sound (of the dripping).

Thus, this haiku is not a juxtaposition of two realistic scenes, as:

"the dripping sound stopped"
and then,
"the cricket song is heard."

Instead, when the poet notices the sound in the here and now, the cricket's sound—suddenly he notices the absence of the sound of the dripping ...

... the sound of nothing.

This is the realm of the mind.

So, also here, due to the effect of (the *kireji*) '*keri*,' "psychological *ma*" arrives.

In this way—via *ma*—arising from the use of *kireji* or *kire*, it becomes possible to open to and explore the nature of the world of the psyche in haiku.

Hasegawa Kai—Selected Haiku

haru no mizu towa nurete iru mizu no koto

water of spring
as water wetted
　water, as is

Hasegawa comments: Almost anything in this world can be wetted by water. However, the one thing that cannot be wetted in this way is water itself. Although water wets other things but cannot itself be wetted, I nonetheless intuit that the water of spring, uniquely, has a special quality in that it can be wetted—though it too is water.

hizakari no kono yo o sugite chô kieshi

in this world
of blazing summer sun
a butterfly disappears

hasaki yori yubi ni sukitoru hotaru kana

from the vertex of a leaf
combed into fingers, firefly

natsu no yami tsuru o kakaete yuku gotoku

summer dark
a red-crowned crane, cradled
as if on my way

fuyu fukashi hashira no naka no nami no oto

deep winter
  within the pillar
    the rushing of waves

Hasegawa comments: Following my university graduation, I began to work as a newspaper reporter in Niigata city. Toward the southwest is the seaside town of Izumozaki, which is the location where Bashô stayed, on a journey he described in *The Narrow Road to the Deep North* (*Oku no hoso michi*); there, Bashô penned this haiku:

araumi ya sado ni yokotau amanogawa

the turbulent sea—
extending to Sado isle
the milky way

In this place in the winter, strong north winds blow all day and enormous dark waves crash upon the seashore. At night, within the dwellings, each massive main pillar resounds due to the roaring sea, whose waves emanate sonically through the ground. [Note: For some 1000 years or more Sado Island was an isolate place of exile for individuals who had been deposed, disgraced, or were considered a threat by those in power.]

Section 1: Theoretical Concerns

3. Uda Kiyoko

UDA KIYOKO

INTRODUCTORY REMARKS

Uda Kiyoko-sensei, President of the Modern Haiku Association (MHA), was awarded the Japan Medal of Honor (Purple Ribbon) in 2002, conferred upon individuals who have contributed academic and artistic accomplishments to the nation at the highest level of merit. She is among the most notable of gendai haiku leaders, and more comprehensively, of literary society in Japan. She has also been active for many years as an international representative, particularly on the Asian continent, initiating cultural and artistic exchange.

A main focus in her poetic endeavors, as can be seen in her publications, concerns how we live, have lived, and will continue to live on the land. Uda recently spoke of her vision of humanity:

> The essence of what I have contemplated, spending time around Satoyama [a celebrated local rural commons, evolved from centuries of agricultural use], seems to be simple: the hope that people would be able to eat self-provided seasonal foods; the hope that people would be able to swim in rivers with drinkable water; the hope that people would be able to feed their children without emergency food provisions (as those provided by LARA), due to the devastations of war (*Satoyama saijiki: Tanbo no mawari de* [Satoyama Saijiki: Ricefield Environs], Tokyo: NHK Publications, 2004, p. 175). [LARA, the "Licensed Agencies for Relief in Asia" provided food to starving children in postwar Japan.]

Our interview took place at the Kakimori Museum-library (*Kakimori Bunko*) in Itami, just outside of Osaka. *Kakimori Bunko*, founded in 1984, houses one of the world's three major collections of haiku poetry and painting. In this interview segment, "Haiku and the Land 1: Toward the Future—A Haiku Ecology," Uda discusses an important aspect of her experience and philosophy, which concerns the roots of human civilization in agrarian society, and the integration of humanity with land, season and cycles of time within the wider ecosystem. Uda also indicates the problem of treating "place" in an affected, or as she puts it, in a "special" way, and hints that for gendai haiku to remain vibrant, it will likely need to move in a direction that incorporates the natural world and ecosystem in essential ways. In "Haiku and the Land 2" Uda comments, "At this point in time, I'm dealing with the problematics of the environment as a major theme in my haiku... so I compose haiku on this theme, as the haiku form is an excellent means for expressing such concerns.

In her haiku and criticism, as well as leadership of the MHA can be seen the continuing evolution of gendai haiku theory and technique, and a longstanding concern with the relevance of poetry to society. Uda has done much to promote women poets, and may represent one of the few poets now living who has combined ecocritical ideas and aesthetics into an innovative poetics.

Please note that parenthetical information in the transcripts indicates clarification by the translators. Example haiku with original kanji and additional commentaries can also be viewed on the accompanying DVD-ROM, and at the Gendai Haiku Website.

UDA KIYOKO—LIFE AND WORKS, IN BRIEF

PERSONAL HISTORY
UDA KIYOKO (b. 1935, Yamaguchi Prefecture), began writing haiku at the age of 19. She became a member of *Shirin* [Lion Forest], and in 1970 joined *Soen* [Grass Park], led by the

INTRODUCTORY REMARKS

haiku poet Katsura Nobuko (1914-2004). From 1976 to 1985 she acted as an editor of the *Gendai Haiku Journal* with Tsubouchi Nenten. In 1985 she became the editor of *Soen*. Uda was a founder of the Osaka Study Group on Haiku History, and is the current President of the Modern Haiku Association (*Gendai Haiku Kyôkai*), is chairperson of "NHK Haiku World," and serves as a judge on the *Yomiuri Newspaper Haiku Column* selection committee.

PUBLICATIONS

HAIKU: *Rira no ki* [Lilac Tree], 1970; *Natsu no hi* [Summer Days], 1982; *Hanto* [Peninsula], 1988; *Zô* [Elephant], 2001, and others. ESSAYS: *Tsubakuro no hibi* [Days of Swallows], 1994; *Hitoba no tegami kara* [Wartime Memories from a Stack of Letters], 1995; *Watashi no saiji nôto* [My Notes on Seasonal-agricultural Events], 2002; *Satoyama saijiki: Tanbo no mawari de* [Satoyama Saijiki: Rice-field Environs], 2004; *Ko-kigo to asobu* [Ancient Kigo, Playfully], 2007, and others. EDITOR: *Katayama Tôshi shû* [The Collected Haiku of Katayama Tôshi], 1984; *Josei haijin no keihu* [A Genealogy of Woman Haiku Poets], 2002, and others. CO-EDITOR: *Josryû haiku shûsei* [The Collected Works of Woman Poets], 1999; *Gendai haiku dai jiten* [The Encyclopedia of Gendai Haiku], 2005, and others.

HAIKU AND THE LAND 1:
TOWARD THE FUTURE—A HAIKU ECOLOGY

Uda Kiyoko (interview), August 3, 2007
Kakimori Museum-library (*Kakimori Bunko*), Itami, Hyogo

RG: In your writings, you emphasize the significance of an ecology based upon agriculture, and compose haiku based on this theme. Could you discuss your "ecological" approach to haiku?

UK: Well, concerning the actual sites of agriculture, these are not particularly special. Rice paddies and other agricultural grounds, on this planet: such places are not special places for visits, that is, on some certain day, at some certain time, in order to compose haiku; in fact, it seems that such agricultural fields have been continuously inhabited by our ancestors, for over a thousand years.

These locales have the purpose of producing food, but as well, they also cultivate human sentiment (aesthetic, ethical, etc.), within the natural habitat. This locale: it is the place where we live, and we have lived—together with dragonflies, frogs, and other living things. As well—this is the place of food: in my philosophy, food is absolutely of the greatest importance!

In any case, here is a place where water, wind, sunlight, and other elements, all of those things for life gather—this is the place of agriculture. And within it, human beings exist in exactly the same way that frogs exist. This locale is not a "special" place. Many haiku poets go to agricultural places like rice paddies, in a "specialized" way, such as for *ginkô* (an excursion for the purpose of haiku composition). However, I feel that part of my body—no—*all the cells of my body*—already exist in rice paddies. So, I think that this is an important matter.

In fact, the climate of Japan seems most suitable to the rice paddy, the ground or earth of rice plants; but not so much for wheat or barley. As you know, generally, cultures may be divided into those of rice, and cultures of wheat and barley (etc.). Wheat and barley need little water; rice wants a lot of water, by comparison. Water is very important, and vast amounts of water are held and saved in the mountains. Then, just at the time when the rice needs water (and fields are needing to be flooded), *tsuyu*, the rainy season comes. And the rice plants grow most rapidly in August, when it is hottest. There is a cycle, a vast cycle, and human beings exist within this overarching cycle. Therefore, for haiku, and haiku themes, I do not think that this activity is particularly "special." There is a sense of natural activity— as natural as breathing.

It is also true that almost all of those places which most Japanese people regard as "natural environment," are related to rice paddies, or places related to the cultivating of rice. Now, please imagine a time when all the rice paddies, and their related places, disappear. Up to this point, we have witnessed such places, without paying them any particular attention. Please imagine a time when all places of rice cultivation become mere soil, lacking plants.

And all such places of rice also play the role of dams for water storage. Rice paddies are dams, but not in the way of "Concrete Dam X," or something else man-made. Rice paddies are dams and biotopes, and I think that, likewise, this is not "special."

In this way, although we may compose haiku on very inorganic and non-representational subjects, yet there is a basis—something essential, isn't there. Yes, it seems true—. In any case, what gendai haiku has mainly explored, to the present, is human emotion and elements related to this general theme. Of course, gendai haiku also esteems scenery; that is, the so-called "natural environment" is taken as scenery, isn't it; this is also important. However, gendai haiku does emphasize human emotion and feeling, doesn't it; expressing itself with subjective creativity. Even so, the essentials of such expressions, I believe—we could say—sometimes exist as trees, as plants, as waters, as winds, and so on.

In my view, if one were to say, "gendai haiku is just: from here to there (indicates a short distance between her palms); but not—here to over there (indicates a large distance)." In my opinion, this would be a mistake.

Haiku and the Land 2:
Ecology, Haiku and the Taste of Experience

Uda Kiyoko (interview), August 3, 2007
Kakimori Museum-library (*Kakimori Bunko*), Itami, Hyogo

Having turned 60, I've been living a more "classical" lifestyle. For example, I use the *uchiwa* (a hand-held fan, for summer), and when autumn comes, I put it away. Then fold the *sudare* (an outdoor bamboo sun-shade) and roll it up. In such a manner, I also arrange autumnal colors.

As I perform these small rituals, I ponder, "Ah, how many times more will I do such things? Contemplating— how many more times shall I do such—I wrote this haiku:

hyakusai wa hana o hyakkai mita sôna

> even at a century—
> cherry blossoms met but 100 times
> the proverb goes

Though a person may live to as much as 100 years, one will only experience cherry blossoms a hundred times. I first heard of this idea from a group of elders in a rice-farming village, when I was farming rice. Farmwork for rice plants is not "everyday work." A farmer once said to me: "Ah, in this year, the amount of water is not sufficient, but we can do this task only once each year. So, however hard we work, this can work can only be done perhaps 50 or 60 times in a lifetime." Farmers live in such a manner and foster such wisdom, I feel.

So it was due to this experience that I pondered that 100 years of life ends with a hundred cherry-blossom viewings (there are such cycles). In a sense then, there is a joy that this existence can be represented in haiku as an act of poetry.

> even at a century—
> cherry blossoms met but 100 times
> the proverb goes

In such a way, haiku enables us to create experimental expressions. For instance, when an urgent situation of choice arises, it is possible to express our ambivalent mental state in an indirect way, via haiku. Sorry, if you'll allow me to show you another of my haiku, I'll present this:

sakuranbo hito hako kaô ka kau mai ka

a single box of cherries
    to buy or
    not to buy

    Cherries are an expensive fruit (here). To buy a box filled up with cherries is a challenging act in the realm of domestic economics. Haiku composition enables one to express an urgent situation of choice: the choice to buy the box or not. To buy the box—? Or not—? In this way there is also a sense of joy, in that this taste of existence can be represented in haiku, as a poetic act ... Choose the 'left' choice, or choose the "right'—Which to choose? There is an analogy: "To be or not to be." This sensibility is a fundamental principle of my approach to haiku.

    At this point in time, I'm dealing with the problematics of the environment as a major theme in my haiku. I feel that we live in the world as if living at the bottom of a vast pot of water [*mizugame*]. However, there is but a little bit left at the bottom of this pot—environmental issues—this is my preoccupation. So I compose haiku on this theme, as the haiku form is an excellent means for expressing such concerns.

    Today, water is of primary importance — water is a most important and problematic issue. In my opinion, being "global" is not fundamentally about being "multilingual," or being absorbed (fascinated) by other cultures. The most "global" issue is water: "anyone-drinkable" water.

    If clean water disappears from the Earth, this planet becomes, really—. Do you know how much drinkable water there is on this planet? What approximate percent is it out of all the water contained on this planet? 7%? 10%? I forget the exact number, but it is very, very small. Do you know the percentage?

[Itô Yûki:] Perhaps about 7% or so? [The answer is, less than 1%.]

So indeed I cannot help but feel that the water at the bottom of the pot is decreasing. When I compose a haiku about such a water pot, it is dealing with the global environmental problem of water (laughs). This is also part of the joy experienced in representing the taste of existence—in haiku. Yes, true—. However, if we take a high-handed attitude in order to deal with ecological issues as a theme, our mode of expression would likely change from haiku to another genre. As well, if unlucky, our haiku may end up as merely an incomprehensible thing.

So, when I scribe "a water pot," I would like to think that readers imagine a pot which contains water; not "the planet Earth" directly, but rather the non-abstract thing: "a vast pot filled with water."

kamezusoko ni mada mizu no aru yuyake kana

    deep in the pot
a bit of water remains—
    twilight glow

So this is a haiku which relates to the topic, I feel. Does only a small amount of water yet remain, at the bottom of the pot? Yes, this might be the sense of it—which is also joy experienced in representing the taste of existence, in haiku. Writing haiku—in fact, sometimes I dare to express my message in a naked way—this brings about yet another form of joy.

Here's (my book), *Satoyama saijiki: Rice-field environs*. The title, "rice-field environs" is not meant to indicate, "agricultural problems." Actually, for me, "rice-field environs" is a good place to meditate. Ecology . . . ecology . . .

[Itô:] "Ecology" the blurb on the book's obi-strip cover says . . .

The publisher arranged that blurb on the book, not me (laughs)! [Taking the book] Ah, yes, it's right—yes, it fits my philosophy. Actually, "rice-field environs" (as a bio-region) represents a small, local area, yet this landscape opens us to the universal. For example (the universal can be drawn) from the question, "Can the *medaka* fish [*Oryzias Latipes*, a fish commonly living in rice paddies] continue to exist or not?"

    deep in the pot
    water remains still—
    twilight
        g
        l
        o
        w

Uda Kiyoko—Selected Haiku

mugi yo shi wa ki isshoku to omoikomu

wheat—
realizing death as one color
gold

nemuri tsutsu fukai e otosu chô no hane

slumbering
drops, a butterfly wing
into a deep well

moteamasu kubi no nagasa ya nashirogan

the unmanageable length of a neck—
rice seedlings chill

(for "rice seedlings chill" see *nashirogan* below)

sanaburi no ichi nichi yuno no yu no atsuki

the day of *sanaburi*
hot springs of Yuno
the heat

(for *sanaburi* and *Yuno* see below)

teki noka kazu dake no nogiku o mochi kaeru

bringing back
wild chrysanthemum—only
the number of enemies

teppen ya kanarazu otoko ga tachidomaru

piled iron :
without doubt
men stop

NOTES

[1] *nashirogan* (a.k.a., *nawashirozamu*, *noshirogan*). In traditional Japanese rice agriculture, during the early spring farmers plant rice grains in shallow trays with soil. In this season, it often becomes chilly and wintery, and this return of cold weather is known as *nashirogan*. Farmers must care for the rice seedlings in this weather. After the young seedlings of rice have grown, they are transplanted into the rice field, and then it is flooded.

[2] *sanaburi*. A folk festival held after rice planting, in early summer. In this festival, village people summon *ta no kami* (the divine *kami* (spirit) of rice) from the heavens, and drink with the divinity. Then, after the drinking with this divinity of food, the people send the *kami* back to the divine heavens once again. This festival has two points of significance: the first is as a refreshment after the very hard work of rice planting. The other is, of course, as a sacred ritual for the divinity of food. The festival of *sanaburi* is a summer *kigo*.

[3] *Yuno*. (Yuno onsen): A famous hot spring (*onsen*) in Yamaguchi Prefecture. In historical documents, this onsen was founded in the late 16th century. In legend however it was founded by the Empress Jungû (169-269 CE).

Section 1: Theoretical Concerns

4. The Disjunctive Dragonfly

The Disjunctive Dragonfly

Introductory Remarks

Contemporary Japanese principles and techniques of haiku have yet to be properly integrated and valued in English haiku composition and thought, as the era when the English haiku itself might provide an effective, autonomous aesthetic basis for critical judgment is only beginning to arrive. Serious interest in haiku in English on the part of the wider literary community is not yet great judging by the small number of relevant journals, and the future of this fledging genre seems in question. Within American haiku groups, there has been a predilection for 'strict' traditionalist-classicist approaches based upon *shasei* stylism. This is not always a bad thing when trying to establish ground rules, definitions, and compositional guidelines for a young sub-genre. On the other hand, many published haiku are formulaic, lack authorial creativity, and possess little sense of language creativity. At this point in time, the old guard which has presided over the North American scene for some decades is being enriched and provoked, if not replaced, by new views and voices, and interest in gendai haiku arriving from Japan is part of this enlargement of the possibilities for, and valuations of, haiku in English.

The future of haiku as an English-language (and international) genre remains unclear, as there is not yet a poet in North America who has found wider recognition through the medium of haiku, and haiku may not be taken seriously as a literary genre until this occurs. Notwithstanding, haiku do not need to first become popular in order to be highly valued; anthologies and critical essays which select fresh and excellent haiku from more expansive critical viewpoints should be of benefit as the potency of this new poetic form is only beginning to be realized.

Recently, Robert Hass (Poet Laureate of the United States, 1995-98), published an edited anthology of classical haiku (*The Essential Haiku: Versions of Bashô, Buson, and Issa*, Ecco Press, 1994), which has drawn greater mainstream attention to the genre over the last decade. In November, 2007 Hass, interviewed on the topic of haiku in *Roadrunner Haiku Journal 7:4*, commented on those qualities in haiku he found influential to his compositional creativity:

> The power of the image, the power of simplicity, the power of discrimination, the implicit idea that anything can contain everything, something about negotiating nothingness in the sense of not ultimately having a place to stand (or sit) in our observation of the world (<http://tinyurl.com/2mrhw7>).

In contemplating the future of the genre in English, Hass added:

> ... Haiku is still acclimatizing itself, in this country, to the cultures of American poetry. ... In so much of poetry and thinking about poetry right now, *there is a good deal of appropriate skepticism about the assumptions behind realism as a literary mode* and therefore about the whole question of what we do when we think to represent nature. *It might be useful to let this tradition—and the range of anti-realist practices from surrealism to language poetics—enter the practice of haiku,* if only to take away the sort of easy wow! poem that tends to be the first stage of our attempts to appropriate the form (*ibid*).

The following paper, "The Disjunctive Dragonfly" offers an expansive theoretical paradigm for haiku in English, illustrated with pragmatic techniques and haiku examples. A starting point of this research was the discovery of a number of innovative haiku which had been negatively critiqued or ignored, as well as participation in discussions with talented haiku poets who expressed frustration regarding opportunities for publication in English.

The Disjunctive Dragonfly:
A Study of Disjunctive Method and Definitions in Contemporary English-language Haiku

Publication history. *Kumamoto Studies in English Language and Literature 47*, Kumamoto University, Japan (2004, pp. 27-66); adapted in *Modern Haiku 35:2* (2004, pp. 21-44); revised and updated, December, 2007 for *Blithe Spirit 18* (issues 1-3).

> Pleasure is the pleasure of the powers that create a truth that cannot be arrived at by reason alone, a truth that the poet recognizes by sensation. The morality of the poet's radiant and productive atmosphere is the morality of the right sensation.
> —Wallace Stevens (1958, p. 58)

Introduction

Over the half-century in which the literary tradition of Japanese haiku has migrated, transformed and burgeoned as an English-language literary form,[1] it is surprising to find that only a handful of primers have been published explicating haiku compositional style in any detail. Recently, closer attention has been paid to the worldwide genre, as witnessed by an upsurge in international conferences, websites and haiku anthologies. In order to further validate and exemplify haiku as expressed in English, investigations into the language-style and linguistic properties of haiku seem timely. While generalist definitions concerning the *what* (definitions of the form[2]) and *why* (e.g. historical analyses) of haiku have become familiar reading, the *how* of haiku method in English has not yet received much attention. How is it that haiku *do* what they do, particularly in English: affect the reader in a manner unlike any other poetic form? The following study seeks to address this question by examining modes of disjunction as a means of determining creative method. As well, by comparing and contrasting modes of disjunction with the prevailing concept of juxtaposition (superposition), it is hoped that ideas such as the insufficiency of the "one-image" haiku, and the limits of "proper haiku,"[3] may be re-examined.

1. Genre Definition

The Problem of the Modern

Existing haiku primers, mainstays of genre definition, are oriented toward beginner-poets, providing introductory overviews of the history of Japanese haiku, with examples of classical and late Meiji-era haiku predominating. The (neo)classical Japanese haiku up to Masaoka Shiki (1867-1902) has served as the aesthetic basis and standard model for composition—historically, such models have been sought for validation. A main element of constraint acting on contemporary haiku composition has emanated from Shiki's late 19th century compositional guidelines, somewhat ironically, as his dicta were themselves partly inspired by western realism.[4] Although there are various additional influences, nonetheless, Shiki's realist dicta for the beginner-poet regarding the composition of *shasei* ("objective sketch of life"[5]) haiku predominate, and selective editorial sensibility has also played a role in maintaining this orientation. Consequently, English-language haiku experimentation has been restricted in terms of both access and publication, as Mountain (1980, 1990) and others[6] have pointed out. The last 120 years of the *modern* Japanese haiku tradition as it might be applied and practiced has been inaccessible to poets writing in English: "*gendai*" that is, contemporary Japanese principles and techniques of haiku, have yet to be integrated and valued in English haiku composition and thought. The era when the English haiku itself might provide an effective, autonomous aesthetic basis for critical judgment has arguably yet to arrive.

GENRE EVOLUTION

The main arc of North American genre evolution begins with Henderson's 1958 *Introduction to Haiku*,[7] followed by his 1967 *Haiku in English*; arriving in 1985, Higginson's *Haiku Handbook* has been a mainstay, offering the reader a variety of English and other-language haiku, and a brief overview of modern Japanese haiku.[8] While such works have spurred the popularization of the genre, there are to date no major publications focusing on newer techniques as they have evolved over the last four decades. Perhaps because the market for haiku primers is small and skillful poets comprise an even smaller group, there has been little further development—for instance, a primer explicating *gendai* haiku approaches and aesthetics, as can be commonly found in Japan.[9] In fact, haiku techniques involving metaphor, allusion, psychological interiority, surrealism, mytheme (qualities evident in both contemporary and classical Japanese haiku) have been critiqued as improper to English haiku form, as Shirane (2000) has discussed. Over the years, "official" definitions of haiku have been challenged with little effect; through recently, fresh approaches are being considered.[10]

A comparative study[11] shows that the Haiku Society of America (HSA) journal *Frogpond* and the *Modern Haiku* journal (the two prominent, longstanding North American haiku print journals), though making recent strides regarding innovation, nonetheless offer less in the way of diversity and experiment compared to some decades past, when the continuum of haiku included notable poets outside the dedicated haiku genre, such as Allen Ginsberg and John Ashbery. Some new as well as established editorial voices have been challenging this situation, suggesting that definitive definitions of haiku may be impossible,[12] and arguing that "standard" guidelines, such as those advanced by the HSA and *Modern Haiku* are problematic (e.g. Mountain, 1980, 2003; Sato, 1999a; Gilbert, 2005, 2007).

Supporting this new trend is the fact of increasing international communication—haiku are now shared worldwide, usually through the medium of English, providing alternative ideas as well as images. A number of skilled haijin have also been evolving new techniques, some of which will be presented below.

2. APPROACHING DISJUNCTION

HISTORICAL OVERVIEW

The following brief historical examination focuses on experiential descriptions of haiku made by "two men who may be called pillars of the Western haiku movement . . ." (HSA, p. 2). R. H. Blyth writes in his *History of Haiku* that the haiku connotes "'a shock of mild surprise', a stab of enlightenment . . . . what distinguishes haiku from other forms of poetry is [its] physical, material, sensational character" (1963a, pp. 2-3). In beginning his *An Introduction to Haiku,* Harold Henderson emphasizes association and suggestion, indicating that the haiku is a poem that "has to depend for its effect on the power of suggestion," in that "only the outlines or important parts are drawn, and the rest the reader must fill in for himself" (pp. 2-3). Taken together, in their mission of delineating and explicating to the west the nature of haiku as a distinct genre of Japanese literature, three primary qualities can be discerned: shock, surprise and absence. From the inception of the English-language tradition, these stylistic determinants have presented somewhat mysterious (nonspecific) properties of disjunction, characterized by either an irruption of habitual consciousness (shock, surprise), and/or reversal of expectation (absence, lack of definite image) in the haiku aesthetic. The sense of disjunction has been subsumed in English under the concept of *kireji* (the "cutting word" a functional concept in Japanese haiku), and juxtaposition, both of which will be discussed shortly.

The idea of disjunction can be equally applied to poetry in general; what is significant for haiku are those types of disjunction used, whether there may be consistent disjunctive styles, and the frequency of occurrence and quality of instances occurring in a single haiku, versus poems in other genres. The extent to which terms such as shock, surprise and absence should properly be ascribed to Japanese haiku is a topic beyond the scope of this paper. What seems relevant to the movement in English is that the foundational terminology presented by Blyth, Henderson, and others revealed a new and exciting aesthetic—new ways of thinking about what a poem could be, and also about what a poem could be for: how it could affect the reader, bringing forth fresh experiences of reality into consciousness, in a new poetic genre.

DISJUNCTION, JUXTAPOSITION AND SUPERPOSITION

JUXTAPOSITION AND SUPERPOSITION AS DEFINED IN ENGLISH.
Disjunction is not a term historically applied to haiku. Haiku elements deemed to be semantically or imagistically non-sequential have been conceptually defined by the terms "juxtaposition," "superposition" or "superposed (section)." The most familiar term, juxtaposition, is illustrated below in the definitions of Lanoue (who has since updated his definition)[13] and Spiess (b. 1921-2002):

> Though it can be presented on the page in three lines, a haiku structurally consists of *two parts with a pause in between. Its power as poetry derives from juxtaposition of the two images* and the sense of surprise or revelation that the second image produces (Lanoue, 2003, para. 4, italics added).

> A nonideational, breath-length poem *aesthetically juxtaposing sensory images*, usually including natural existences tinged with humanity or faint humor, that evokes intuition of things' essentiality (Spiess, quoted in Gurga, 2000, p. 75, italics added).

The necessity for juxtaposition, as implied in the above definitions, rests on the use of *kireji* in the Japanese haiku; *kireji* will be discussed separately, later. "Superposition," a term advanced by Ezra Pound as a motif of Vorticism remains resonant as an influence in haiku (as in poetic thought generally). Rachel Blau Duplessis, commenting on Pound's well-known "In A Station of the Metro,"

> The apparition   of these faces   in the crowd :
> Petals   on a wet, black   bough .
>   (Pound, 1913, p. 6)[14]

debatably accepted as haiku these days, writes:

> Two discourses—documentary/social (which is abstract or realist) and lyric/poetic (symbolist) are brought into one configuration and are made to interact. "The 'one-image poem' is a form of superposition, that is to say, it is one idea set on top of another" (Duplessis, 2001, p. 89; quoting Pound, 1914, p. 467).

Duplessis suggests that "two discourses" become "one configuration" and "are made to interact." Does the concept of superposition (more or less synonymous in function with juxtaposition) alone explain why "one configuration" presumably arises in the reader's mind? What is the alchemy which welds the dialectic of "two discourses" into a "one-image poem"; what draws the two images into fusible interaction, forcing or forging coherence? It may be that coherence occurs in Pound's poem through the disjunction of images caused by what is absent. I would like next to view this poem as a near-approach to the habitually expected—the prosaic sentence—adding the missing elements needed to create normative sentence structure:

> The apparition of these faces in the crowd: [they are (like/as if)] petals on a wet black bough.

Approaching Disjunction

In the "filled in" example, although the connective phrase "they are (like/as if)" has been added to the end of line one, two separate and distinct images remain: 'apparition of faces' / 'petals on a bough.' A juxtaposition between these two images occurs due to the colon, which creates two separate (dependent, juxtaposed) clauses. However, the property of disjunction has now been practically eliminated through the addition of grammar parts: (personal-pronoun+*be*-verb[+simile]). Adding these parts *imparts a clear, overt relational identity* to the two separate images.

The point here is that superposition (or juxtaposition) alone does not *intrinsically* provide poetic power. Rather, it is the force of disjunction acting on the reader's consciousness which is the primary motif impelling successful juxtaposition. Disjunction is then, *a priori*. Notably, most haiku structures mime or deform prosaic sentence structure as a formal element, allowing for haiku play. As an aspect of this play, the experience of disjunction, paradoxically, generates or compels coherence. As can be seen in the above "filled in" example, which shows juxtaposition with only very weak disjunction, lacking disjunctive power the sense of poetry is lost. Particularly in haiku, the reader enters the disjunctive "gap" (or gaps) and in a sense re-authors the poem.

Superposition

The term "superposition" as used to describe a basis for haiku has been recently presented in English translation, via Kawamoto's *The Poetics of Japanese Verse*, which examines Japanese haiku technique, form and meter in some detail. He illustrates the primary appeal of haiku:

> The main appeal of a *haiku* lies in the operation of a dynamic segment, which—while drawing the reader's interest through powerful stylistic features—remains only a single layer that offers little indication of the poem's overall significance (or

else gives only an ambiguous clue). . . . We will refer to this part as the "base section." Similarly we will use the term "superposed section" to refer to those evocative phrases which . . . work upon and in conjunction with the base sections in order to furnish the reader with clues to the poem's overall significance. . . . A segment of the base [may] simultaneously function in the role of the superposed section (Kawamoto, 2000, pp. 73-4).

This is a refinement in the detailing of traditional haiku form which takes us further into method—a "dynamic segment," known as the base section of the haiku, draws interest, while paradoxically withholding significance—this relates well with Henderson's "only the outlines." Kawamoto incorporates the idea of absence into the dynamic segment, which "offers little indication of the poem's . . . significance" or imposes ambiguous clues. The "superposed section" is "evocative" (coherence or resolution may be implied); nevertheless, readers must arrive at their own sense of how the haiku coheres. Notably, in describing the superposed section, we find it contains not a single "phrase" but rather "evocative phrases:" there is a notion of plurality. As well, "a segment of the base may function in the role of the superposed section"—this description invites a conception of superposition as a technique that is motile, nuanced and diverse, when compared with other extant descriptions in English.

As Kawamoto indicates, juxtaposition alone is not enough to confer poetic power. Incompleteness, absence and ambiguity are necessary; these are among the properties impelling disjunction. Because modern haiku is primarily text-based, the means for creating disjunction involves the application of literary-poetic techniques.

Having parsed and contrasted in brief the concepts of disjunction and juxtaposition, it might be asked, if disjunction is in principle more fundamental than and necessary to coherence than juxtaposition in haiku, therefore in terms of the action of the haiku on reader consciousness, is it possible for a haiku to possess little or no imagistic *juxtaposition* (for instance, in a so-called "one-image" haiku), while retaining a strong sense of *disjunction*? And further, is it possible to create haiku of excellence in this manner? In the next sections, a number of examples will be provided. First, an exegesis of a "one-image" haiku will follow, presenting four primary disjunctive types; Section 4 will offer a typological nomenclature with haiku examples of 13 additional disjunctive techniques (making a total of 17 types).

The term "one-image" is a bit of a misnomer, as in most cases the reader can find more than one image in such haiku. As applied by Spiess, "single image" (1976, p. 27) or "one-image" haiku, imply something rather different than Pound's sense of image-overlay, as discussed by Duplessis. One of the basic requirements for the English-language haiku, as heretofore editorially determined, has been the necessity for the polar "juxtaposition of two [and only two] entities" (Spiess, 2001, p. 60); that is, objects or images in the poem. Single (or one-) image haiku, and other types as well, do not accede to this juxtapositional requirement. The topic will next be considered from the perspective of disjunction.

3. The Disjunctive Dragonfly

In this section, a "one-image" haiku by Jim Kacian (Kusamakura International Haiku Contest, 2003: Third-place Prize), will be analyzed:

my fingerprints
on the dragonfly
in amber

The 'dragonfly' haiku contains a selection of elements based on an inward poetic aesthetic. The main images are novel and captivating; in terms of images alone, this is a fine microcosmic *shasei*, much in the manner Shiki has elucidated, as at first glance the haiku presents a realistic impression. However, this haiku goes beyond *shasei* and realism, utilizing four semantic modes of disjunction: 1) <u>perceptual disjunction</u>; 2) <u>misreading as meaning</u>; 3) <u>overturning semantic expectation</u>; and, 4) <u>linguistic oxymoron</u>. We can find no *kireji* or clearly defined "traditional" juxtaposition of images; in its form, the haiku is strikingly similar to a simple declarative sentence. What makes this short declaration an excellent haiku?

    Semantically, haiku often mime or deform prosaic sentence structure (a proposition or complete thought, as discussed in Pinker, "Section 2," 1994). It may be said as well that a sentence (proposition) need not be formed only of prose. At the beginning of a sentence, we habitually recognize a noun following a first-word pronoun as subject (e.g., "My fingerprints ..."), and then look for a verb; last, an object. This structure follows the SVO grammar of English. 'Dragonfly' puns upon or irrupts habitual constructions of the textual proposition in several ways. First, "my fingerprints on the dragonfly" is a highly idiosyncratic imagistic collocation—fingerprint-on-dragonfly approaches the surreal, the monstrous, or the taxidermic. In any case, the image is an irruption of naturalism. At the same time, the reader's suspension of disbelief is sorely tested. Perhaps we misread the collocation? Overall, the play between reading and misreading, between the plain existence of nouns as known things, and the strangeness (alternativity, idiosyncrasy) of collocation creates a *perceptually disjunctive* tension, resulting in a form of semantic paradox which can be called *misreading as meaning*, as the process of misreading, in itself, powers the reader's poetic experience and the poem's significance. Actually, misreading as meaning occurs at a number of levels in the poem, as will be further illustrated.

    Next, *semantic expectations* are overturned. As mentioned,

at the beginning of a simple declarative sentence, is familiarly found a noun following a first-word pronoun (the subject) then the verb, last an object (e.g. "Her shoes are black.": pronoun+subject noun+verb+object). So, the subject (fingerprints) of the haiku needs or seeks a verb and an object. The second line ("on the dragonfly") may (impossibly) take on a verbal quality, due to expectation, or becomes simply a question mark, an unknown, while in the third line there is a definitive preposition and strongly placed object ("in amber"). Semantically then, "fingerprints...in amber" may tend to be what is first cognized as a subject-object pair. This is the implicit semantic expectation. But, how can a fingerprint be in amber, which is often thought of as a kind of rock. Does the poet *really* mean inside, within? We expect that fingerprints, which can only exist in relation to surfaces, be *on* and not in them. So, the fingerprints (as subject) carry definitive existence, yet semantic expectations are overturned, as the relational object (in amber) is in doubt.

This haiku acts like a set of nested Chinese boxes. There are layers of image-schemas, each created by an active misreading. Experiencing the misreadings is great reading fun, creating a subtle nuanced humor, which does not diminish over several re-readings—as habitual language expectations tend to reassert themselves strongly. The world created by the haiku seems to hover between the realistic and fantastic or surreal. The haiku idea gradually congeals much like tree sap into amber, as attention is clarified, caught, and fixed within, the poet's fingerprint upon it, as the dragonfly becomes the subject of "in amber" and we realize that the fingerprints only *seem* to be on the dragonfly, as the poem's protagonist gazes acutely through the translucent gold substance, perceiving both fingerprints and dragonfly in an overlaid landscape, the prehistoric dragonfly within translucent amber. The reader's semantic process crystallizes as a metaphor of the geologic processes of deep time to which the poem alludes. This reading process may take only a few seconds, yet the disjunctions remain as landmarks or "markers," indicating coherence.

The process of entering and absorbing this haiku is multiple, full of accident, incident and play. As with many of Kacian's haiku, typical descriptive analytical devices such as the parsing of fragment and phrase, juxtaposition, etc., seem reductive, if applied as formal determinants. In fact, we can locate no precise *kireji* (cutting word) or juxtaposal polarity. An additional nuance of disjunction has to do with the prepositional grammar, as the relational image "fingerprints...amber" normatively takes the preposition "on" (i.e. "my fingerprints are on the amber"). This is *linguistic oxymoron*, in the sense that fingerprints are ascribed to being on a dragonfly, and a dragonfly is ascribed to being in a rock—not where they are usually found, in haiku language or the natural world of the outdoors. There is a dual-disjunctive quality of linguistic oxymoron concerning the neighboring prepositions "in" and "on": "fingerprints on a dragonfly" is bizarre, while fingerprints in a dragonfly might be horrorshow. Haiku pun within the haikai tradition, done in a contemporary manner, the ironic humor deepens, as misadventure interweaves with lucent amber and deep time; poetic elements and imagistic layers clash and fuse, impelled by strands of misreading.

There are several varieties of disjunction used in excellent haiku, and perhaps additional modes could be teased from the above example. Importantly, disjunction is not, strictly speaking, paradox or juxtaposition, because the effects are not cognitively dualistic—the alchemy is that of *impossibles*. Disjunction, as intended, serves to indicate a poetic process happening in the reader's consciousness—disjunction is motile, having no fixed point of realization. Disjunctions appear and fall away, alternately reveal and hide themselves, depending upon the moment of reading.

4. A Typology of Disjunction

Space does not permit a lengthy demonstration of disjunctive typology. It is hoped that the manner of discovery presented here could be easily enough applied by the sensitive reader or poet—readers are no doubt natively aware of disjunction in haiku, but have not had an available nomenclature to articulate types. In addition to the four types described above, 1) <u>perceptual disjunction</u>; 2) <u>misreading as meaning</u>; 3) <u>overturning semantic expectation</u>; and 4) <u>linguistic oxymoron</u>, the following 13 types propose additional categories. Each set of examples is preceded by a category "signpost" titling the most prominent disjunctive quality (as haiku typically contain more than one "moment" and type of disjunction), followed by a brief comment:

5) <u>Imagistic Fusion</u>

> my head in the clouds in the lake
> (Ruby Spriggs in Kacian et al, 1998)

> the shadow in the folded napkin
> (Cor van den Heuvel, 1977)

> forgotten for today by the one true god autumn mosquito
> (Lee Gurga in Gordon, 2003)

> autumn mist oak leaves left to rust
> (Marlene Mountain, 2003)

Imagistic fusion compresses semantic meaning, images, rhythm, and sometimes orthography, irrupting the reader's habitual means of parsing grammar, phrases and images. The disjunctive aspect fuses disparate images into one complex, while at the same time, paradoxically, creating separations due to reading/misreading. So, "head-clouds-lake" in Spriggs becomes a multiple reflection of self as experienced in the evoked scene, *and* cross-layering of: / sky / self-as-mirror-image / water / *and* consciously remains text, due to the extreme brevity and velocity obtaining in the rapid rhythm and short line. It seems van den Heuvel's "the shadow in the folded napkin" hovers in its own shadow: as though the text shadows its representation—imagistic fusion combines with one-line brevity to create a sense of insubstantiality in the read text. A unique, collocatively fused image, "one true god autumn mosquito," and the introjection of "the one true god" as subject is highly disjunctive in Gurga; semantic expectation is artfully reversed as the poem's object remains unknown until the last word of this longer one-liner; and, what variety of space-time is "today" for a god? This haiku (as with many here) exhibits disjunct temporality. The fusion of the abrupt and impossible collocation, "mist oak" creates strong disjunction in Mountain—a nuanced sense of misreading rapidly evolves, aided by the repeating strong-weak cohesive rhythmic pull of (to emphasize): "*autumn* mist *oak* leaves *left* to *rust*." Imagistic fusion works quite effectively with the single line and shorter haiku, as the velocity of the eye scanning across the text enhances the technique.

6) Metaphoric Fusion

> the river
> > the river makes
> of the moon
> > > (Jim Kacian in Mainichi Shimbun, *Anthology*, 1997)

In this unusual example, the (seeming) juxtaposition of the first-line fragment with the following phrase is irrupted as one discovers the first line is not the alpha but rather the omega-point of the poem (reversing semantic expectation). A second reading may yield a sense of three disjunct fragments without juxtaposition (a poem made only of fragments). Considering the last two lines as the phrasal element (the superposed section), out of what seems textually and imagistically to be two rivers and their juxtaposition, a fusion arises as synthesis: the naturalistic river in the second line metaphorically "makes" of the moon a second river (the river of the first line); finally, natural and metaphoric images combine, resolve and fuse into the traditional image of moon on water: moon river on "river" river. In this way, a poem which at first glance may seem elemental and static releases a flowing metamorphic power, quite in keeping with its riverine imagery; a highly nuanced haiku, informing our understanding of the relationship between realism and metaphor. Experiencing this haiku, readers may find it difficult to understand proscriptions which warn against the use of metaphor. Metaphor has created some of the very best English-language haiku, when evoked through the sense of disjunction rather than through grammar parts.

Another example of metaphoric fusion occurs in Virgilio's "lily" haiku further below, which uses the disjunctive technique of rhythmic substitution to impel the imposition of an "impossible" metaphoric reality — this haiku has for some decades been considered among the most influential in the tradition.

7) Symmetrical Rhythmic Substitution

    letting
        the cat in
        the fog in
                    (Vincent Tripi in Ross, 1993)

    an empty elevator
    opens
    closes
                    (Jack Cain, 1969)

Rhythmic repetition combines with lineation, creating

disjunctions yielding a light, humorous effervescence. In the above examples brevity also plays a role. "Substitution" refers to word substitutions occurring in symmetrically repeated rhythmic patterns. Neither of these haiku contain *kireji* in the traditional sense. Rather, the symmetrical substitution evokes a quality of superposition (image layering) and jump-cut, filmic "snapshot" action, as cat/fog, and opens/closes arise both as identities (two sides of the same coin), and are paradoxically separated by the disjunctive "jump cut" technique. These haiku contain not one but two juxtapositions, of varying intensity.

8) <u>Concrete Disjunction</u>
    (orthography, punctuation, placement), and
9) <u>Rhythmic Disjunction</u>

    a barking dog
    little bits of night
                    breaking off
                        (Jane Reichhold in Ross, 1993)

    fog.
    sitting here
    without the mountains

                      (Gary Hotham in Kacian et al, 1998)

    stuck to the slab
    the   i
    of the frozen f sh

                    (David Steele in Kacian et al, 2002)

There have been numerous orthographic concrete experiments relating to lineation, phrase, word, and letter placement. The above haiku were chosen for ease of reproduction on the page, as well as effectiveness. Reichhold's haiku extends the idea of *kireji* past the breaking point, to create a broken-off fragment—the concrete disjunction pulls the image/line fragment back into the poem. Beyond the obvious orthographic pun, the broken-off third line has a sonic dimension as "breaking" has assonant rhyme and similar rhythm to "barking," so it seems the broken night is, at the same time, the "bark bark" of a dog. This is emphasized by the circularity of the poem, which knits together the broken fragments of both "night" and the third line. Hotham's haiku seems at first glance to have merely replaced the usual dash or colon signifying *kireji* with a period. However, the use of a period for *kireji* in the first line is idiosyncratic and creative. Its use, combined with extreme concision, propositionally yields a one-word, three-letter sentence. Thus the fog, as a resonant image, splits off from the rest of the haiku, returning to settle as elemental weather all about the following phrase. In Steele's haiku the 'i' (eye) of the fish seems to be misplaced! Each of these haiku has a strong sense of rhythmic disjunction, a natural consequence of concrete disjunction.

10) **The Impossibly True**

>A spring cliff—
>in my cup
>tears of a bird
>
>>(Koji Yasui, 2003)

>Lily:
>   out of the water . . .
>   out of itself.
>
>>(Nicholas Virgilio, 1963)[15]

>Sucking in the blue sky
>a cicada hole
>disappears
>
>>(Natsuishi Ban'ya, 1999)

The introjection of an "impossible" image may be one of the distinct features separating *gendai* haiku style from the *shasei*-oriented neo-classical: realism is imploded. Or is it?

Realism itself is a form of appearance, as the the "real" is given not only by objective sensation (hearing, seeing, touching, etc.), but also by the way in which sense data are synthesized in consciousness to create "real" experience. Just as a dream can be sensed as vivid reality, it is not only the "outer" senses alone that dictate "the real." Internalized judgments ("stances"), subtle though they may be, existentially validate experience. Poetry in its widest sense deforms or irrupts habitual literalism—challenging or irrupting habitual validations of the real. In the school of Archetypal Psychology, James Hillman discusses the ego (the sense of the literal "I") as the literalizing function of the psyche — stating that the ground of psychic life is non-literal. Hillman advances the intriguing psychological notion that mind is fundamentally poetic and metaphoric in nature.[16] This may be good news for poets, providing a clue as to why haiku often impart a powerful and nearly instantaneous reality-sense. As well, what may be taken as literal reality by one culture, or one individual, may not be literal (that is, "real") to another—haiku "realism" is not ultimate truth, or a best representative of sincerity (*makoto*) by any means, as some critics have implied.[17]

What the above haiku provide is an imagistic paradox generating a deeply inward psychological, philosophical and/or mythic contemplative sense. The key disjunctive aspect in these haiku lies in the cutting edge between the reader's knowledge of the impossibility of the superposed images and the contrary sense, brought by poetry, that the resultant whole is real (true) and believable. Literal and metaphoric sensibilities cannot entirely merge (except mystically or pathologically), yet paradoxically, in these haiku they present as coterminous. Haiku of the impossibly true reveal that real-ism is a subset of reality. It is notable in this regard that "poets such as Wallace Stevens use the word 'reality' without shame, acknowledging that 'its connotations are without limit.'"[18] Incorporating realism within a larger field, haiku of the "impossibly true" penetrate to the deeper layers of identity and self, providing a glimpse of the ground of poetic being—"poems that create a truth that cannot be arrived at by reason [or realism] alone" (Stevens, 1958, p. 58).

11) Displaced Mythic Resonance, and
12) Misplaced Anthropomorphism

> I shall help the dawn
> give birth
> to its colors
>
> (Alain Kervern in WHA, 2003)

> Entering a dream
> of that Great Fish of the South
> wanting to cry out
>
> (Natsuishi Ban'ya, 1999)

> coming to rest
> the tossed pebble
> takes a shadow
>
> (Bruce Ross in Kacian, 1998)

Living in an age of logical positivism we live in an age between myths, an idea Joseph Campbell pursued in his last work, *Inner Reaches of Outer Space*, suggesting that the future holds a return to mythic thinking which will incorporate science within its wider skein. Poetry easily enters the mythic dimension, as its roots are preternaturally archaic—poets continually return to origins, do "violence" to language (irrupt, deform), in order to "give purer meaning to the words of the tribe" (Mallarmé, 1999, p. 92), an idea discussed at length by Octavio Paz (1991). Mythic *resonance* in haiku is displaced because our cultural concepts of the real tend to determine helping "the dawn give birth" or the "Great Fish of the South" as idle fancy, yet haiku form and intention gives these motifs something more: a mythic landscape evinces belief, perhaps subconsciously. One of the dynamic properties of haiku is the ability to rapidly, shockingly irrupt habitual thought. Here, this poetic power becomes marvelous, as fundamental cultural assumptions are challenged by a deep, some would say healing, archaism. Helping "the dawn give birth" hints at shamanic reality, while a "tossed pebble" anthropomorphically "takes a shadow" for its own, as if possessing autonomous will. While this image may be attributed to a naïve sense of childlike projection, it is the disjunctive, paradoxical sense of the image being both a kind of fancy and sincere seeming that allows the anthropomorphic metaphor to rise above pathetic fallacy. The act of "taking" in the Ross haiku provides a stronger anthropomorphic sense than animism might allow (see "Elemental Animism" below); in such haiku, whenever a natural element possesses an anthropomorphic aspect it will also inherently exhibit the quality of animism.

Each of these haiku contains both mythic and anthropomorphic qualities, though to differing degrees. The Natsuishi haiku is primarily mythic: the protagonist enters a dream of the mythic image itself. This sort of haiku has been repeatedly dismissed as "deficient" due to reliance upon the surreal (*viz.* lacking in substantial, believable images to base sensation upon); however, the impact and effective evocation of a realized mytho-archaic reality is undeniable. The haiku succeeds in presenting a novel mythic aspect of "the impossibly true."

13) The Unsatisfactory Object

> Athlete's foot itches—
> still can't become
> Hitler
>
> (Hoshinaga Fumio, 2003)

> leaves blowing into a sentence
>
> (Bob Boldman in van den Heuvel, 1999)

In these haiku, the object cannot possibly satisfy the subject. Beyond the obvious pun, Hitler, an object of both "athlete's foot" and the implicit "I" in Hoshinaga's haiku, stretches the subject-object continuum. The playfully dark, ironic metaphor of "becoming Hitler" remains disjunctive, allowing a sense of depth to enter the haiku, partly created through allusion (a quality heretofore proscribed for haiku). Due to itchy feet, the author cannot smartly click his heels or march in goose-step: the poem presents a disturbing psychosocial complex indicating the will to power or assumption of dictatorial authority hidden in persons or society (and confessional poet). In Boldman, the naturalistic reality of leaves blowing into a shape, say a line, would be a curiosity; the conversion of matter into pure semantic being stretches the sense of subject-object agreement. Both of these haiku through their use of unsatisfactory objects activate intertextual metaphor, a sense of metaphor which is neither implicit in the text nor semantically conclusive.

14) <u>Pointing to the Missing Subject</u>

>   he said he could not gather
>   peonies in meadows—
>   Geraldine does not live
>   (Shyqri Nimani in WHA, 2003)

>   counting down the goodness of man:
>   from the sixth
>   obscure
>   (Hoshinaga Fumio, 2003)

The focal-point of these haiku seems to be on a subject that is either indistinct or missing: the subject is not allowed or able to solidify or cohere. A very difficult technique, as an indistinct subject will in general create a haiku lacking in poetic direction—it will be unclear what images to base sensation upon. In the first haiku, a "not" at the top and bottom of the poem frame the peonies with absence. The suddenness of the name of the departed as the first word in line three shocks: the name is both a presence and absence. The subject "he" cannot be imaged (is unknown); as well, the sudden shift from passive/past to active/present voice is irruptive. In this meditation on death, the mentioned yet missing subject reaches us beyond image or name—an offering to life attended by deeply felt tragic emotion. Hoshinaga's haiku, ending with "obscure" seems to echo with multiple dimensions of obscurity—of goodness and its measurement, of finding goodness, and the sense that in the human realm, such findings are uncomfortably moot. The obscurity of the subject is instigated from the unusual syntax of the leading phrase "counting down the goodness," an idiosyncratic collocation combining the act of counting with an uncountable noun, an ironic linguistic pun (linguistic oxymoron). "Sixth" is significant: it is "definite," a whole number, but to what type of subject does it refer, exactly? Again the successful use of allusion is seen in Hoshinaga's style. The mystery of the subject as well as the sense of profound question in the haiku keeps the reader involved.

15) <u>Semantic Register Shift</u>

> winter
> in a world of one color
> the taste of peaches
>
> (Wendy Smith in Kacian et al, 2002)
>
> in my ordinary clothes
> thinking ordinary thoughts—
> peach blossoms
>
> (Hosomi Ayako, in Kacian et al, 1997)

Here the linguistic concept of register shift (register, i.e. when context results in a commonly recognizable speech style) is borrowed, to indicate a sudden, irruptive shift in the perceptual landscape of the haiku. Haiku normatively have juxtaposition, which also creates a sudden conceptual shift, but in this case, semantic register shift implies something more innovative. In Smith's haiku, the fragment *and* first line of the phrase (the first and second lines) lead to a vast world of white snow (or simply, white), but the last line creates a semantic/perceptual shift from seeing to taste, winter to summer, white to peach, external to internal: changes of semantic register. Similarly, the symmetrical rhythmic substitution occurring in the first two lines of Hosomi's haiku moves from the skin (clothes) of the body to psychological interiority, and in the last line irrupts into the unadorned, exterior blossom. In both haiku, the disjunction of semantic register shift lends resonance to an exotic poetic fusion: there is winter, white, in the taste of peaches; "ordinary mind" clothing peach blossoms.

16) <u>Elemental Animism</u>

> Between two mountains
>   the wings of a gliding hawk
> balancing sunlight
>
> (David Elliott in van den Heuvel, 1999)

> last piece
> of a jigsaw puzzle . . .
> filling in the sky
>
> (John Stevenson, in Kacian et al, 2001)

> clouds
> blowing off the stars
>
> (Penny Harter in van den Heuvel, 1999)

Elemental animism is somewhat related to displaced mythic resonance and misplaced anthropomorphism, in that natural elements such as clouds, trees, weather, stars, etc., which are habitually taken in western culture as dead, without soul, inanimate, become animated. The quality of animation may be subtle, as in Elliott's haiku; the hawk simply does "something" with sunlight, as the poet or reader perceives it subjectively. However, there is a nuance—the verb also ascribes to sunlight the improbable quality of being balanced (as a compound noun), which, lying autonomously in the third line, lends a subtle sense of animism. Likewise, the improbability of the sky being "filled in" creates animistic nuance. Last, the more overt pun of "clouds blowing off...stars" carries an anthropomorphic as well as animistic aspect—one "elemental" acting animistically upon another.

17) Irruptive Collocation

Table 1 lists unusual, idiosyncratic and creative collocations occurring in the 26 haiku presented above:

TABLE 1. EXAMPLE COLLOCATIONS

Word Collocations	Phrasal Collocations
mist oak fog. sitting cicada hole sixth obscure balancing sunlight	fingerprints on the dragonfly god autumn mosquito tears of a bird out of itself help the dawn takes a shadow sucking in the blue counting down the goodness

Collocational function in haiku is the subject of a separate study; preliminary results indicate that unusual, creative and idiosyncratic collocations occur at a higher frequency per total number of words in the haiku genre than in any other poetic form. The usage and frequency of unusual or idiosyncratic collocational types may be a defining feature. In whatever type of literature, such collocational types, particularly idiosyncratic and creative types, are disjunctively irruptive in function.

DISJUNCTIVE QUALITIES

In this paper, 17 disjunctive types have been presented. They are shown in Table 2, along with a tentative functional definition of disjunction:

TABLE 2. DISJUNCTION: FUNCTIONAL DEFINITION AND TYPES

DEFINITION	Disjunction: The root-semantico-linguistic principle impelling juxtaposition, superposition, possessing multiple types, each related to specific poetic and formal functions and techniques which irrupt habitual consciousness and concept; may supervene more traditional functional stylism, such as fragment/phrase, juxtapositional dualism, *kireji*.
DISJUNCTIVE TYPES	
1) Perceptual disjunction 2) Overturning semantic expectation 3) Misreading as meaning 4) Linguistic oxymoron 5) Imagistic fusion 6) Metaphoric fusion 7) Symmetrical rhythmic substitution 8) Concrete disjunction 9) Rhythmic disjunction	10) The impossibly true 11) Displaced mythic resonance 12) Misplaced anthropomorphism 13) The unsatisfactory object 14) Pointing to the missing subject 15) Semantic register shift 16) Elemental animism 17) Irruptive collocation

5. DISJUNCTION, SEMANTIC KIREJI AND HAIKU FORM

SEMANTIC KIREJI: DYNAMISM AND INTERTEXTUALITY

As has been shown in the above examples, disjunctions, whether they are metaphoric, collocational, imagistic, orthographic, rhythmic, mythic, existential, etc., create in the reader's mind what may be termed *semantic kireji*— irruptive elements that create degrees of dislocation, segment images, pose absences, or delimit mere outlines, thereby impelling juxtapositions (plural as well as singular).

Notably, such juxtapositions may rest upon "impossibles" rather than polarities between image-complexes. As Kawamoto suggests, that most important technical aspect, interplay of dynamism and significance, may occur intertextually, a process occurring in the dynamic space *between* reader and poem.

The dynamic of disjunction affects the action of metaphor and allusion; these generally succeed as intertextual implications, rather than being overt (in haiku, the addition of the terms *like* or *as (though/if)* are usually unsuccessful). Haiku dynamically cohere through disjunction, and generally speaking do not avoid, temper or support disjunction with conceptual "handles" such as overt simile, metaphor, explanation, or philosophizing; techniques commonly found in other poetic forms. As a result, by disjunctively irrupting habitual thought in a highly concise manner, haiku achieve a powerful contextual paradox, challenging the literal and engaging an active re-authoring of the poem by the reader.

SEMANTIC KIREJI: EMULATION AND SENSIBILITY

Emulation and imitation are dissimilar.[19] When Blyth and Henderson translated the Japanese haiku, they usually replaced the *kireji*, an evocative Japanese *word*, with punctuation, or utilized lineation alone to indicate the cutting word. Direct imitation of *kireji* is not linguistically possible for English haiku; however, an application of analogues miming the function of the original is, obviously, possible. By emulation is meant *mimesis*, literally, the replication of the "animate sense," sensual life, or psycho-somatic activity residing in the original.[20] Virgilio's "lily" haiku uses a colon *and* stretched ellipsis *and* a period, creating a secondary pause after the second line, and then ending with a final stop. We can appreciate how well this works in English, yet it has no linguistic counterpart in Japanese: an example of a creative approach to *kireji*, arriving in a new language.

A variety of novel techniques have likewise been applied in English relating to modes of *semantic kireji*—a sense of "cutting (word)" which arrives through (usually multiple) disjunctive qualities. Looking through haiku journals, there are a substantial number of haiku without punctuation—*kireji* is signaled from within the text. Because the division caused by "traditional" *kireji* rests upon processes of irruption and disjunction, one can look to these deeper fundaments, in terms of emulation. What is relevant is that a "B-should-equal-A" type of direct-imitative analogue—the replacement of, say, a (Japanese) *ya* with a dash, or lineation—may be effective, but it is only one possible mode of emulation, and not necessarily the "model" emulation, if there is a desire to emulate mimetic sense—the spirit of the original, rather than the flesh.

6. Expansive Definitions

Disjunction as Literary Dialogue

Considering the wider field of poetic literature in English, as an imported literary form, haiku has remained on the margin, though the haiku aesthetic is found by innuendo, as haiku has had a major impact on the arts. Nonetheless, core issues of haiku, such as the manner in which the haiku aesthetic relates with poetic form, have often been discussed using exclusionary Japanese terminology with reference to (neo)classical Japanese models. Such practices have created an intellectual chasm, orphaning the genre. Viewing haiku through the lens of disjunction allows for greater relationship and colloquy with the literary world, without the need to limit comparative poetic models outside the haiku genre to the "near haiku" (a.k.a., haikuesque). For example, a disjunction of "unsatisfactory object" can be found in the following excerpts (1) and (2) of poems by two Hispanic poets:

Like wet cornstarch, I slide
past my grandmother's eyes.
                    (1) (Lorna Dee Cervantes in Purves, 1993)

in your home
we were cast
as rugs

sometimes
on walls
                    (2) (Francisco Alarcón in Purves, 1993)

In the first two lines of Cervantes' poem "Refugee Ship," "slide" has several layers of meaning, in terms of who's doing the sliding (the grandmother or the poet), and of allusion; in Alarcón's "Letter to America," the same disjunctive technique catalyzes poetic power. In both cases, the direct use of simile and metaphor is evident. Poems (3) and (4) below have been recently published in *Noon: Journal of the Short Poem*, whose editorial landscape extends the haiku form into the short poem, and the converse, anthologizing what may be a new poetic genre, as well substantiating the influence of haiku principles and techniques in contemporary poetry:

stone

mirror
fogged with
breath

of stone.
                    (3) (Glass, 2007)

brightening after rain—
pale marks
on the grimy whitewashed wall
where rungs were
before the ladder was thrown away
                    (4) (Rowland, 2007)

In Glass, subject becomes object as "mirror" is sandwiched into the middle-distance of the poem, time, and space of the uroboric "stone" presenting a disjunction of "unsatisfactory object." In Rowland (4), the missing subject (ladder rungs) appears as a *memento mori*. The sense of disjunctive gap is heightened through temporal disjunction between the first and last lines.

These poems are not haiku, yet similar disjunctive techniques are shared with the haiku form. Finding additional examples of continuity may provide for the cross-pollination and hybridization of genres, aiding exploration and experimentation. As well, further studies of the English haiku may yield unique perspectives illuminating other genres.

MAKING IT NEW

Those involved in appreciating and composing haiku have long been dedicated to the haiku spirit, as Bashô first exemplified. Ideas of disjunction, particularly as methods that supervene stricter views of juxtaposition (one-image haiku, *kireji*, etc.), will not appeal to everyone. And there is a danger in losing poetic power through arbitrary definition, in poetic containers which do not properly support haiku form. Strong or multiple disjunction can certainly produce terrible poetry. Disjunction, a variety of sensed qualities and techniques, only becomes effective via poetic creativity. The goal of introducing the concept of disjunction is not to supplant traditional practice, but add dimension, and allow for a wider range of variation and experiment—in keeping with the spirit of Haruo Shirane's definition of haiku:

> Echoing the spirit of Basho's own poetry . . . *haiku in English is a short poem, usually written in one to three lines, that seeks out new and revealing perspectives on the human and physical condition, focusing on the immediate physical world around us, particularly that of nature, and on the workings of the human imagination, memory, literature and history.* . . . this definition is intended

both to encourage an existing trend and to affirm new space that goes beyond existing definitions of haiku (Shirane, 2000, p. 60).

Looking at the haiku presented in Sections 4 and 5 above, it can be seen that they diverge in various ways from the prevailing definitions of haiku (illustrated in Section 2). As Shirane indicates, it seems timely to open the form.

DISJUNCTION AND THE SENSE OF DEPTH

While there is much to be garnered from the Japanese tradition, the English-language tradition has arisen in a separate literary environment, with its unique influences, needs and concerns. This paper has sought to address the problematics of definitional restriction, technique, and validation of the contemporary English-language haiku through an examination of disjunctive modes, for the purpose of providing new analytical and compositional perspectives. Disjunctions cut across fragment/phrase and formal *kireji* parsing: a haiku may cohere through its disjunctive attributes alone. Disjunction invites supra-realist possibilities—the contextual field is as wide as consciousness: disjunctive magnetism and the play of disjunction-versus-coherence is a taproot of haiku.

Disjunction has at least three dimensions of velocity: centrifugal force (the reader is thrown out of the poem and image, even out of language); gravitational force (the reader is drawn into interior contemplation); and, misreading as meaning (a falling out of, and recovery of meaning). Disjunctive method relates to the *kireji*-concept as *semantic kireji*, helping to catalyze the reader's aesthetic perception of haiku as an artform, and disjunction also evokes a sense of depth. Mistake, breakdown, irruption: these attributes partake of the wound, whether that wound be to habit, form, function, or stable reality. As has been brought to light in the field of depth psychology, it is through such wounds that we deepen.

Acknowledgements

I wish to thank poet, editor and Red Moon Press publisher Jim Kacian; this research has benefited from his literary insight, poetics, and colloquy. Discussions with Philip Rowland (Tamagawa University) have improved my understanding of the relationship of haiku with wider issues of poetics and aesthetics. Masahiro Hori (Kumamoto Gakuen University) has provided insight into his innovative literary corpus-collocational methodology, Rinzai Zen practice, and haiku researches. Insightful conversations with Judy Yoneoka (Kumamoto Gakuen University) inspired my interest in applying linguistic approaches to haiku. I am also greatful to co-translator/poets Kanemitsu Takeyoshi and Itô Yûki (Ph.D. cand., Kumamoto University), comrades in arms. And my profound gratitude to Hoshinaga Fumio, founder and *sensei* of the *HI-HI Gendai Haiku Circle* of Kumamoto, who has revealed the living heart of contemporary Japanese haiku through his poetry and personage.

Endnotes

1. "It was roughly the decade of the 1950s that saw the real beginning of what may be called the haiku in the Western world" (HSA, 1994, p. 5). (I am American, so likewise are most of the citations and references in this paper. While fairly familiar with contemporary haiku composed worldwide in English, I am less familiar with the haiku history, small presses, etc., on other continents. Notwithstanding, there is a broad similarity in haiku composed in English, in the west.) In this paper for brevity the term 'English haiku' will at times be substituted for 'English-language haiku.'

2. The frontispiece of each HSA Frogpond journal through 2004 gives the pre-existing definition (1973-2004): "1. An unrhymed Japanese poem recording the essence of a moment keenly perceived, in which Nature is linked to human nature. It usually consists of seventeen *onji*. 2. A foreign adaptation of 1, usually written in three lines totaling fewer than seventeen syllables." (It should be noted that *"onji"* is an archaic linguistic term, being supplanted in Japan by the 1930s, and it has become unknown in Japanese. The most appropriate term is *"on"* (as: "This haiku has 17-*on*"). The new (2004, Autumn) HSA definition reads: "A haiku is a short poem that uses imagistic language to convey the essence of an experience of nature or the season intuitively linked to the human condition"; this definition is problematic and in some ways is a backwards step, as it lacks specificity, and introduces culturally problematic language (Gilbert & Rollingstone, 2005; Gilbert, 2008). As this essay takes a historical approach, The HSA 1973-2004 definition (termed "HSA definition" throughout this essay) is used.

3. From a lecture by Hiroaki Sato (1999b), in which "proper" is described in broad strokes: "American haiku writers have tended to move in one direction . . . [they] have tended to move with a few guiding principles, while Japanese haiku writers have not. To judge by the [pre-2005] HSA definition, one of the principles for American haiku writers is associated with Zen-like enlightenment ('the essence of a moment keenly perceived'); it is as if the brevity of the form has to be equated with the temporal briefness of the matter to be described" (p. 1). Also see Spiess, 2001 and Gurga 2000, for their delimitations of "proper."

ENDNOTES

4. Selected haiku in the journal *Modern Haiku* are mainly of the naive-realist *shasei* variety. In a recent interview, the nationally known reviewer and haiku critic Hasegawa Kai referred to the problem of naive-realist haiku, coining the term "*garakuta haiku,*" i.e. 'junk haiku,' stating that this mistaken idea of haiku has "created a nearly stagnant situation" (Hasegawa, 2007). Nearly a decade ago, the *shasei* approach was defended by an essay in *Modern Haiku*, advancing the idea of a triune hierarchy or schema of haikai: at the top 'haiku,' followed by 'senryû,' and at the bottom 'zappai': "seventeen syllable poems that do not have proper formal or technical characteristics of haiku ... if we look at all of what is presented today as 'haiku' a large number of so-called haiku are, like zappai, imaginative or imaginary" (Gurga, 2000, pp. 62-63). In the years since Lee Gurga penned his essay, much has changed. In fact, one only need glance at Gurga's 'mosquito' haiku in the disjunctive category, "Imagistic Fusion" of this paper, to observe the poet's evolution. Gurga concurs (personal communication, August 2007) that 'imaginative or imaginary,' applied in a blanket negative sense requires emendation. Usage problems concerning the term 'zappai' in English by the HSA (untruly implying verity with Japanese haiku sensibility) are discussed in the Chapter, "Cross-cultural Problematics."

Research in English into the modern senryû movement (covering the last 120 years) is nearly nonexistent. Over the last century, *gendai* (modern) senryû has developed in parallel with *gendai* haiku in Japan—this includes the banning of its presses, persecution and torture of its poets during the war-time period (*cf.* Itô, 2007)—obviously, for more than composing 'mere wit.' Excellent senryû poets such as Ônishi Yasuyo are acclaimed as poets per se, not merely as "senryû poets."

5. *Shasei* (translated as "objective sketch of life") refers to Masaoka Shiki's concept of *tokyoakkan byôsha* (objective description). Shiki's haiku philosophy is indelibly linked to naive-realist-inspired haiku, which include the first and second stages of his critical development: *shasei* and "selective realism." His third stage, *makoto,* indicates a potential increase in subjectivity, yet remains connected to realist determinants. Shiki died young and unfortunately his doctrine of *makoto* was not fully articulated. Tsubouchi Nenten, who recently published a book (in Japanese) on Shiki's life and work, suggests that Shiki

did not mean for his *shasei* stylism to be discerned as one offering intrinsically profound insight, but was articulated more along the lines of skillful language play and consciousness shift. Tsubouchi discusses Shiki-led speed games whose participants would vie to see who could pen the most ku before a stick of incense burned down, and used the term "automatic writing" to describe the participant experience of these and similar events: all-nighter writing 'raves,' etc. (*cf.* Tsubouchi, 2007). After Shiki's death, his ideas were spun in particular by Takahama Kyoshi to accord with ultranationalist perspectives (for further research into this topic an excellent paper on the New Rising Haiku movement by Itô Yûki, 2007, see "Note 1" in the Preface to this book). An overview of Shiki's critical evolution can be found in Ueda, 1983; also see Anakiev, 2003.

6. Analyses of this point may be found in Shirane, 2000; Sato, 1999. Marlene Mountain has a series of historically illuminating essays on her website, including a record from 1976-77 concerning 'haiku wars': " . . . a lot of people were die-hards. It got pretty bad. People started hating each other. . . . People divided up, chose sides, like children do in a game. But it wasn't a game. War broke out" (Mountain, 1990).

7. *Cf.* "Henderson's [1958] *Introduction to Haiku* . . . has remained an excellent beginning source for understanding Japanese haiku and by extension for determining what English haiku might be"(HSA, 1994, p. 6). Yasuda (1957) needs to be included here; however, the author's concept of English haiku compositional form was too idiosyncratic to be of longstanding influence.

8. Between 2002-2004, primers were published by Bruce Ross, Jane Reichhold and Lee Gurga. *Gendai* haiku concepts and technique, and the validation of non-*shasei* haiku are not presented in the above volumes. As of 2007, not a whole lot has changed. Jim Kacian is seeking publication for his haiku primer; having read some preliminary segments, it is eagerly anticipated.

9. A Japanese-English bilingual primer briefly outlining the history and nature of *gendai* haiku is available from the Modern Haiku Association of Japan (2001). *Gendai* approaches are considered part of the haiku literary culture of present-day Japan, and have

ENDNOTES

been integrated into children's education, as in the book *haikukyôshitsu* [Haiku classroom], for Elementary School children learning haiku (Natsuishi, 2002). Recently, the massive five-volume "Gendai Haiku Saijiki" was published by the Modern Haiku Association (*Gendai Haiku Kyôkai*; MHA); the fifth volume is a *muki kigo* or "non-seasonal season word" dictionary. Six collected articles concerning kigo are available (*cf.* Gilbert et al, 2006).

[10.] Mountain writes: "I find it odd . . . that after all these years there are still those who 'push' certain Japanese rules and moods. It is one thing to study the various eras of haiku and related genre—they and the poets are different—and quite another to *pick-and-choose aspects from the past and expect them to apply to all contemporary writers around the world.* While debate can be a great learning experience I will always wonder what Western haiku would be today had it gotten started in other ways— lineation and [syllable] counting only two of the problematic areas (1992a, Section 5, "foreward/foreward/foreward/foreward," para. 16). "The later terms 'political haiku' and Rod Willmot's 'psychological haiku' did a lot of good for haiku. They were ways of speaking to so-called new content, feelings and attitudes which had begun creeping into pure haiku (of which there are none) . . . Given the complexity of adopting even adapting any foreign art it seems that we would have been better served in haiku had final-sounding definitions come after a larger body of our work"(1992b, Section 99, "unaloud haiku contents," para. 3). Swede's indicative research was gathered from two surveys conducted in 1980 and 1997, concerning lineation. He writes: "Despite the efforts of some to promote one-, two-, and four-line haiku as well as visual [concrete] haiku, the combined use of these forms has actually gone down . . . to an overall average of 6.6%" (1997, p. 71).

[11.] The following is a quantitative and qualitative comparative analysis of the two large-circulation North American haiku journals, regarding *shasei*-style haiku published in the journals, in 2003. Both present a majority of *shasei* haiku. Surveying *Modern Haiku* (*34:3*) Autumn, and *Frogpond* (*26:3*) Autumn, five categories were determined: 1) total haiku listed in the section(s) "Haiku and Senryû"; 2) *shasei*; 3) formulaic *shasei*; 4) non-formulaic *shasei*—that is, shasei with innovative disjunctive elements— formal and/or content elements, psychological, animistic, etc., placing them outside of the *shasei*-oriented field; 5) non-*shasei* haiku. (Note: inferior senryû are included within category 3) formulaic *shasei*.) Haiku-translation sections were not included. Counts can be considered approximate; numbers are rounded-off to the nearest whole number:

Modern Haiku	Frogpond
1) 146	1) 149
2) 139	2) 124
3) 133	3) 71
4) 6	4) 53
5) 7	5) 25
Non-*shasei* haiku = 3%	Non-*shasei* haiku = 17%
Formulaic *shasei* = 91%	Formulaic *shasei* = 48%
Non-formulaic *shasei* = 3%	Non-formulaic *shasei* = 36%
Total *Shasei* = 95%	Total *Shasei* = 83%

Considering the excellence Shiki demanded, the judgment of 'formulaic' here is likely to be forgiving (cf. Ueda, 1983, pp. 19-28). It may be seen that both journals contain, overwhelmingly, *shasei* haiku—in the last few years, the scope of these journals has broadened somewhat. As well, journals are reliant on their submissions, and the haiku genre maintains a small following. Nonetheless, editorial restriction has been a major genre-limiting factor, over the decades.

[12.] *"My current definition of haiku is that haiku can no longer be defined"* (Mountain, 1992b, p. 99). "'Today it may be possible to describe haiku but not to define it" (Sato, 1999a, p. 73).

[13.] Following the publication of the 2004 version of this paper and convivial communication, Professor Lanoue has a new definitions page (Lanoue, 2007). My apologies for the illustration of his historical definition; however, his earlier definition remains relevant, as it reflects the *shasei* stylism prevalent in published haiku, to the present.

[14.] The lines have no spaced-out words in the 1916 version. The most commonly published revision (Pratt, p. 50) of the poem uses a semi-colon. Whether a colon or semi-colon is used, the issues concerning superposition (juxtaposition) and disjunction remain the same.

15. "[This haiku] has very possibly had more influence on the direction taken by Western haiku than any other single haiku" (Haiku Society of America, 1994, p. 9). An extended analysis of Nick Virgilio's 'lily' haiku can be found in the Chapter, "Plausible Deniability."

16. "*Soul is imagination* . . . releasing events from their literal understanding" (Hillman, 1983, p. 27; 1989, p. 122); reality is imaginal, a "seeing through: . . . the subject studying itself by means of the fictions and metaphors of objectivity" (*ibid*, 1989, p. 18); "the most fecund approach to the study of mind is through its highest imaginal responses" (*ibid*, p. 10); imagination has itself been articulated as "the poetic basis of mind" (*ibid*, p. 10).

17. In 2003, Terry Eagleton penned this critique of realism: "If realism is taken to mean 'represents the world as it actually is', then there is plenty of room for wrangling over what counts in this respect. . . . Artistic realism, then cannot mean 'represents the world as it is', but rather 'represents it in accordance with conventional real-life modes of representing it' . . . the world is itself a matter of representation. . . . To describe something as realist is to acknowledge that it is not the real thing. We call false teeth realistic, but not the Foreign Office. If a representation were to be wholly at one with what it depicts it would not be representation. . . . No representation, one might say, without separation. . . . all realist art is a kind of con trick . . . realism is calculated contingency. . . . representational art is from one viewpoint the least realist of all, since it is strictly speaking impossible. Nobody can tell it like it is without editing and angling as they go along (Eagleton, 2003, pp. 17-19). For a reconsideration of the relationship of the concrete and abstract in English haiku, see Rowland (2002); a paper addressing this topic is in Gilbert, 2008.

18. Rian Haight (Northwestern University) quoting Wallace Stevens (1958, p. 24). Personal communication, November 13, 2003.

19. In the English-language haiku, an example of where an imitative idea has failed is syllable-counting. Five-seven-five syllable

counting began as an idea of imitation, but was found to be a poor emulation of the original. This discovery was not suddenly brought to light by scholars, or if so, was not well promulgated— it was made serendipitously by poets, who began using fewer syllables in their haiku as a consequence of discovering a more effective, poetically powerful, means of evocation. It has been shown that the use of fewer syllables serendipitously provides a more proper emulatory template of the Japanese haiku then the "traditional" 5-7-5 count (*Cf.* Gilbert and Yoneoka, 2000).

[20] "The essence of mimesis is somatic, visceral, a shared physic element wherein we feel the action, the wounding, the marking of a body, in our own being" (Slattery, 2000, p. 13). "Whalley refuses to translate mimesis as 'imitation,' and instead keeps the transliterated Greek because the English noun seems to denote an object of some sort, while Aristotle's word refers to a process, not a product" (Richter, 1998, para. 2). For more on mimesis see the landmark 1953 work by Auerbach.

References

Anakiev, D. (2003). "New Tools: The Dimensions of the Line." *Frogpond: Journal of the Haiku Society of America, 26:3*, pp. 61-64.
Auerbach, E. (1953). *Mimesis: The Representation of Reality in Western Literature.* Princeton University Press.
Blyth, R. H. (1949-1952). *Haiku, vols. 1-4.* Tokyo: Hokuseido.
———. (1963a). *History of Haiku: Vol. one.* Tokyo: Hokuseido.
———. (1963b). *History of Haiku: Vol. two.* Tokyo: Hokuseido.
Cain, J. (1969). *Haiku Magazine, 3:4.*
Campbell, J. (1988). *Inner Reaches of Outer Space: Metaphor as Myth and as Religion.* New York: Harper Collins.
Duplessis, R. B. (2001). *Genders, Races, and Religious Cultures in Modern American Poetry, 1908-1934.* Cambridge University Press.
Eagleton, T. (2003, October). "Pork Chops and Pineapples." *London Review of Books 20*, (book review of *Mimesis: The Representation of Reality in Western Literature*), pp. 17-19.
Gilbert, R. (2006). "Kigo and Seasonal Reference: Cross-cultural Issues in Anglo-American Haiku." *Kumamoto Studies in English Language and Literature, 49*, Kumamoto University, Japan, pp.29-46. Revised from *Simply Haiku 3:3* (Autumn 2005). Accessed 25 November 2007, http://tinyurl.com/24hbap.
———. (2007). *Gendai Haiku Website.* Accessed 25 November 2007, http://gendaihaiku.com.
———. (2008 February). "Plausible Deniability: Nature as Hypothesis in English-language Haiku." *PALA 2007 Conference Proceedings.* Accessed 18 February 2008, http://tinyurl.com3xtu5o.
Gilbert, R., et al. (2006). *Six Collected Kigo Articles.* (website). Accessed 25 November 2007, http://research.iyume.com/kigo.html.
Gilbert, R. and Rollingstone, T. (2005). "The Distinct Brilliance of Zappai: Misrepresentations of Zappai in the New HSA Definitions." *Simply Haiku, 3:1.* Accessed: 25 November 2007, from http://tinyurl.com/yrp358.
Gilbert, R. and Yoneoka, J, (2000). "Haiku Metrics and Issues of Emulation: New Paradigms for Japanese and English Haiku Form." *Language Issues: Journal of the Foreign Language Education Center.* Prefectural University of Kumamoto, Kumamoto, Japan. (Online as: "From 5-7-5 to 8-8-8"). Accessed: 25 November 2007, from http://www.iyume.com research/metrics/haikumet.html.

Glass, J. (2007, Autumn). "stone." *NOON: Journal of the Short Poem, 5*. Tokyo: Noon Press, p. 8. (*NOON*, a limited-run journal, is available through noonpress@mac.com.)

Gordon, C., (Ed.). (2003). *ant ant ant ant ant: issue six*. Portland, OR: Chris Gordon.

Gurga, L. (2000). "Toward an Aesthetic for English-language Haiku." *Modern Haiku, 31:3*, pp. 59-75.

Haiku Society of America. (1994). *Haiku Path: The Haiku Society of America 1968-1988*. New York: Haiku Society of America.

Hasegawa, K. (2007) "Cross-cultural Studies in Gendai Haiku— Hasegawa Kai, interview excerpt 2." (ed., trans. R. Gilbert) *Gendai Haiku Online Archive*. Accessed 25 November 2007, http://gendaihaiku.com/hasegawa.

Henderson, H. G. (1958). *Introduction to Haiku: An Anthology of Poems and Poets from Bashô To Shiki*. New York: Doubleday. An updated version of *Bamboo Broom, 1934*.

———. (1967). *Haiku in English*. Tokyo: Tuttle.

———. (1971). "Letter to Anita Virgil." Quoted in *Haiku Path: The Haiku Society of America 1968-1988*, pp. 46-47.

Higginson, W. (1985). *Haiku Handbook: How to Share, Write and Teach Haiku*. Tokyo: Kodansha.

Hillman, J. (1983). *Archetypal Psychology: A Brief Account*. Woodstock, CT: Spring Publications.

———. (1989). *A Blue Fire*. New York: Harper Collins.

Hoshinaga, F. (2003). *Kumaso-Ha*. (Trans. R. Gilbert and T. Kanemitsu). Tokyo: Honami Shoten.

Itô, Y. (2007). *New Rising Haiku: The Evolution of Modern Japanese Haiku and the Haiku Persecution Incident*. Winchester, VA: Red Moon Press. Published online with an additional Addendum in *Simply Haiku, 5:4* (Winter, 2007). Accessed: 25 November 2007, from http://tinyurl.com/yrka65.

Kacian, J. (2003). "my fingerprints." *Kusamakura International Haiku Contest* (third-place prize). Kumamoto, Japan: Kumamoto City Government.

Kacian, J. et al., eds. (1997). *The red moon anthology of English-language haiku*. Winchester, VA: Red Moon Press.

———. (1998). *Snow on the water: The red moon anthology of English-language haiku*. Winchester, VA: Red Moon Press.

———. (2001). *The loose thread: The red moon anthology of English-language haiku*. Winchester, VA: Red Moon Press.

REFERENCES

———. (2002). *Pegging the wind: The red moon anthology of English-language haiku.* Winchester, VA: Red Moon Press.

Kawamoto, K. (2000). *Poetics of Japanese verse: Imagery, structure, meter.* Tokyo: University of Tokyo Press.

Lanoue, D. (2003) *About haiku.* (Webpage). Accessed: 8 November 2003, from http://webusers.xula.edu/dlanoue/issa/abouthaiku.html.

———. (2007). *About haiku.* (webpage). Accessed: 25 November 2007, from http://haikuguy.com/issa/abouthaiku.html.

Mainichi Shinbun. (1997). *daiichikai mainichi ikutai shyôsakuhinshi.* [First Mainichi anthology of winning selected haiku]. Tokyo: Mainichi Shimbun.

Mallarmé, S. (1999). "A tomb for Edgar Allen Poe." *To purify the words of the tribe* (trans. D. Aldan). Troy, MI: Sky Blue Press.

Modern Haiku Association, eds. (2001). *Japanese haiku 2001: Japanese-English.* Tokyo: Modern Haiku Association.

Mountain, M. (1980). "One-image haiku." *Frogpond: Journal of the Haiku Society of America, 3:2* (as Marlene Willis). Accessed: 25 November 2007, from http://www.marlenemountain.org/essays/essay_oneimage.html.

———. (1990). *self-interview circa 1976/77: discussions.* Accessed: 25 November 2007, from http://www.marlenemountain.org/essays/sinterview_discussions.html.

———. (1992a). *from the mountain/backward, section one.* Accessed: 25 November 2007, from http://marlenemountain.org/backward/ftm_backward_1.html.

———. (1992b). *from the mountain/backward, section two.* Accessed: 25 November 2007, from http://marlenemountain.org/backward/ftm_backward_2.html.

———. (2003). *Frogpond: Journal of the Haiku Society of America, 26:1.*

Natsuishi, B. (1999). *A Future Waterfall: 100 Haiku from the Japanese* (trans. Natsuishi et al). Winchester, VA: Red Moon Press.

Natsuishi, B. et al (2002). *haikukyôshitsu* [Haiku Classroom]. Tokyo: Shueisha.

Paz, O. (1991). *The Bow and the Lyre: The Poem, the Poetic Revelation, Poetry and History* (trans. E. Weinberger). Austin, TX: University of Texas.

Pinker, S. (1994). *The Language Instinct: The New Science of Language and Mind.* New York: Penguin.

Pound, E. (1913). "Contemporania." *Poetry: A Magazine of Verse, 2:1.* Accessed: 25 November 2007, from http://rpo.library.utoronto.ca/poem/1657.html.
———. (1914, Sept.). "Vorticism." *Fortnightly Review, 571,* pp. 461-71.
———. (1916). *Lustra.* London: Elkin Mathews.
Pratt, W. (1963). *The Imagist Poem.* New York: Dutton.
Purves, A. (1993). *Tapestry: A Multicultural Anthology.* New York: Simon & Shuster.
Richter, D. (1999, Winter). "Aristotle's poetics: A translation with commentary" (review of G. Whalley's book). *University of Toronto Quarterly, 42:4,* pp. 416-19.
Ross, B., ed. (1993). *Haiku Moment: An Anthology of Contemporary North American Haiku.* Tokyo: Tuttle.
Rowland, P. (2002). "Avant-garde Haiku." *Frogpond: Journal of the Haiku Society of America, 25:1,* pp. 47-59.
———. (2007, Autumn). "brightening after rain." *NOON: Journal of the short poem, 5* (as Philip Lansdell). Tokyo: Noon Press, p. 73. (*NOON,* a limited-run journal, is available through noonpress@mac.com.)
Sato, H. (1999a). "HSA definitions reconsidered." *Frogpond: Journal of the Haiku Society of America, 22:3, pp.* 71-73.
———. (1999b). "Divergences in Haiku." *HSA Lecture,* September 18. Accessed: 25 November 2007, from http://www.marlenemountain.org/mminfo/revsofmm/ofmm_divergences_hsato.html.
Shirane, H. (2000). "Beyond the Haiku Moment: Bashô, Buson, and Modern Haiku Myths." *Modern Haiku, 31:1,* pp. 48-63.
Slattery, D. (2000). *The wounded body: Remembering the markings of flesh.* New York: State University of New York.
Spiess, R. (2001). "A certain open secret about haiku." *Modern Haiku, 32:1,* pp. 57-64.
———. (1976). "The problem of the expression of suchness in haiku." *Modern Haiku, 7:4,* pp. 26-28.
Stevens, W. (1958). *The necessary angel.* New York: Random House.
Swede, G. (1997). "A history of the English haiku." *Haiku Canada Newsletter, issues, 10:2 & 10:3.*
Tsubouchi, N. (2007). "Cross-cultural studies in gendai haiku— Tsubouchi Nenten, interview excerpt 1." (Ed., trans. R. Gilbert). *Gendai Haiku Online Archive.* Accessed 25 November, 2007 from, http://gendaihaiku.com/tsubouchi.

References

Ueda, M. (1983). *Modern Japanese poets and the nature of literature.* Stanford, CA: Stanford University Press.
van den Heuvel, C. (1977). *Cicada, 1:3.*
van den Heuvel, C., ed. (1974). *The haiku anthology,* 1st ed. New York: Doubleday.
———. (1999). *The haiku anthology,* 3rd ed. New York: Norton.
Virgilio, N. (1963). *American Haiku, 2.*
WHA (World Haiku Association). (2003, October). *The second world haiku association conference program & haiku anthology.* (Ed. Ban'ya Natsuishi). Saitama: World Haiku Association.
———. (2003). *Anthology of haiku poets.* Accessed: 25 November 2007, from http://www.worldhaiku.net/poetry.htm.
Yasuda, K. (1957). *The Japanese haiku.* Tokyo: Tuttle.
Yasui, K. (2003). *Kuhen* [Haiku Psalms], (trans. B. Natsuishi and E. Selland). Tokyo: Chûsekisha. Accessed: 25 November 2007, from http://www.worldhaiku.net/poetry/jp/k.yasui.htm.

Section 2: Multicultural Issues

Prefacing Remarks

5. Tsubouchi Nenten

6. Hoshinaga Fumio

7. Kigo and Seasonal Reference

8. Ônishi Yasuyo—Gendai Senryû

9. Cross-cultural Problematics

10. Yagi Mikajo

11. Stalking the Wild Onji

12. Afterword

MULTICULTURAL ISSUES

PREFACING REMARKS

This book has been divided into two sections, "theoretical concerns" and "multicultural issues," yet there is quite a bit of overlap. The intention of the first section has been primarily to present two main approaches to haiku theory: recent western-oriented academic approaches to literature, such as ecocriticism, literary linguistics, consciousness, and cognitive studies, and the second approach has included a presentation of novel theoretical concepts. Hasegawa Kai reorients the idea of "cutting" and its importance to an understanding of non- or para-realism in haiku (regarding *ma*) in his discussions on the centrality of *kire*, showing that *kire* is at the core of the haiku tradition. A historical view of haiku in the west and a re-conceptualization of haiku was also presented, in considering disjunction as a fundamental aspect of haiku (and fundamental to juxtaposition). Discussed also was the relationship between language features (disjunctive techniques, plausibly-deniable hypotheticality, MUMS, metaxic ambiguity, etc.) in haiku and reader consciousness.

Just as my publication on disjunction occurred prior to an acquaintance with Hasegawa's thought ("semantic kireji" being akin to *kire* and *ma*), in a similar way, Uda Kiyoko's involvement in ecocritical concerns predates western academic organizations and codified approaches. That such theoretical concerns and perspectives autonomously and contemporaneously arise in different forms, cultures, and languages seems to mark the contemporary zeitgeist, as multicultural influence has become the norm. It should also come as no surprise that Hasegawa has studied Ezra Pound and Imagism, along with Bashô.

The last 150 years have seen paradigmatic changes in culture, technology, lifestyle, war, art, health, scientific concepts, etc., so immense they are hard to overstate. Haiku poets have responded in complex ways in integrating haiku poetics with this evolution. While multicultural influence and a mixing of cross-cultural modes has been part of the modern, gendai haiku poets have also sought anew the roots of Japanese cultural history, indigenous ethnicity, locality, and spirituality in a quest for relevance, wholeness and humanity. The following Section presents thematic elements which include Tsubouchi Nenten's discussions of *katakoto*, *haigô* and *kigo*; Hoshinaga Fumio's discussion of *kotodama shinkô* and the indigenous Kumaso tribal spirit; Ônishi Yasuyo's overview of gendai senryû; Yagi Mikajo's radical ecocritical-feminism; and as well, papers discussing *kigo*, *zappai*, and haiku terminology in a multicultural context. Each of these Japanese terms remains culture-specific, yet the poetic intentions are universal. It is this universality of poetic intention which makes such terms and conceptions accessible and hence multiculturally available.

Section 2: Multicultural Issues

5. Tsubouchi Nenten

TSUBOUCHI NENTEN

INTRODUCTORY REMARKS

Tsubouchi Nenten is an acclaimed gendai poet, critic and innovator, notable for his unique creative vision. Emeritus Professor, Kyoto University of Education, and currently a Professor teaching at Bukkyo University, Kyoto. Our interview took place in his research office, on February 15, 2007.

In the first interview segment, "The Poetic Self 1: *Katakoto*—Fragmentary Language in Haiku," Nenten discusses *katakoto*, which can be translated as fragmentary or "broken" language (literally, "baby talk"), as a sourcepoint of haiku creativity. He also touches upon *dôshin*, "childlike or innocent mind," contrasting this idea with his conception of *katakoto*. In the latter part of the transcript, Nenten discusses the manner in which *katakoto* can be seen to be at the heart of the Japanese aesthetic: intrinsic to notions of "imperfect beauty."

In the second interview segment, "The Poetic Self 2: *Haigô*—Masaoka Shiki & Haiku Persona," Nenten discusses the relationship between *haigô* and persona. Historically, haiku poets have used *haigô*, "pen-names" to create multiple personae, each an autonomous creative entity; this psychological process is both a central aspect of Nenten's compositional approach and an integral part of the haiku tradition. Masaoka Shiki is also discussed in this regard. The second part of the transcript focuses on Shiki's sense of language play as a core concept of his *shasei* ("sketch of life") approach to haiku. Nenten suggests that the *shasei* was never meant to be seen as a poetics of profundity: Shiki's main disciples and later poets having distorted his primary intention, with the result that the low contemporary critical valuation of

Shiki's thought represents a misunderstanding of his approach. Nenten thus sheds new light on the significance of Shiki's creativity.

Please note that parenthetical information in the transcripts indicates clarification by the translators. Example haiku with original kanji and additional commentaries can also be viewed on the accompanying DVD-ROM, and at the Gendai Haiku Website.

Tsubouchi Nenten—Life and Works, in brief

Personal History

Tsubouchi Nenten (1944—; born as Tsubouchi Toshinori, Ehime Prefecture). Studied Japanese literature at Ritsumeikan University where he received an MA degree, and became a scholar. Acted as editor of the Journal of the Modern Haiku Association, *Gendai Haiku*, 1976-1985. In 1986 founded his own haiku circle and journal, *Sendan no kai*. Emeritus Professor, Kyoto University of Education, and Professor, Bukkyo University. Tsubouchi Nenten is also a committee member of the 'Study of Rivers' in Japanese Literature [*Nihon bungaku ni okeru kasen*], and a member of the Modern Haiku Association [*gendai haiku kyôkai*].

Publications

Haiku: *Asa no kishi* [Morning Riverbank], 1973; *Haru no ie* [House of Spring], 1976; *Waga machi* [My Town], 1980; *Neko no ki* [The Cat's Tree] (1987); *Hitomaro no tegami* [The Letters of Hitomaro], 2003, and others. Books: *Masaoka Shiki: Haiku no shuttatsu* [Masaoka Shiki: Beginning of the Haiku Journey], 1976; *Haiku kôshô to katakoto* [The Oral Culture of Haiku and Katakoto], 1990; *Haiku no yûmoa* [Haiku Humor], 1994; *Furo de yomu haiku nyûmon* [An Introduction to Haiku], 1995; *Kaki kû Shiki no haiku sahô* [Biting a Persimmon: Shiki's Haiku Manner and Method], 2005, and others.

The Poetic Self 1:
Katakoto—Fragmentary Language in Haiku

Tsubouchi Nenten, Bukkyo University, Kyoto

[Note: One of the core concepts of Tsubouchi Nenten's haiku aesthetic involves his coinage of the term *katakoto*, discussed in "Plausible Deniability, Section 2.1" as, a "functional compositional-stylism of missing syntactic elements and semantic language-gaps in haiku form . . . *katakoto*: 'fragmentary or "broken" language' (*lit.* 'baby talk'), Tsubouchi Nenten, 2007."]

Examining so-called "juvenile" poetry, the poetry of children—in Japan, from antiquity, concerning the quality of *dôshin* (a childlike, innocent mind), children have been thought to possess this capacity—so they have been considered to be natural poets, as Kitahara Hakushû writes. However, I don't think that children possess *dôshin* (in relation to poetic composition), as children do not have an adequate vocabulary. In fact, children rather tend to express themselves in "impossible" expressions, in short, *katakoto*-like expressions. And therefore from the viewpoint of adults, these expressions can appear to be extraordinary, shocking—and such works are often quite excellent. In any case, this is my viewpoint on the matter.

Short-form poetry such as haiku is, in a sense, *katakoto*—it tends to be *katakoto* by its very nature. Thus, if we are able to call forth some of the poetic power of *katakoto*, it is possible to create a much more powerful poetry. Regarding the excellence of children's expressions, Bashô and others certainly observed this; but —why are they so good? It may be that a "*katakoto*-like Japanese language" exists, or the magic of such a kind of thing. Especially, in the case of haiku, we often cannot articulate our most fulsomely eloquent expression, due to formal brevity. So, haiku must be possessed of *katakoto*, by its very nature. This is how I think of it—but perhaps not so many others would agree with me! (laughs)

Actually, this quality of *katakoto* may also be a characteristic aspect of Japanese culture. For example, when people view and have a festive party under the moon—you know, in the celebrated book, *Essays in Idleness* (*Tsurezuregusa*, by Kenkô, 1330-32 CE), there is a renowned section which relates that while viewing the full moon is worthwhile in itself, viewing the partial moon truly represents an apotheosis of moon viewing. There is exactly this sort of notion in Japan: that the waning moon is "imperfect"; an imperfect moon for viewing, hence an imperfect moon. But something imperfect (lacking or missing some element)—how shall I say this—there is a cultural tradition of finding beauty within the sense of *katakoto*.

In like manner, haiku also seem to flow within this stream.

The Poetic Self 2:
Haigô—Masaoka Shiki & Haiku Persona

Tsubouchi Nenten

The "*hai*" of haiku ... "*hai*" means, literally, "not human." Concerning this topic, it is my belief that—how to say this—the "not human" quality is related with a way to enrich the poetic self, as author. That is, a person—a self—if there is a self—within the poetic-creational realm, is typically a lone (isolate) self. An isolate author.

By contrast, originally, traditionally, in the haiku world poets used pen-names, that is, "*haigô*." And in this manner, they obtained different selves. Take for example a poet I really like, Masaoka Shiki. Shiki used more than 100 pen-names. Yes! And in doing so, the pen-name becomes a kind of mask, persona—so that the personality is changed—it's true. This was once the traditional haiku poet's, so to say, "way" (mode, path) of creation.

As well, as you know, in the feudal class-structure found in the Edo era (1603-1867), when poets gathered such situations could become incommodious, uncomfortable. (Lower classes had no surnames, and samurai surnames could easily reveal rank as well as family history.) So, to hold a joyous and expansive haiku party, for all in attendance, by utilizing *haigô*, all participants become equal. You know, there is a saying, "*haikai* is for freedom" (qtd. in Bashô's *Kyoraishô*). All are equal. Yes, I believe this tradition is really important. So, having not only a usual self with a usual name; being not only an individual human being — but several personalities within a poet's psyche: this can make one's haiku much more interesting. And this is my philosophy.

To discuss this a bit more, from the early-modern era, haiku poets became "actual-name" oriented. For most then, having a pen-name constitutes nothing but a minor genre-attribute. Furthermore, using only one's real name causes a poet to become isolated (alienated); tends to cause restriction, compositional limitation. I ponder this in some corner of my mind.

A further, personal, point—I am called "Nenten." As you know, "Nenten" is a *haigô* that was conferred upon me by my friends. The kanji ('nen'+'ten') can also be pronounced as (Toshinori) my actual name. And, when I absorb my "Nenten-*haigô* self" into hippos, and perceive and feel as a hippo (laughs), I am *a totally different personality* from my usual self when I do this. I become a man like a hippo.

And from within such a mind, perceiving society and nature: I am doing just this. It's a process which is, in a word, interesting, isn't it? I both persist in and recommend this method. (laughs)

RG: In your (2005) book, *"Kaki kû Shiki no haiku sahô"* [*Biting a Persimmon: Shiki's Haiku Manner & Method*], you discuss Masaoka Shiki with real passion. For instance, the manner in which you described Shiki's deathbed pain, and so on. Reading such examples, I feel that you have some unique insights concerning Shiki. Could you please comment on this topic?

TN: Ah—let me see—Yes, Masaoka—Well, the modern era of Japanese haiku began with Masaoka Shiki (1867-1902). However, contrary to what you might believe, the evaluation of Shiki is not high among haiku poets. In fact, Shiki is considered to be shallow, superficial, on account of his short life. And although Shiki innovatively advocated *shasei* stylism (a realist, objective "sketch of life"), his *shasei* are considered to be merely external; that is, he did not succeed in achieving a profound realm of poetic philosophy. This is the majority opinion.

However, I am opposed to such a valuation of Shiki. Hmm, what to say—Should a haiku poet attain to a deep, profound realm, via the method of *shasei*? I really doubt such a notion. Indeed, examining literature of the modern period, Japanese literature in particular has a strong, even singular tendency to seek profoundness or inwardness. However, in narrowly pursuing such a theme, we may also lose something.

I feel that Shiki cherished exactly that something which we tend to lose. So—What is it, would you ask me? It is, in my opinion, the enjoyment of LANGUAGE (words).

That's it.

And, in Shiki's case, he had his own philosophy, regarding the composition of poetry: Language composes worlds via combinations; just like playing blocks. His idea derives from the fact that he began his poetic career based upon his study and composition of poems (*kanshi*), written in Chinese characters. (Kanshi are structured by ideogrammatic lines having the appearance of 'block' combinations.) Shiki became enthusiastic about this compositional method. He adopted it to haiku, and composed quite a number, taking many topics for his haiku. And for each topic, he composed 10 haiku as part of his formal compositional style.

Then, whenever he and his friends would gather, he lit a stick of incense, and they would write as many haiku as possible before the incense went out. This may seem merely playful—but the process requires intense concentration. As a result, something of the unconscious is revealed: this is similar to a kind of automatic writing, the automatic writing of the surrealist poets, I believe.

However, unfortunately, this aspect of Shiki's compositional method was regarded as that of a person who was always just, and merely, "playing." This was the view of later generations. As well, his youthful companions, Takahama Kyoshi and Kawahigashi Hekigotô respected Shiki, but likewise also regarded Shiki as being too playful.

Later, Kyoshi insisted that *shasei* should be re-conceived as a deeper, more profound method (than evident in Shiki's actual approach). As a result, for haiku, *kachôfûei* (*shasei*, composed with traditional Japanese sentiment and proscribed season words) was advocated (by Kyoshi), as a means "to grasp the origin of the world through *shasei*."

In the tanka world, Saitô Mokichi and other tanka poets stated that, "*Shasei* is the method to grasp '*sei*' (life): life itself." In such ways, the disciples of Shiki re-oriented *shasei* towards the profound. This might be an acknowledged viewpoint; however, I tend to doubt this view—And—is this new viewpoint I'm speaking of regarding *shasei* true, or not? If we deepen *shasei* too much, won't we loose the sense of language (word) "play," and a host of related qualities? This is my opinion.

So, as for Kyoshi's thought, my feeling is that we needn't regard Shiki's approach as immature, as a result of his early death.

Tsubouchi Nenten—Selected Haiku

harukaze ni haha shinu ryûkakusan ga chiri

to the spring wind
mother dead, herbal medicine
scatters

suichû no kaba ga moemasu botanyuki

a wallowing hippo
burns—
snowflakes

botanyuki are large snowflakes or snowflake clusters, known also as 'snow flowers.' *botan* is a peony.

batta tobu ajia no sora no usumidori

flying grasshopper asian sky a washed-out green

sakura chiru anata mo kaba ni narinasai

cherry blossoms fall—
you too must become
a hippo

haru o neru yabure kabure no yô ni kaba

in the spring—
lying down desperate, as
a hippo

In this final example, elements of the original Japanese are retained, in order to reveal qualities of language play, which are important to Tsubouchi's haiku aesthetic. This type of stylism has stymied attempts at translation. A brief cultural note follows the haiku, giving an abbreviated explanation of the un-translated phrases.

sangatsu no amanattô no ufufufufu

in march
amanatto:
u fu fu fu fu

NOTES

[1.] In Japan, March (*san-gatsu*) is the end of the business year, full of fresh energy, yet somewhat sad with the departure of the old and familiar. There is a saying in this regard: *deai to wakare no kisetsu* (the season of meetings and farewells).

[2.] *amanattô*—is a traditional Japanese confectionery, made of sweet, fermented azuki beans and sugar; the word-feeling of 'sweet natto' reminds of "*natto*," a unique food, with a pungent aroma, which is a kind of "power food" or "soul food" (vitality-enhancing).

[3.] *u fu fu fu fu*—For us, this onomatopoeia evokes the image of a group of older women eating the sweets together—in Japanese "*ufufu*" is a small laughing voice, made with a slightly opened mouth, that is, a kind of modest, small-voiced chuckle. Or, it is perhaps the poet, who enjoys this traditional sweet?

[4.] The haiku also has a sense of personification: it seems as if amanattô is itself offering a modest chuckle. This haiku is among the most well-known of Tsubouchi Nenten, and is often cited.

Section 2: Multicultural Issues

6. Hoshinaga Fumio

HOSHINAGA FUMIO

INTRODUCTORY REMARKS
Hoshinaga Fumio has developed a unique approach to haiku. As a native of Kumamoto Prefecture in Kyûshû, he is especially concerned with local tribal history and culture, and has discussed the possibility of ressurecting both nature and culture through poetic language. Hoshinaga was recently selected as one of 25 outstanding national *gendai haijin*.

In the first of two interview segments (August 2006, Kumamoto), "Sacred Language in Haiku 1: *Kotodama Shinkô*," Hoshinaga begins his discussion of *kotodama shinkô*, the "miraculous or sacred power of language," his primary approach to haiku composition, by describing a recent trip to a local village ceremonial festival (*matsuri*) in the Amakusa Islands, in Kumamoto Prefecture. Reading aloud several of his most recently-penned haiku, we learn how insects too may "become divine." Hoshinaga introduces an ancient word of the Hayato Tribe of Central Kyûshû, *kamuagaru* (to rise to heaven / become or unite with *kami* (gods)), as a key critical concept of this haiku series. Through decades of historical research into the animistic and indigenous roots of his local environs, Hoshinaga has developed an approach to haiku which weds the lifeways and spirituality of pre-history to contemporary language and style, in order to resurrect or revive the heart-sense of his culture—and by extension our own.

In the second interview segment, "Sacred Language in Haiku 2: 'Becoming Divine,'" characteristics of location, in time, space, era and "person" are discussed in relation to inherent powers of nature, including creativity, originality, uniqueness, and healing. The discussion broadens to the meaning and description of *kami* and the relation between *kami*, the natural world, and "the aura or environment of mind." Hoshinaga next discusses the possibility of representing *kami* (the divine, sacred) via language, particularly in the haiku genre. Within the sacred locale of *matsuri*, all beings (a frog, a dragonfly, etc.) "have the opportunity to unite themselves with the sacred cosmos." Hoshinaga suggests such an ethic may constitute a primary taproot for haiku composition and practice.

The third text is a transcript of a published audio interview, "The Miraculous Power of Language: A Conversation with the Poet Hoshinaga Fumio," slightly abridged here, which took place in Kumamoto, at my home on January 20, 2004. Please note that parenthetical information in the transcripts indicates clarification by the translators. Example haiku with original kanji and additional commentaries can also be viewed on the accompanying DVD-ROM, and at the Gendai Haiku Website.

HOSHINAGA FUMIO—LIFE AND WORKS, IN BRIEF

PERSONAL HISTORY

HOSHINAGA FUMIO (b. 1933, Kumamoto Prefecture). Graduated Kumamoto University, 1956 with a degree in Japanese Literature. Became a High School teacher at Dai-Ichi High School in Kumamoto, and began his haiku career in 1967, joining Kaneko Tohta's *Kaitei* group. In 1983, he founded his own haiku circle and the journal *HI-HI*. Hoshinaga is a member of the Modern Haiku Association [*gendai haiku kyôkai*].

PUBLICATIONS

HAIKU: *100/67* [100/67ths], 1967; *68' Natsu* [Summer, 68'], 1969; *Onibi* [Devil Fire], 1970; *Ôkami matsuri* [Wolf Festival], 1973; *Higo kiga-kô* [The Great Starvation in Old Kumamoto], 1975; *Genjitsukan* [Parhelic Halo], 1986; *Shikijin* [Color Dust], 1998; *Kumaso-Ha* [Kumaso Tribe], 2003. Also, numerous essays in the *HI-HI Journal* and elsewhere, published plays, poetry in various genres, public lectures, and others.

Sacred Language in Haiku 1: *Kotodama Shinkô*

Hoshinaga Fumio

RG: Could you share some of your recent haiku?

HF: Yes—these are my latest works. I'll read some now.
   The other day I went to Amakusa (Amakusa Islands, Kumamoto Prefecture) and enjoyed a festival known as *Mushioi Matsuri* (the "Casting Out of Insects" festival), which celebrates the autumn harvest. Many in the participating local communities attach numerous flags onto tall poles, hoisted and carried high in the air. There are perhaps seven colors of flags, which are moved in a swaying dance to symbolically cast out bugs—. Symbolically chasing out the bugs which get caught in the rice paddies, is at the same time a prayer for the productiveness of grain, and as well an expectation for a rich autumn harvest.
   These are the haiku I composed while at that festival:

mizu wo kiru tonbo ga sui to kami ni naru

flicking off water
 a dragonfly quickly
 becomes divine

mushioi no kane sumu hodo ni naku hodo ni

the 'casting out insects' bell
 approaches transparency
  approaches weeping

kamuagaru mushi yo oyama ni nemu saite

  insects rising to heaven, I call—
on the mountain silk trees blossom

"*Kamuagaru*" means rising to heaven (an ancient indigenous word); insects are spiritualized, and become heavenly. An appellation of insects—these haiku! Actually, there were no insects to be seen, but there are many bugs flying around inside my aged head! (laughs) Anyway, I was watching the festival poles swinging, and thinking about such bugs being chased off by the flags, to the heavens they might meet—or so I envisioned.

The approach here is related to *kotodama shinkô* (the miraculous power in words), which is a religious or sacred belief in the mysterious power inherent in language. We can say this is *reiryoku* (*rei*: "ghost/spirit"; *ryoku*: "power; the power of *pneuma*, 'spirit'"); the word has *pneuma*—the power of spirit in it. By speaking a word, the event or thing indicated by that word can occur in the real world (a mirroring of a mutual identity).

For example, if I say, "Professor Gilbert, I deeply wish and pray for your successful journey to England." These words offered for your journey have a sense of prediction, intuition. Within this language there is a *pneuma*, a mysterious power—a sense that the prophecy will indeed come into being, in your successful future travel.

As well, it may be expected that positive things will happen if I spoke positive words; however, bad things might happen, speaking negative words. Concerning this sort of concept of language as prophecy, there is a term, *norito* in Japanese, used for the case in which good or positive things will happen; by the way, have you ever prayed at a Shinto shrine? [RG: "Yes—"] Shintô priests chant *norito*. I think you have read, no, actually heard this chanting?

RG: "Read . . . ?"

HF: Oh no, not actually read . . .
Have you heard, when a Shintô priest performs purifications: they chant such words. That is, those words

which collect positive energies only. We call this *norito*. When you collect evil words, this is called *jyuso*, cursing. Cursing—So, for example if I said negativistic words such as, "You will be kicked in the teeth"; such words also have a mysterious power, and bad things could happen. These ideas pertain to the roots of *kotodama shinkô*.

Actually, *kotodama* language was used in the Manyô era (8th century Japan was known as the land of *kotodama*). Such language existed even earlier, probably based on *Yamato kotoba* (Japanese tribal language). Japan was, as well, deeply influenced by Chinese culture and language; Japanese kanji characters originated in Chinese characters, hence Japanese culture was quite deeply influenced by this.

However, prior to this time, Japan also possessed a richly complex classical language. There existed a wide range of indigenous cultural groups, and the language spoken was pure, classical Japanese. This was *Yamato kotoba*. In fact, there has been a traditional attitude, that has considered the purity of *Yamato kotoba* as a matter of especial cultural pride. This pride was, more likely than not, nationalistic—there is such an aspect as well, concerning *Yamato kotoba*.

To take an example of this idea, the word *kamikaze* is well known around the world. In this word there inheres the idea that in the case of a national crisis *kami* (gods), through their power, help the nation. I think you are aware of this notion? In the Kamakura era of the Middle Ages (1192-1333 CE) Mongolia attacked Japan. This invasion is known as *genkô*. The Mongolian army led by Genghis Khan's grandson attacked Japan, and there were two separate attempted invasions, both occurring during typhoon season. Powerful winds battered the ships on these occasions and as a result Japan remained unconquered!

So, we can see that *kamikaze* has become such a wind. In situations of national crisis, kamikaze will blow to help the nation: "*kamikaze*" is such a thing. For instance, at the last

Football World Cup, Japanese supporters had bandanas (*hachimaki*) tied around their heads with "*Kamikaze Japan*" written on them (in kanji). They prayed that Japan would win, with some delight, as if the kamikaze had blown. I think this example reflects a social reality; a cultural expression of *kotodama shinkô*.

Japanese people have a mentality or sensibility to pray to *kamikaze*. The sacred exists in words, and "*kamikaze*" includes such an intention. So I think that when we say the word "*kamikaze*" we have an expectation that something divine will rescue us from difficulty. Or, we anticipate this. So, I think that one reason for my *kotodama shinkô* approach to haiku is that I maintain a certain posture: I would like to protect and nourish something that is unique within Japanese culture, within the art of haiku.

RG: Would you say that good haiku use *kotodama* well?

HF: If we were to say that "good" means not: "moral" but "art," then in that case, I think so. Hmm, and I would not necessarily say every genre pursues (an excellence of *kotodama*), because situations are so varied; however I think that, at least those who wish to preserve the uniqueness of Japanese culture may have a stronger inclination to engage in this way. I do not mean to say that poets lacking a sensibility of *kotodama shinkô* would be unable to write successful poetry. And, I don't know how many Japanese poets are aware of *kotodama shinkô*, in any case. Nonetheless, I think most Japanese have an abiding sense of this language deep in the roots of their consciousness when they write poetry in Japanese.

Sacred Language in Haiku 2: 'Becoming Divine'

Hoshinaga Fumio

RG: Good haiku evoke truly distinctive landscapes. Do you think that a well-depicted world within haiku would have to be unique—unlike any other thing?

HF: Yes—after all, each meeting takes place only once in life. If you compose from a sense of this unique, singular location: myself standing here—everything meets only once, ('one meeting: one lifetime'—a proverb of Rikkyu) in time and space; this meeting must be unique.

RG: And the inherent power of nature felt in such places as countryside shrines ... [HF: Yes—] originates not from the shrine buildings, but in natural presences—such as, a sacred grove of trees?

HF: Yes indeed. And, for example—we can see that Japan has a wide variety of Gods (*kami-sama* in polite form of address): and for instance, "that" shrine heals your eyes—and this shrine eases the pain of hands and legs. Each and every *kami* which inhabits a locale has its distinctive originality, creativity, uniqueness: definitive character, neighborhood, and modality of existence. Now, to take an example of a fountainhead (plentiful and near to Kumamoto)—do you think that the atmosphere of the fountainhead itself evokes a feeling of sublimity?

RG: The atmosphere itself?

HF: Yes, definitely, the atmosphere—

RG: A fountainhead, and the surroundings—

HF: Yes, the trees as well—this seems true. So we can regard "*kami-sama*" to mean not only "one" but also, I may say, the entire "canvas" of *kami*, the aura or environment of *kami*, we call this "*kami*" as well. There are a great variety of activities, objects and things which are concomitant to *kami*. If you are able to grasp such phenomena, it is possible to compose radiant haiku.

RG: Do you mean to say, it is possible to represent something like kami—a representation—a part or aspect of kami—via language?

HF: Yes, it is possible, yes. Returning to the "dragonfly" haiku example which I read before (in "Sacred Language 1," above), a dragonfly becomes divine (*kami*) as it flicks water off. This isn't essentially "composing" *kami*, of itself, but rather grasping the *Mushioi Matsuri* ("Casting out of Insects" festival) symbolically, and thus integrating *kami*.

When we go to *matsuri* (sacred festivals), we all—are becoming divine (*kami*) . . . all . . . all . . . all beings—gathering in one place, become divine. In Japan, the attendants of the sacred festival are called: "*zen-nan-zen-nyo*" (in Buddhism: "noble sentient beings"). All the attendants become divine; even if they are a dragonfly, a snake, even a frog—anything. All are becoming divine (becoming *kami*).

The integral whole—microcosm and macrocosm—holding all divine beings (souls), every kind of creature; we call this *kami*.

RG: In Western thought, within the historical Judeo-Christian tradition, God is alone. And though a divine soul can be possessed by human beings, other creatures do not possess a divine soul. This is a difference—.

HF: Yes—I suppose, from a global viewpoint however, similar religious notions (as I described) must exist in the world. In any case, all grasses and all trees conceive *kami* (divinity); such a notion is found within Japanese sensibility. All living things can be(come) *kami*, when they meet with *kami*, and join their being in their prayers to *kami*. Of course—actually, a dragonfly, a frog—do not join their hands in prayer; yet they are within the sacred locale of the festival. They are present, and thus have the opportunity to unite themselves with the sacred cosmos.

Therefore, they can become divine, can't they?

The Miraculous Power of Language:
A Conversation with the Poet Hoshinaga Fumio

Publication. *Modern Haiku, 35:3*, Autumn 2004, pp. 27-45.

Introduction

Spending time with Hoshinaga Fumio is like spending time in warm sunshine, as his beaming smile and youthful energy radiate expansively. At seventy, among many literary activities, Hoshinaga leads some dozen haiku circles around our Kumamoto, Kyûshû, area. Over a forty-year career he has garnered numerous commendations, and was recently selected as one of 25 national poets in *Haiku Grove: An Anthology of Meritorious Haiku* (*Haiku no hayashi*, Honami Shoten, 2003); his knowledge of both modern and traditional haiku is extensive. Along with research interests in Japanese language and history, Hoshinaga has been concerned with the local history and deep tribal past of Central Kyûshû, a concern which frames his latest effort, *Kumaso-Ha*, a ninth haiku collection published by Honami Shoten in autumn 2003. The creativity of the haiku in *Kumaso-Ha* are striking: many are innovative in approach, presenting social and philosophical perspectives with deeply humane insight. Most also use *kigo* (though *kigo* with a difference) and are written in 5–7–5-*on* or in a less formal 17-*on* form, echoing haiku verities. Hoshinaga often employs free-meter and orthographic fragmentation to create a fusion of rhythmic elements and psychological concept, a style unique in his work.

We were joined in our conversation by Shinjuku Rollingstone, *haikaishi* (haikai poet), a mutual friend and interpreter, instrumental to our communication. I wish also to thank Shinobu Yamaguchi of Kumamoto University, who produced a draft transcript from the recorded material.

Interview

RG: I'm looking forward to our talk, as readers in English are not familiar with your life and your haiku. Could you say a few words to introduce yourself and your haiku style?

HF: I began studying haiku in 1967, so it's been about forty years now. In the beginning, I learned traditional haiku, following and sticking to, so to speak, a conservative form. At the time I started to write haiku, avant-garde haiku was becoming a major movement. Especially, Kaneko Tohta published the haiku magazine *Kaitei*, and many young people became intensely interested.

In fact, Tohta's soft-cover book, *Kon-nichi no haiku* [Today's Haiku] was something like a bible for young people. From that book, I began to discover *gendai* (modern, contemporary) haiku. I published my first book of haiku after studying and writing for just one year. The title is 100/67 that is, one hundred sixty-sevenths. A "one hundred haiku collection" in '67; 100/67^{ths} in Japanese is called an improper fraction (*kabunsû*), and this term also has also has another meaning: "big head" (laughs). And not a proportionally big head, but a big head—out of all proportion. I felt that I wanted to write haiku from my heart, not my head; I thought that my published haiku collections were out of proportion because they were written more from my head. . . . Now I've published nine books of haiku, and I feel I'm getting closer to my heart. That's it.

RG: May I ask, what was your experience as a child, growing up?

HF: I was born in 1933. When I was in the sixth grade of Elementary school, World War II ended. So until that time, I was a nationalistic, militaristic child in a militaristic environment. After the war, with the advent of democracy, gradually I discovered what I had not been able to see—

what had somehow been hidden behind society. That's why I cannot believe *anything* I see: there must be some hidden meaning. That's the way I grew up. Even though I was writing traditional haiku, I thought there must be something hidden behind it. So, it was very easy for me to shift over to *gendai* haiku.

And, I'm an impoverished tenant-farmer's son. I learned after I had become an adolescent that the wealthy landowner of our farmland was a famous traditional-haiku poet; this circumstance contributed to my despising such a sort of "representative" poet. These are some of the factors that drove me to write *gendai* haiku.

RG: What might be frustrating or dissatisfying about traditional haiku?

HF: Hmm. Not frustration or dissatisfaction, so much as antipathy towards authority and power.

RG: Do you mean then, that you feel restricted, concerning traditional haiku?

HF: Yes. I have repellence, revulsion exactly against the formal rules and approach, kigo, and various formal necessities. [Reads the first poem from 100/67]:

> ni-ju oku kônen no gishô   omae no B-gata
>
> twenty billion light-years of perjury: your blood type is "B"

HF: I have a lot of misgivings, so I want to make visible these misgivings in myself. These misgivings are not directed toward typical persons, but rather towards any kind of authority. This kind of repellence or revulsion drives me to write haiku! [Laughter.]

RG: So, in this first haiku, we have the word "perjury" . . .

HF: "Twenty billion light-years" is almost an infinitely long distance... I had been fooled for so long, concerning any and every fundamental thing—without knowing any fundamental thing in the first place. Blood-type B is rare in Japan; Type A is happier, but Type B carries a sense of melancholy. So, I felt my rebelliousness or revulsion could not be not blood-type A—it must be blood-type B.

RG: In North America, we don't really focus on blood types, so it's difficult to grasp the meaning of this haiku. The haiku you mention brings up a different question. In many of your haiku, such as "twenty billion light years," you create a deep, interior psychological feeling, or seem to allude to a mysterious subject. The power of psychological allusion seems uniquely creative in your work. Could you comment on this theme?

HF: I write about or touch upon human heart and feeling, by creating human mental images. The human mental image does not have a typical form, such as a cake cut into four quarters—a mental picture is not like that — it has no form. For example, though I don't like to talk about this, my mother attempted suicide when I was in my first year of high school. I don't know the reason. This was just an attempt, but in the next week something in her mind or spirit was terribly, unusually troubled, and at the end of that week she passed away. I have mixed feelings—both love and hate. Santôka also lost his mother to suicide. I cannot cut the love and hate apart, separate them. And I cannot tell if this light is bright—is dark. When you eat cake it's bright, but when I get a difficult question—it's getting dark! [Laughter]

So that is why my approach may be very difficult to understand for some people. In any case, there's no doubt psychological influence is an aspect of my work.

SR: [looking at Hoshinaga's first anthology] "*Cho-sen*," is written in roman letters—this is challenging in Japanese...*cho* means butterfly, doesn't it. What does this butterfly mean?

HF: *Cho-sen* is the name of my first major haiku collection. My hometown is named Sen-cho—and cho-sen means challenges, as in challenging traditional haiku. Also, cho-sen means 1,000 butterflies spreading their wings. Cho-sen also means "rebellion, provocation" and additionally, *cho-sen* represents the world of beauty and the mixed or "upside-down" (ambivalent) feelings I have towards my hometown — it is also a classic symbol of Japanese beauty. So, I cannot love purely—there is both love and hatred—I'm the kind of man who can't love *that* way. I have loved in a "winding" way.

SR: Is that love and anger, or love and sadness? Love—and, what?

HF: Love and hatred... This book is dedicated to my wife, who passed away some years prior. To this day: did I love her, didn't I love her? Maybe I loved her, but I'm not sure. Perhaps I didn't really love her.

SR: You—didn't love your wife?

HF: No. I feel deeply sorry.

Disharmonies lead to harmonies

RG: It seems that, in a mysterious way, through your poetry, ambivalent feelings are fused. From your haiku a deep sense of harmony arises.

HF: Hmm. Thank you for your compliment. At the beginning, I didn't intend to write mysterious haiku! Well, in language words always have an order, and as I mentioned before, there is also ambiguity (ambivalence). The beauty of disharmony may appear—which might seem mysterious in some sense, but perhaps it's not really that mysterious? Disharmonies lead to harmonies.

RG: Disharmonies lead to harmonies—that's very interesting.

HF: Thank you. When I wear clothes, I usually try to coordinate them. However, some people do not do things this way. Lately, in a modern fashion trend, with some skirts one side is short, while the other side is long—but there is harmony: that is interesting.

RG: Now, I'd like to ask two questions regarding your comment, about the disharmony of words. For instance, it seems that in a simple sentence like "The dog is sleeping," we don't have a feeling of disharmony, rather the opposite. But there are different levels to the meaning; we could say that just by reading this sentence we've made our world a bit darker—we've eliminated various poetic realities as consciousness encounters a literalistic sensibility. In this simple sentence we accept realism. Maybe my point is that, in a way it seems harmonious but perhaps in a sense, realism, or literalism, has a kind of disharmony. What do you think?

HF: Yes, I know what you mean: I agree with you. I feel suspicious towards what is generally believed to be right or true—generally.

RG: So, in your poetry, you don't write "the dog is sleeping,"—you give us the feeling that something about language is a little uncomfortable—cause us to feel or sense some disharmony in language.

SR: The way your poetic language speaks—it seems that being language is not easy.

HF: This might be. Words (languages) have been overworking themselves. Here is part of the postscript I published in *Cho-sen* (penned in January 1968):

> I do not believe the truth that the sea is blue. That I believe it is blue: an encompassing state of affairs that limits as blue, via the comprehension of my eyes: I believe *only* that. Though it is inconvenient, I wish to compose haiku with a free posture towards truth, that is, with reference to the encompassing situation. With this thought, I've been writing haiku freely, selfishly, for half a year. This is the result of my selfish six months. . . . As a matter of fact, there is a vast wilderness of lyricism beyond these haiku: the wilderness I failed to capture with a dull, sleepy-faced rebelliousness. This book reminds me afresh—I must start again with a clean slate and to this end, I cast out this book with good grace.

So, this is the root-principle of my haiku. As a result, my order and usage of words, syntax, etc., will change and diverge from that of ordinary daily usage. I believe it is both such usage and rhythm that makes my haiku well-balanced—even though language is, generally speaking, overworked, fatigued. In any case, rhythm creates balance and helps readers to understand a haiku. I try to compose in very understandable rhythms. Definitely, in my haiku, rhythm is a very powerful and important element.

SR: Does rhythm help sustain a sense of harmony in your haiku?

HF: Yes. Even though language has been overworked, through it's just my own opinion, I try to create good rhythm and well-balanced haiku. That is why I believe that my haiku have euphony.

The Miraculous Power of Language

SR [to RG]: He has confidence in rhythm in his haiku—that's why English translation is really difficult! [Laughter.]

Image and rhythm

HF: [writing on a piece of scrap paper,] I told my grandson, "if you wish to know my work, please remember only this one haiku of mine:"

ika hakka aka deka hôka kinsenka

squid   peppermint
Red detective   arson
marigold

[aside: *ika* is squid (unusual kanji implies "crow bandit"—in Chinese legend squid feast on crows); *hakka* is peppermint (a homonym is 'catching fire'); *aka* (red) implies "anti-establishment/communist" esp. in relation to *deka* (detective/ plainclothes /thought police: *deka* arrest *aka*), also as slang used by Meiji era thieves. More recently film star Matsuda Yusaku famously played a *deka* ('rebellious/outlaw cop/ detective'); *hôka* is arson, and *kinsenka* (*Calendula officinalis*) is a large bright-orange marigold, which in Chinese legend is a 'gambler's flower,' whose petals radiate outward like bursting fire. In Japan, the flower is dedicated to the spirit of ancestors, and planted (prob. also in Hoshinaga's village) on farms to prevent plant disease—a consequence of crop disease might be fearful starvation. When praying to ancestors, and at cremation ceremonies, *kinsenka* is offered.]

HF: *ika hakka akadeka hôka kinsenka*. Reading this poem, the rhythm of each word was considered carefully. From the beginning, the first image is "white," then "arson," then "blooming flower." This order or connection yields aesthetic feeling (*bishiki*), which is pretty strong—but this is just my opinion. Then, "communist," to detective, and then to arson—finally, blooming marigold, perhaps like a fireworks.

[Hoshinaga used the onomatopoeic *pa* for blooming, which connotes a "bursting out;" also the words *hana* ("flower") and *hanabi* ("fireworks") are closely related, sharing assonance and a common kanji. Peppermint is a bursting out of flavor, Red / detective (revolutionary / secret police) implies a bursting out of revolution and authoritarian violence; arson, a bursting out of flame and crime; finally, the bursting out of *kinsenka*; each phrase connotes color, from white to red to a metaphoric rainbow.]

As you can see in this haiku, I've been working very hard in creating a sense of euphony. Of course, it might be playful at the same time. One also needs to be shown how to read "detective" (*deka*) as it's an unusual reading of the kanji.

RG: Reading this, first of all, I feel humor: the rhythm is stable, but concept and image are quite disjunctive—it's the rhythm that causes the images join together, creating one world: a sense of coherence. There is also an abstract visual element, which recalls color-field painting. The literal meaning doesn't seem to make sense, yet you can't remove a single element.

HF: That's right. You know, there is the traditional Japanese song "Goodbye Triangle" (which everyone knows) that goes like this: "goodbye = triangle; see you = square; square = tofu; tofu = white; white = rabbit" [*sayonara sankaku, matakite shikaku, shikoku tôfu, tôfu shiroi, shiroi usagi . . .*]—pairs connect by sound, or meaning, or shape, etc. I got the idea from this song. Images are changed one by one, but they also have various connections, at the same time.

These might be just techniques of language, but I believe there is also a sense of aesthetic beauty (*bishiki*) working within the lines. "Goodbye triangle; see you square; square tofu; tofu white; white rabbit"—each group in this song has a meaningful connection with the following group. No one knows how long the song will continue in this cyclical way. I wanted to somehow adopt the idea into my haiku.

SR: I think your haiku have really got rhythm.

HF: There is rhythm in my haiku—yet, language may be being overworked ...

RG: This question concerns a completely different topic. Since approximately ten percent of Japanese people live in the Tokyo area, and many haiku poets are from that area, could you say something about being a poet of the southern island of Kyûshû, and how living in Kyûshû and Kumamoto Prefecture has influenced your writing?

HF: Haiku is a centralized art. For instance, looking at the *saijiki* (haiku *kigo* or season-word dictionary), the *kigo* focus only on the Kyoto or Tokyo (Edo) locales. There are no "local" *saijiki*: you cannot find local characteristics in the *saijiki*. Given such a situation, local people have a sense of inferiority, when regarding the "center" of the tradition.

This type of inferiority-complex provides a kind of energy for my creation. So to "wave a flag" on Kyûshû—this is how I assert my existence and identity as a local resident and a living being. The sort of nature that is written in the *saijiki* is fake or false; it's not *real* for me. And, real things I feel in Kyûshû—no one can take this away—my haiku have arisen from this.

RG: I can't say whether every haiku that you have written has *kigo*, but it seems that most do. So, since *kigo* are found in the *saijiki*, how do you work with them or experience them in composing your haiku?

HF: It is difficult to explain. It's going to be a long story! I believe each haiku represents a slice of life. To make a cross section, you need time, and place, and person. To make a cross section of life, it must be *human*, and have a sense of place and, of course, time. There are reasons why those three things are necessary. First of all, you need "person" to reveal or present a cross section of *life*. Then, you also need to show the place and period (time) in which the person lives. In creating haiku, I want to infuse my work with all three of these elements.

It is necessary to *recognize the period* in which you live—that is "time." For example, I live now in the Heisei period in Japan, but if I lived in a certain year in the Shôwa period, I would need to recognize the period through myself. One needs awareness or perception of time, or era. And "place:" where do you live, *where do you belong to?*

First, there is perception of time or era; then, where you are, where you are breathing—and then, how do you relate to your era and place—this is the essence of compositional structure or intention; an important matter for a person, and writer.

Kigo is very useful and convenient for creating a sense of place (where) and time (when). For example, "chrysanthemum" which is *kigo*. "Chrysanthemum" definitely shows a season of autumn. It displays clearly—this is autumn; the time. In the *saijiki*, "chrysanthemum" belongs to autumn. So you can instantly establish the time, "autumn," and also image a place where chrysanthemum is in bloom, for example, a house garden or a garden party. So, chrysanthemum reveals "place" as well. We can say that a *kigo* is just one word—but this one word can speak volumes.

Finally, *how a person lives* in the time and the place; makes a relationship with the time and place—you can describe or express a cross section of life just by identifying "person." I can express a cross section of life with *kigo*—so *kigo* make it much easier to compose haiku. From this point of view, *kigo* is very useful and symbolic language. This is why ninety percent of my haiku contain *kigo*.

RG: So you don't use *kigo* so much to reflect upon or connect to traditional haiku, but more because *kigo* have a kind of poetic power, the capacity to evoke the elements you've mentioned . . .

HF: Yes, *kigo* describes "what" and where I am. This is the power or energy of *kigo*.

RG: So, *kigo* carry a sense of environment, a sense of location in time and space . . . When I look at this poem we translated into English,

> *nigemizu e sengo no chichi wo oitsumeru*
>
>   toward the mirage of water
> the postwar fathers
>   chasing after . . .

the *kigo* we translated is mirage: "mirage of water," and as you were saying, it gives a tremendous power to the haiku. Though in English we can't say what this kigo means—we don't have a connection to the various *saijiki* references (or any standard *saijiki*) in English—yet it seems a central image. What I want to say is that in traditional Japanese haiku, this *kigo* would never be used in the way you have used it.

HF: Yes, this use of *kigo* is more of a symbolic element.

RG: That's what I was musing about earlier, in terms of finding allusion in your oeuvre. This *kigo* doesn't seem real, that is, realistic, as in realism.

SR: You feel *kigo* through your heart (inner sense), not through seeing, touching, and so on.

HF: Yes. You have to experience the *kigo*. If you have never experienced "mirage of water" in your life, you can't have written this haiku. I've had a lot of experiences with mirages of water! That is why I can write this haiku! Especially, while I'm driving ... [laughter]

When I was small, "mirage of water" was very mysterious. I wondered what the forward movement was, but it never reached an end. I've had this kind of experience. I have *real* experience, *real* experience of *kigo*. This is why I can write haiku. It seems that I make haiku with my brain, but I can say I make *kigo* with my *real* experience, my sense of reality.

RG: Yes, not from having looked up a *kigo* in the *saijiki*— for instance: "Oh, today is April so-and-so, I'd better find a spring kigo to use in my haiku." You don't have that kind of process.

HF: Absolutely not. Never! I've just written this haiku:

hari motte kagayaku nikutai no porutogaru

with a needle   sparkling   the metaphysical flesh of Portugal

There is no *kigo*. I like this haiku, but because there is no *kigo*, it doesn't have a sense of scenery—there is no background behind this haiku. If haiku has *kigo*, it can also show its background scene or time. However, if a haiku does not have *kigo*, like this one, you cannot see the background. There is no environment—just naked haiku— naked myself, in this haiku. I like it, but I don't write this kind of haiku very much.

RG: So, for English speakers—we don't have a *saijiki* or a long history of *kigo*, centralized *kigo*, or season words concerning nature that are directly related to earlier literature. In English, *kigo* is usually something not human (or human associated), something from the natural world— a flower, weather, seasonal image—some kind of environmental image, or seasonal reference.

HF: Yes, I've read many Japanese-translated English-language haiku, and I often feel that they are naked, without a background, such as we've discussed, as haiku, in my feeling.

RG: However, we recently translated an English-language haiku into Japanese [by Jim Kacian], and it had four *kigo*, one from each season in it!

HF: Ha-ha! Well you know, you can find the same kind of haiku in Japanese!

SR: I know a Japanese *haijin*, Kennosuke Tachibana, who likes using double-*kigo*. He just wants to express as much as he can.

HF: I know what he means.

RG: So, because we use simply a seasonal reference or image in English—do you think that using a seasonal reference is important in English-language haiku composition—though, strictly speaking, this use is not what is meant as *kigo* in Japanese haiku? It seems as though you're suggesting that an environmental quality is really quite important, and it arrives through *kigo*. Would you recommend methods which convey, if not nature, a sense of "environment" behind the haiku?

HF: Yes, using a seasonal reference may be a good hint or suggestion for an English-language haiku writer, but sometimes you have to write naked.

RG: Traditionally, haiku are associated with nature. Do you think this connection is important in *gendai* haiku?

HF: Yes, the Japanese sense of nature is in harmony, or the harmony of—person (human being) and nature—no separation—in in its widest sense. Without the sense of harmony with nature, Japanese literature would become very weak. So to write about nature—from that position—embodies traditional haiku, and my position is the same.

Nature and Haiku

RG: This brings up a question, in terms of the sense of, or need, for harmony. Are there now challenges, living in our industrial, technological world, in terms of writing honestly about nature in haiku?

HF: Is this a question about haiku specifically, or more a question regarding social problems and conditions?

RG: I think perhaps it could be a problem for haiku, specifically regarding relating with nature, and more generally, any genre of poetry which takes nature as its subject.

HF: This involves *kotodama shinkô*, the miraculous power of language: something that is worshiped in Japan.

RG: Oh, really? Could you say more?

HF: There is a saying: "There are eight million Japanese gods." In any aspect of nature, gods exist. For instance, there is a tree close to this neighborhood — a tree known as *ichirigi*. A sacred rope surrounds the base of the tree. Even in the tree a god exists; so we worship this tree. I don't describe just the tree, but rather the tree infused with spirit: this involves *kotodama*. I do not want to use the word just for describing "as it is," but want to touch behind the word, further, deeper.

RG: The energy or miraculous power behind the word—language, the word can carry that power . . .

HF: Even when I compose a strongly imagistic (pictorial) haiku, I want to create a haiku in which the reader can feel more than a *shasei* (realist sketch). A deeper perspective. Is this enough of an answer to your question? I have been seeking something beyond the merely sketched (described) thing.

RG: Yes, thank you. How can we be sincere to our world, and still write about nature as "pure" or beautiful? I can mention two examples: if we write about a beautiful dawn, which is also a polluted sky, or that nearby mountain which now happens to have a microwave tower—it seems that the spirit or energy of nature is somewhat destroyed in that place.

HF: I can answer the question in this way. You meant, when you see the beautiful dawn, you also find destruction in it, didn't you? Well, I could say that I want to rehabilitate nature using *kotodama*.

RG: That's what I was wondering, because I feel just such a power in your poetry.

HF: Thank you very much. There are many ways to protect nature, or rehabilitate nature—for instance, social movements. But in my case, I am a professional of language, so I want to rehabilitate nature with language.

RG: Maybe also, you want to rehabilitate language with nature?

HF: Yes, definitely! And to rehabilitate nature with language. I think contemporary American Indians may also act in a similar regard. They have been able to preserve and revive their ruined world in the American continent through the propagation of language—through *kotodama*. I feel some resonance with contemporary American Indian culture. Now they are reviving their language, and through this, associations with nature. Reviving a sense of their real culture.

I mean, their voice has been greatly destroyed to date, yet they still have faith in their own beliefs, like a kind of animism, incorporated within their own original language. I think they re-create (re-make) what they lost, which is their culture. You know, here in Kyûshû, the Kumaso, the ancient tribe of central Kyûshû, have been conquered and eradicated, but in my haiku, I want to rebuild, revive the Kumaso world—the era of the Kumaso and the essential nature of the Kumaso. [. . .]

Kumaso culture has been totally ignored in contemporary school education. The Ainu people have abandoned their culture by learning Japanese in the public educational system. In a similar way, I think the Kumaso people renounced Kumaso culture. In any case, it is true that we lost Kumaso culture, but we may still have something that originally came from the Kumaso, for example, words from the Kumaso dialect. You know, we can find the sound of 'kuma' even now, as in Kuma-gun (Kuma county) and Kumagawa (Kuma River), which implies that Kumaso culture still remains. I feel something painful in my bones, which is caused by the conquest and defeat of the Kumaso by the Yamato. We were forced to Japanize and become Yamato, just like the Ainu have been Japanized. I want to rehabilitate or resurrect our abandoned culture and nature somehow.

RG: Could you discuss your new haiku anthology, *Kumaso-Ha* in this regard?

HF: *Kumaso-Ha* is a kind of challenge to rehabilitate the beaten tribes of history. To make a long story short, *Kumaso-Ha* is my challenge to resurrect ourselves, who were conquered by the Yamato, through the use of language. ["*Kumaso-Ha*" has multiple references, as the name of an ancient tribe of central Kyûshû, Hoshinaga's school of haiku, and a quality of haiku spirit.] You know, the people of Kumamoto Prefecture may have hardly ever considered, or would even believe, that their ancestors were conquered by the Yamato.

However, it is possible to say that this is true—we were conquered by other people. When Japan invaded Korea, Koreans were forced to speak Japanese, so there is still strong anti-Japanese sentiment. The same situation must have occurred to the Kumaso as well.

SR: Do you know the people of Amami Island, Kagoshima? They were not allowed to use more than one kanji character for their family names. People in Okinawa or Amami also have the strong feeling that their cultural ancestry was ruined or destroyed by the Yamato.

HF: Yes, that's true—I think people in Kumamoto may be pretty tolerant or generous in a sense, but people in Kagoshima believe that they were conquered.

SR: Didn't they think they won a victory against the early Meiji-period government? [The samurai rebellion portrayed in *The Last Samurai* radiated from the southernmost Kyûshû prefecture of Kagoshima.]

HF: [Laughs.] No! They surely think they were defeated. Because they believe their ancestors were defeated; I think this is the direct cause of the Hayato tribe [Kagoshima samurai] rebellion.

SR: I feel I'm a citizen of Kumamoto who has the character of the Kumamoto area, a so-called *higo mokkosu*, but I doubt I'm a Kumaso.

HF: [Laughs.]

SR: So, we are saying that the Satsuma (a.k.a. Kagoshima) people descend from the Hayato tribe, while Kumamoto people descend from the Kumaso tribe; and these were two different cultures. Contemporary Kagoshima people will say of each other, "you are of the Satsuma-Hayato tribe." They have that Hayato identity. As a Kumamoto person, I don't have Kumaso identity, but, Hoshinaga-sensei, I think you do.

HF: I was born near Yatsushiro (about an hour's highway drive south of Kumamoto); this was on the road of return that the victorious Yamato warriors took after they conquered the Kumaso. It was on this road that the *shiranui* [a mysterious fire rising from the ocean] was seen. So some people may think the Yatsushiro area does not belong to Kumaso anymore. The definition of the Kumaso area is a matter of concern for me. In any case, Kumamoto culture has been conquered by the center. So I would like to be a Kumaso-Ha!

RG: So, it seems that the center—the centralized concept or category—is a kind of death: gray, dark: centralized ideas, centralized opinions. The heart of poetry, by contrast, is unique, creative action.

HF: Well, haiku bows to centralization generally. So, I don't know about you, but I'm holding out against this trend—I don't care at all about the center.

Why did you become a haiku poet?

HF: I don't think I'm a *haijin* [haiku poet], because I may be a *haijin* [maimed person]! [Hoshinaga is punning on a kanji-variant homonym] [Laughs.] When I'm asked about my job, I am unwilling to say "I'm a *haijin*." You know, there are *kajin*, which means "*haijin*" as a job title. When I write articles for newspapers, you know I can say I'm a *kajin* or *haijin*. However, I don't really like using *haijin* for my professional work. And I'm still not sure if I've become a *haijin* or not. I had wanted to be a literary artist since I was a child. I had always wanted to write something.

During much of my career, when I was teaching in school, I was unable to write longer pieces. So, early on, I wrote a radio drama about Santôka, *Ushiro sugata no shigure te yukuka* [the title is taken from among the most-famous of Santôka's free-style haiku]:

a retreating figure: rain drizzling off and on

which won a prize. This was some time before he became famous [Kumamoto was Santôka's home for some years]. It was not very common to write about Santôka, or produce radio drama at that time. Then I was asked by the professional theater group of Kumamoto City to write a play. It was titled *Kiki-mimi kôjintô* ["Listening to the Speech of *Kôjintô*." *Kojin-san* is a *kami* of Western Japan, with local manifestations].

Actually this play was interesting, I'm not sure if you know this or not, but the *senain no eki* (the main historic samurai rebellion) occurred in year ten of the Meiji period. Before this event there was the *jinpuren*, another rebellion, which was instigated by the rebel group known as *fuheibunshi*, just right here, in Kumamoto. You know there is the *sakurayama* shrine around the corner from here, which was built and founded in remembrance of the *fuheibunshi*. The *kôjintô no ran* [kôjintô rebellion], which was the original material of my play, occurred just after the *senain no eki* and attempted *jinpuren* coup d'état.

But, the *kôjintô no ran* did not actually quite happen, as the group was stopped before they could commit their action. They prayed to the god *kojin-san*, and tried to rebel, utilizing the god's power, receiving messages from the god, which was, by the way, very similar to the *jinpuren* idea or belief. Although it was a small group, they were eager to change society, and remarkably, allowed farmers to join. Because I myself am the son of a tenant farmer, I wrote a script which focused on the farmers in the group. I like the play very much. As you can see, I had wanted to write something for long time.

As a high school teacher, I found that teaching haiku to young people was very difficult. Haiku had become "senior citizen" literature, and it was very difficult to teach this "senior citizen" genre! If I said *tôyama ni hi no ataritaru* ("there is the sunshine on the barren mountain"), my students wouldn't understand such a haiku. So, I decided to study haiku on my own. By composing original haiku, I was able to teach in a more inviting way. This was the beginning. It was for this reason that I joined the traditional (*dentô*) haiku group, to begin with.

After six months, I became bored with traditional haiku! Sometime after I became bored, I found a *gendai* haiku group in Kumamoto and joined them. *Gendai* haiku enabled me to express all of my ideas or unclear thoughts and feelings. And so I discovered, "Oh, I can write! I can devote myself and my life!" Since that time, I have been composing haiku.

RG: I wonder, since you could have written, simply, contemporary poetry, why did you keep your focus on the genre of contemporary haiku? Was it because you were very inspired by haiku, or because it was simply the best possible form for poetic composition?

HF: Well, I wrote contemporary poetry also. I wrote both *gendai* haiku and contemporary poetry. I'm not sure Americans can understand this, but in Japanese literature, there is a kind of caste system of poetry. At the top is contemporary poetry (*shi*), followed by tanka, then haiku, then senryû.

RG: Is this still true?

HF: Yes, to an extent. Haiku will probably never be seen at the same equal level as *shi*. However, *gendai* haiku has been getting more popular, so it is now considered to be at a higher level than tanka. [Laughter.] The traditionalist order has remained, basically, unchangeable. At any rate, I thought it was amusing and never agreed with that sort of ranking and, further, wasn't happy about it. I tried various genres in Japanese literature because I wanted to do everything equally. I joined poetry groups and writers' groups without caring about the order ranking inherent in Japanese literature. I just wanted to say "haiku is not in third place," but rather, "all genres are the same." However, I think *dentô* (traditional) haiku is still in third place.

RG: There is a kind of discrimination against senryû as well?

SR: Yes, once I read a haiku by Nishiyama Soin, for example (the founder of *Danrin haikai*). Someone said "that is senryû!" "No," I said—that is haikai—which came before senryû. "Who wrote that haiku?" the person asked. "Nishiyama Soin was Bashô's master, so there was no senryû at that time," I said. Then he understood.

HF: Yes, it's true. Haikai originally meant "humor, humorous." Haikai is the root of haiku, and also the root of senryû.

RG: Related to the topic of *gendai* haiku, in English-language haiku, we have a young art form—the main tradition is only about sixty years old. Since being exported from Japan, there has been a strong focus on the classical masters while the contemporary tradition has remained largely unstudied. As a result, there is much respect and honoring of the classical writers and tradition. Although there has been this respect for traditional haiku, compositional approaches have been largely limited to varieties involving pictorial realism. Can you give some advice as to how one might liberate oneself or expand beyond the *shasei* (realistic sketch)—whether one is Japanese or actually, from any country?

HF: I don't know if I could give you advice, but, sentences will likely become shorter and shorter, especially in languages used for international communication (internet, email, etc.). I've been thinking that haiku will endure. Because, as technology has advanced, time has been disappearing—everything is becoming shorter and shorter—fragmented. You know, e-mail is very short, isn't it. Shorter sentences (phrases) will increasingly be used to create *uta* [song, poetry, or haiku]. You know, contemporary poetry (*shi*) has been decreasing in popularity recently. In the 1950s, shortly after the war, people grieved for their lives and for society and wrote long-form poetry. Well, it could be said this era was an epitome of modern poetry, in terms of composition and popularity. Since that time, phrases have become shorter and shorter, and particularly since the time of the university disputes, and social repulsion towards public order, *gendai* haiku began to increase in estimation. So, I think if you create haiku or make short poetic phrases, sentences with confidence, they will in the future become international, worldwide *uta*.

For instance in e-mail, or cell-phone mail, people are using very short sentences but sometimes also infusing a lot of meaning. Haiku will be similar—influenced by the short poem and such changes in communicative styles. I think that contemporary Japanese haiku will continue to have even more commonality with the short-form poem, and haiku in the future may exist purely (defined) as a one-line poem, or a short-form poem. So I think Japanese haiku has commonality with short-form poem or one-line poem forms.

SR: Haiku will be developing purely as a one-line poem (*shi*)?

HF: I think so. As a short-form poem or one-line poem. But the question of how you can infuse the very short form with *kotodama*—is the key to how much and how multi-dimensionally you can express your feeling in haiku, or short-line, or the one-line poem. I have never tried, but for example, in e-mail people might just say "send me money!" And, a short sentence (short e-mail) is sometimes enough to express your feelings in a manner equivalent to a love letter.

RG: If someone wishes to expand their compositional ideas beyond pictorial realism in haiku—could you offer any advice?

HF: This is a very difficult question, so I'm not sure if I can answer properly or not. A short poem is limited as to words. So, you have to use your intelligence to infuse a lot of information, meaning, feeling. Well, adopting realism is okay, but it was a brief, temporary movement. Although not written, if you use the energy of *kotodama*, as I said before, if you use the "double sides" of words, the surface and deep world, as in *kotodama shinkô*, you can constellate a deep and multi-dimensional message, in a short form. The short poem will continue to exist in this century, with the power of *kotodama*.

RG: The powerful short poem. So, in a way, could we say, you don't think: "I'm a haiku poet," but rather, "I'm a poet, and I write in a short form," is this the way you think of yourself, as a poet?

HF: That's right. I don't like to use the term "haijin" as applied to myself. Simply "poet" is enough. If I must choose "haiku poet" or "writer of short poems," I want to say "I'm a poet" rather than "I'm a haiku poet." I am called haijin, not poet, because my poem style is haiku. Yet I remain hopeful that we can fairly say that the tanka writer, the senryû writer, the contemporary poet—is simply the same poet, short or long.

RG: Thank you for speaking at such length and so openly about your life and career.

HF: It's my hope that Japanese haiku may be read by many people outside Japan, and I'm very happy that some of my own haiku have been translated into English in *Kumaso-Ha*. I deeply appreciate it.

Hoshinaga Fumio—Selected Haiku

nigemizu e sengo no chichi wo oitsumeru

    toward the mirage of water
the postwar fathers
        chasing after . . .

gamu kande   tekii wo kande   shônen shoka

chewing gum
chewing on enmity—
the summer rebel

nawatobi no wa ni higurashi ga haittekuru

into the jump rope's spinning ring a cicada jumps in

haru no ki ni noboru   sensô ga meru made

the spring tree—
I climb until I can see
the war

hô saku yo ichi ni san de shinu ga kureba

from magnolia blossoms
   1 . 2 . 3 : if
     death comes

rokkugatsu wa mizu yori   kodoku wa kabe yori   ku

june   is from water   solitude from the wall   : comes

siriusu ga yane ni   shôwa ga sono ura ni

Sirius over the roofline
        Showa: beyond

kan no mushi naku kara   kantsubaki pota-pota

so irritated the
              winter camellia flutter down

eki mae de mabushii jidai to ippai yatta ga

near the station
drinking with the dazzle
of the era

takenokoyama kara muhon no to ga deru kaze ni deru

from young bamboo mountain rebels take off
                        –   against the wind

Section 2: Multicultural Issues

7. Kigo and Seasonal Reference

KIGO AND SEASONAL REFERENCE

Publication: *Kumamoto Studies in English Language and Literature 49*, Kumamoto University, Kumamoto, Japan, March 2006 (pp. 29-46); revised from *Simply Haiku* (Autumn 2005, vol 3 no 3).

INTRODUCTION

This paper explores conceptions of kigo with the goal of clarifying differences in the approach and meaning of kigo (Japanese "season words") across two distinct literary cultures. One area of debate in Anglo-American haiku criticism has concerned the importation of kigo as a necessary concept for haiku practice. As haiku in English has no abiding kigo tradition, in some quarters the genre has been described as lacking in artfulness and depth.[1] Attempts have been made to institute kigo practice, largely via the publication of saijiki (season-word glossaries); however, there is little evidence of poets having sought out these works, over the last several decades. So, can it be concluded that the implementation of a kigo practice and culture is unlikely if not impossible, outside of Japan, and if true what might this imply about the haiku tradition in English?[2] A second issue concerns the function of kigo terms within Japanese poetry. As viewed from the Anglo-American perspective, the kigo of Japan seem to convey a naturalistic indication of season, but little more. With the above considerations in mind, some of the challenges involved in instituting a kigo culture in English-language haiku will be investigated within a cross-cultural context. As a further note, language issues relating to kigo will be discussed for readers unfamiliar with Japanese.

Parsing kigo and seasonal reference

When we look for seasonal reference in English haiku, a non-season-specific nature image, such as "migratory birds" would likely not meet the definition, as we cannot determine a single season for migration, which occurs in both spring and autumn. This fact points to the prevalence of naturalism as an expectation within English-language haiku. Nature[3] in English-haiku literary culture generally accords with naturalist views, else the image will not be given credence, and the poem will thereby suffer. Another way to put this is that in order for the reader to enter the poem, the images presented need to be experienced or intuited as "true" within a prevailing cultural context. In this light, it might come as a surprise to the English-haiku poet that "migratory birds" (*wataridori*) is an autumn kigo in the Japanese tradition. Birds arrive from Siberia to winter in Japan, departing in the spring;[4] nonetheless, in the culture of kigo, migrating birds migrate only one way, in one season.[5] This fact offers a first clue that seasonal reference in English and kigo as found in Japan do not rest on the same conceptual basis.

To clarify the discussion, "kigo" will henceforth indicate the Japanese haiku tradition, while "seasonal reference" will indicate the tradition in English. I would like to show how the two terms "kigo" and "seasonal reference" represent different entities, in terms of both intention and culture; that the conceptual base of kigo is its culture, rather than its season, and that it is the culture of kigo which is the context through which kigo has arisen as a literary fundament. The use in English of "season words/seasonal reference" as a translation of "kigo" seems a reasonable first choice, as "season word(s)," is the literal translation. However, some confusion arises when by the idea of "season word/reference," it is imagined that the context of seasonal reference in English equates to that of Japanese haiku, and by implication, that the literary contexts are virtually identical. What has been missing from discussions of kigo to date is their cultural context, which reaches to the heart of their expression. It is this aspect which is not easily translated along with the kigo terms themselves.

Two haiku in English: Treatments of "no season"
Two representative haiku in English which lack seasonal reference will next be presented, to see how these poems might be treated if an English-language kigo culture were implemented. In this case, existing Japanese kigo culture will be used as a model.

> between silent moonlit hills
> something waiting
> to be named
>
> Leslie Giddens (in *Blithe Spirit*)

> the river
>   the river makes
> of the moon
>
> Jim Kacian (in *Mainichi Shimbun*)

In both poems, as a reader, I receive a powerful though secondary sense of season; my impression is subjective, as the season is not given. In Leslie Giddens' haiku, reading the last phrase, "something waiting to be named" I reflect on origins, on seeds waiting to be born, on the origins of names, envisioning these moonlit hills as hills of deep winter or winter's end. The first part of the haiku, "between silent moonlit hills" grounds the poem's primary impression in the natural world (with "silent" implying a witness). Yet "moonlit hills" itself is not specific enough to yield a seasonal reference. In Jim Kacian's haiku, there are two rivers and a moon in the text—though one river is a metaphorical river of moonlight (a 'river of the moon'). We do not find these natural, primordial elements of "river," "moon" or "moonlit hills" to be seasonal references in English, as they encompass our planet in time and space, extending beyond seasonal division. It seems the power inherent in both of these haiku lies in their indication of a non-human-centered imagination—a native wildness, wilderness. In this sense, they resist humanistic inclinations to connote seasonal division. This would seem an exo- or even contra-humanistic power inherent in haiku.

How might these two poems be treated, if translated into a traditional Japanese-haiku form? Considering Giddens' haiku, would "moonlit hills" be kigo or not? Searching for "moonlit hills," in the saijiki, a kigo cannot be found, though "moon" by itself indicates autumn;[6] this seems unnatural—the moon, just as with, say, a river or mountain, is a primordial element in Anglo-American literary culture.

Importantly, in Japan we would not know for certain whether "moonlit hills" has existence as kigo or not, without first checking a saijiki. In the Japanese context, a given haiku may remain unresolved by the reader prior to the lookup process, as the poem may not be fully understood or even taken in prior to consulting a separate text. This mode of reading presents a sharp semantic and cultural contrast with that of haiku in English. In that there is "moon(lit)" in the haiku, and "moon" itself is a kigo, autumn would be the season by default.[7] The kigo "moon" envisions the moon of autumn moon-viewing (*tsukimi*). So, "moon" is not just any moon: in Japanese haiku, it is a kigo moon: nature becomes reified as an artifact of culture. The bilingual saijiki published by the University of Virginia offers this explanation:

> Since ancient times, the natural phenomena favored above all by Japanese poets have been the triplet "snow, moon, blossoms" (that is, cherry blossoms). The moon appears in all four seasons, of course, but in both classical poetry and haikai it has been firmly associated with autumn, so that unless otherwise specified, "the moon" means the autumn moon. One reason for this is that as "blossoms" is the pre-eminent image of spring and "snow" is that of winter, the

moon came to connote autumn. No less important a reason, surely, is that the moon seems to shine with a special clarity in the months of autumn.[8]

There is found a kind of symbolic, poetic culture implicit in natural phenomena, with certain phenomena assigned to certain seasons, partly for reasons of aesthetic balance, or due to historic antecedents, etc. In terms of kigo, the seen moon is related to a kigo culture in which the moon is part of a series of literary conventions and cultural associations (including myth and legend)—irruptions of naturalism. Such does not imply that kigo lack depth, quite the contrary; yet at the same time, kigo is a culture which a naturalist would take exception to. In any case, we find that Giddens' haiku has no seasonal reference in English, but acquires the autumn kigo "moon" in Japanese.

In Kacian's haiku, imbibing the fullness of the river and brightness of the moon, I sense a brilliant, warm summer night—the enfolded metaphoric image of the moon unwraps as if were at its fullest, brightest apotheosis. Again, the moon figures prominently, and as with Giddens' haiku, there is no adjectival modifier for "moon," so moon becomes the kigo in Japanese, and we have a poem of autumn. Luckily "river" (without a modifier) is not kigo, as in traditional haiku only one kigo is allowed per poem. A modifier might be, *risshun no tsuki*, "beginning-of-spring moon." Here, "moon" is adjectivally modified to connote a different seasonal kigo. Since, for kigo, every named phenomena pertains to a specific season, and often a timeframe within a season (early, middle, late), modifiers are often used to locate phenomena (e.g. river, moon, rain) within that season—so, we cannot use "moon" if we mean to indicate a moon of spring, as we can with "moon" for autumn. An autumn moon is a very brief word of 2-*on*, (*tsuki*), while the early-spring moon above (*risshun no tsuki*) is a phrase of 7-*on*. This is another way in which the given seasonal reference becomes an attribute of kigo culture. In the extremely short 17-*on* haiku form, an early-spring moon seems verbose compared to the non-adjectival autumn moon. Generally speaking, in kigo culture the moon is never a moon in the empirical sense of simply being— uncontained by the filters of season, collocation, literary and linguistic verities, as determined through historical precedent.

Looking at our two haiku, what might be lost by moving them into an imagined formal kigo system, in English? It seems unlikely that their authors wished or needed to posit a specific season—though season is hinted, at a distance: the precise distance of the reader's imagination in meeting the poem. As a reader, I sense the power and purity of nature, image, natural life-force in these haiku; a sense of the purity of not-me, of nature and earth beyond seasonal division. It is tempting to say that a seasonal reference would reduce these poems. And yet it is hard to imagine a kigo culture in which the moon would be absent! Here, the question of kigo versus seasonal reference becomes entirely secondary—in either culture or language.

The argument against kigo in Japan was first advanced in 1912 by Ogiwara Seisensui, who saw kigo as an artificial restriction befitting only beginner poets. The term for haiku lacking kigo is "*muki haiku*." However, we cannot rightfully apply this term to haiku in English (such as those above) which lack seasonal reference. It would seem that all English haiku are *muki* from the Japanese point of view, as the context of kigo culture does not exist. Rather, in English we have haiku with or without seasonal reference.

In the case of *muki haiku* the haiku poet must either explain they are *muki*, or be known to write *muki haiku*. Otherwise, as in the haiku examples above, we will find a specific season, even if the poet wishes the season to be *muki*. At issue is the treatment in a Japanese context of a haiku which appears to have kigo—which the author does not wish to be "read" as having such—while still considering it as haiku, and not a senryû variant (as senryû do not read with kigo). These issues are not confronted in English, but immediately would if a kigo culture were implemented. Various modern poets have offered solutions to the problematics of kigo. Natsuishi Ban'ya has for instance introduced system of keywords, a transformation of kigo culture into a suggested keyword culture. Along a similar line, last year the delightfully oxymoronic Modern Haiku 'No Season' Season-word Glossary [*gendai haiku saijiki muki*] was published (it likewise utilizes a keyword system).[9] From an Anglo-American perspective, problems relating to the use of kigo in Japan and the consequent desire to transmute kigo culture may not be readily apparent.

A Kigo Project in English

Recently, the World Haiku Club (WHC) began a "worldwide kigo project" in English, which will collect "viable kigo." The prospectus, written by its President, Takiguchi Susumu, states:

> The real issue is whether or not finding local season words pertaining to specific climatic and cultural zones or countries in the rest of the world would be possible, plausible, desirable, useful or necessary in terms of making what is written as haiku more like haiku or better haiku. The fact that many poets have thus discarded or dismissed kigo (some have even condemned it as being no more than a weather forecast and not poetry) as inapplicable or irrelevant has damaged haiku outside Japan and denied it cultural and historical depth.

Certainly, this view posits the need for kigo in English, as it implies that some number of poets have up till now been writing faux haiku—that they could be writing something "more like haiku or better haiku," with approved English kigo. Consequently, the result of not having or rejecting a potential kigo tradition is damage and "cultural and historical" superficiality. What exactly is the damage implied—that of the reputation of haiku in English, as viewed from Japan? The statement seems to reflect an opinion held by traditionalists who consider haiku, in whatever language, as something less than artful if lacking kigo. As for the denial of historical and cultural depth, this seems a thorny problem. It is true that in many mediocre haiku, the formulaic stylism of seasonal-reference-as-weather-forecast is rife. But then, to look fairly at any literature we ought to examine the best it has to offer, not the worst—there are quite a few excellent haiku not only lacking kigo but without seasonal reference—in both English and Japanese. So we enter into the zone of kigo politics: that without kigo—and consequently a definitive, accepted agency-published glossary of kigo to follow—we cannot have cultural or historical depth.

> after the bombing
> ruins of a bridge
> linked by the fog
>
> Nebojsa Simin (in *Knots*)[10]

In this haiku, which arguably possesses historical and cultural depth, "fog" may or may not connote season; in any case, the felt season here is war. It is any season, the season of hell. In Japanese, "fog" (*kiri*) is kigo. Its use as kigo in this haiku would subvert the traditional sense of kigo, at the very least. What does "spring" (as the kigo season of fog) have to do with this poem. At most, the kigo would imply an additional level of irony. The predominant aspect of this natural element lies in its insubstantial "as-if" character, in contrast to the violent machinations of humankind, rather than in any presumed seasonal quality.

Imagining a future saijiki in English, how are modern haiku to be treated—how is the contemporary vision of haiku to be expounded? Looking through various Anglo-American season-word projects, what can be witnessed is factory work, specimens, taxonomy. Starting points for focus

Delimiting Kigo

perhaps, but a work of genius will likely be required before poets will tote that season-word glossary along.

Delimiting kigo

It can be argued that kigo do not exist outside of the saijiki in any real sense. Below, Tsubouchi Nenten broaches the issue delicately when he comments, "The saijiki is only one standard of kigo; kigo are always being born and have died within the nexus of haiku poets." Quite true, although until the new term is officially documented and published in an approved saijiki, has it come into definitive existence as kigo? There is a difference between being born and arriving. The "death" of a kigo may occur these days as a function of disuse, but it's hard to shake kigo out of electronic dictionaries with so much cheap memory available. It seems fair to say that in Japan kigo don't simply exist, they must also be published—a kigo without a saijiki is like one hand clapping. This is part of the existential dilemma of kigo—their necessity for editorial approval, publication, and hence institutional exclusivity. Their bureaucratization—factors which have in part caused a number of Japanese haiku poets to subvert or revolutionize kigo use, as mentioned. The Kyûshû poet Hoshinaga Fumio comments, "Haiku is a centralized art. For instance, looking at the saijiki, the kigo focus only on the Kyoto or Tokyo (Edo) locales. There are no 'local' saijiki: you cannot find local characteristics.... I have repellence, revulsion exactly against the formal rules and approach, kigo, and various formal necessities" (Gilbert 29-34).[11]

There is a question of source points for a kigo culture in English, if they are to reflect literary history and cultural depth. Looking to Japan for conceptual models, the oldest kigo originate in Chinese literature. In a like manner, should multicultural perspectives be considered mandatory in English-haiku culture? The first major Japanese saijiki collections were published in the Edo period, centuries after the earliest poetic anthologies (*Manyôshû, Kokin Wakashû*). Following a similar line, should medieval flower language or Elizabethan poetry be consulted for primary sources? Might historical literary "conversations," the round of succeeding generations of poets' and critics' reinterpretations of earlier works, be a central focus? The dimension of literary reference has not yet been investigated; as an example, Edgar Allen Poe's 1843 story "The Gold Bug" features a fantastic, poetic insect, a type of scarab beetle (*koganemushi*); would this be a likely candidate? Certainly, by lending literary dimension, such conceptual moves would begin to erode the cyclopean stranglehold of naïve realism within the contemporary season-word tradition. On the other hand, these artificially wrought creations may prove entirely spurious. Even accounting for future conceptual evolution, is the Anglo-American genre putting the cart before the horse, in self-willing a glossary of official terms into being? To the present, season-word collections have not included discussions of conceptual relevance within the wider cultural context of contemporary Anglo-American literature.

CONFABULATIONS—
KIGO/SEASONAL REFERENCE: OPPOSED TO HUMAN NATURE?

Writing in 1986, Cor van den Heuvel published an influential preface to the second edition of *The Haiku Anthology* (a leading anthology of haiku in English), reprinted at the front of the current third (1999) edition. These sentences have occasioned some confusion:

> It seems useful to me to keep the two genres [haiku and senryû] distinct in somewhat the same way the Japanese do—haiku relates to Nature and the seasons, senryû relates to human nature. Traditionally, the Japanese have ensured this by insisting that to be a haiku the poem must have a season word (kigo), while a senryû does not. (xlv-xlvi)

Indeed, one reason for the popularity of senryû from the Edo period on was that a saijiki became unnecessary. Yet, although haiku is considered a "serious" literature, its roots are likewise to be found within the inclusive humor of the haikai genre. (A recent book (in Japanese) by Tsubouchi Nenten, *Haiku Humor*, addresses this topic.) The above quotation was written at a time when a focused awareness concerning modern Japanese haiku was just beginning to be cultivated in English. Some 20 years later, the categorization of haiku as relating to nature—and senryû with human nature—is reductive. While there is a locus to each form, interpenetration, synthesis and fusion are evident.[12]

From the traditionalist point of view, there may be an insistence that haiku have kigo, but it is not the case that "the Japanese... [insist] that to be a haiku the poem must have a season word." This has not been true within the last 100 or so years. The contemporary Japanese tradition does not find unanimity regarding *muki haiku*. We have the term "*muki haiku*" itself, which would be an oxymoron according to the above dictum. As well, "kigo" is being conflated with "Nature and the seasons"—as opposed "to human nature (senryû)." Given that numerous examples of anthropomorphism exist in haiku (e.g. from Bashô, "even the monkey / needs a raincoat"), it might be that the duality posed between "nature" and "human nature" is lent credence via a somewhat bald statement regarding genre separation. Significantly, senryû, lacking kigo, often contain seasonal reference. One does not need kigo to indicate season, as English haiku well reveal. In this manner English haiku and Japanese senryû seem similar. In any case, the projected duality between "nature" and "human nature" seems at variance with the intentionality of Japanese haiku.[13]

KIGO: ECOCRITICAL PERSPECTIVES
Might having just "seasonal reference" and "non-season" haiku serve well enough in English. In the first American magazine devoted expressly to haiku, James Bull wrote: "If

there is to be a real 'American Haiku' we must—by trial and error—work out its own standards" (lxi). In a young tradition, these standards yet remain in flux.

Japanese haiku relate to a prevailing literary culture of nature, a culture of psychological space, and a culture of consciousness. Conversely, in the English tradition we have, primarily, realistic objectifications of nature: to paraphrase Joseph Campbell, we live in an age between myths. There seems a problem in English-haiku criticism concerning the prevalent idea that kigo equals nature. This seems a misreading of kigo. As mentioned in the Hoshinaga Fumio interview, "kigo [may be] more of a symbolic element. . . . [The writer may experience kigo] through your heart (inner sense), not [only] through seeing, touching, and so on" (Gilbert 40). Contemporary kigo stylism provides an environment which may be symbolic, surreal, impressionistic, disjunctive. Such subversions of naïve realism approach the mythic, so the archaic may be divined within, as much as the modern. Thus, it may be asked, what is the true intention of kigo?

As a young genre, the English haiku has a unique opportunity to forge a refreshed sense of culture with regard to nature: there may be more relevant philosophical issues at hand than the question of how to connote season words. A question yet to be addressed in English haiku is, "what do we mean by nature?" Pulitzer-prize winning poet and essayist Gary Snyder has been pursuing this topic over a lifetime. In his ecocritical essay "Unnatural Writing" he comments,

> There is an older sort of nature writing that might be seen as largely essays and writing from a human perspective, middle-class, middlebrow Euro-American. It has a rhetoric of beauty, harmony, and sublimity. . . . Natural history writing [is] semi-scientific, objective, in the descriptive mode. Both these sorts are "naively realistic" in that they unquestioningly accept the front-mounted bifocal human eye, the poor human sense of smell, and other characteristics of our species, plus the

assumption that the mind can, without much self-examination, directly and objectively "know" whatever it looks at. (163-64)

These comments may serve as a relevant critique of haiku. Snyder asks the reader in his introductory remarks to carefully examine the nature of human awareness, to question habitually unquestioned characteristics of reality. Perhaps it is not kigo which will link us as international practitioners of haiku, but a deeper understanding of the contemporary ethos of our respective literatures. The central issue for haiku in English may not be so much related to kigo and cultural superficiality (the WHC thesis), as with a central question Beat writers such as Snyder first articulated in the 1950s: "How do we grow our own souls?" That is, how do we grow our own culture.

TSUBOUCHI NENTEN: KIGO AND THE NATURE OF TRUE INTENTION

Tsubouchi Nenten refers to several modes of kigo reification in locating the treasure of kigo to haiku: its "true intention." The following quotation is taken from his *An Introduction to Haiku* [*Haiku Nyûmon*].[14]

CONCERNING THE "GLOSSARY OF SEASONAL TERMS FOR HAIKU COMPOSERS (SAIJIKI)"

There is a measure of covenant in kigo. This covenant can be described as one's true intention or true sensibility. For example, considering "spring wind" (*haru kaze*): there is a word, *shunpûtaitô* (from the Chinese: "wind blowing mild and genial") which can be applied to human character. It is made of four kanji characters: *haru* (spring) and *kaze* (wind) plus the compound (*taitô*), meaning calm, quiet, peaceful wind. It is a true intention of the spring wind. The true intention is a tradition of the spring wind used by the waka, the Chinese poem, and the haiku, etc. So, the single (*kigo*) word is a distillation wrought by tradition representing the true intention of *kigo*. The saijiki elucidates (glosses) the

true intentions of such words. In a nutshell, an expression such as "lonely spring breeze" (*sabishii haru kaze*) does not exist as *kigo*.
What?
So, when the spring breeze is felt as lonely, "what am I going to do"?
In this case, the spring breeze: it's calm and warm; however, I feel that it is lonely—nonetheless, there is no way to concretely express this. Here is my haiku,

harukaze ni haha shinu ryuukakusan ga chiri

to the spring wind
mother dead, herbal medicine
scatters

Concerning this haiku, in this case the spring wind blows calmly and peacefully. However, the person (figure) who exists in the wind is looking at the spring breeze feeling sad, because their mother has died. Because the spring breeze is calm and peaceful, the person's mind (heart, feeling) is also (sensed as) fleeting—as unreliant as the herbal powder that scatters to the wind.
Recently, there are people who make muki haiku; concerning kigo, the external, objective world is divided into four seasons as in a mechanism or system; that is to say, the external, objective world of four seasons (for kigo) is something like wearing spectacles (blinkers). For example, the tomato and the cucumber appear in the market all the year round, though the kigo (for those vegetables) is summer. When the external world is delimited in this way at the four seasons, the delimitation marks the rhythm of life. You ask me are kigo man-made? Yes, exactly. There are originally no four seasons in the natural world, but humankind delimits the natural world at the four seasons, and so it happens that kigo arise, as one result.
In a word, kigo is a culture. Because there is a culture, there are generally trends, but sometimes the change is drastic. . . . The saijiki is a collection of kigo; however, the entries in the saijiki do not cover all kigo. The saijiki is only

one standard of kigo; kigo are always being born and have died within the nexus of haiku poets. (50-54)

A MEASURE OF COVENANT

Tsoubouchi points out just above that "the single (kigo) word is a distillation wrought by tradition representing the true intention of kigo." In this sense, each kigo possesses a complex alchemy, every term a multidimensional surface measured within a literary cosmos. Modern haiku writers often subvert or otherwise alter the means or methods of kigo presentation in their compositions; at the same time, most continue to utilize the transformative poetic power inhering in kigo culture, the "environment" spawned by a millennium of kigo. This environment includes nature and culture, objective and subjective, fact and fancy—the topoi of psyche; that is, "reality" as given by the cultural connotations of the terms. As seen above, Tsubouchi is not discussing the true intentions of seasonal reference, but rather the true intentions of a wellspring of literary, philosophic and spiritual culture. What are these true intentions? And, what are the intentions of Anglo-American haiku, regarding kigo?

Would it be best to avoid amassing kigo terms-to-be altogether, and seek first the heart of kigo, its "true intention," as Tsubouchi above implies. Perhaps only at such a juncture will the tradition in English have acquired the needed measure of insight required to move it further toward new sensibilities, expansions of dimension, regarding the actual words of a proposed kigo world. Whatever words they might be, these upstart kigo, they would be marked but not delimited by haiku—as kigo represent a more extensive culture than that inscribed by any single literary genre. Kigo are not a subset of haiku, but the obverse: haiku utilize the historical culture and tradition of kigo, in which the haiku genre participates.

From the perspective of the Anglo-American genre, as with all unique cultural treasures, kigo may be an achievement witnessed, studied and admired, rather than possessed. It is also quite possible that poets and critics will proceed along an entirely different line. In fact, it seems unclear how to proceed regarding the birthing of a kigo culture in English. Likely, poets themselves will open us to new haiku vistas, yet there also exists a need for further research and understanding.

ENDNOTES

[1.] See "A *kigo* project in English" in this paper, for a critique along these lines by Takiguchi Susumu.

[2.] In this paper "haiku in English" (in shortened form, "English haiku") is considered to be largely synonymous with Anglo-American haiku. While the English haiku is a worldwide phenomenon, judgment of quality has generally been evaluated upon the basis of the Anglo-American haiku tradition.

[3.] For the sake of brevity, in this paper "nature" indicates the outdoors; particularly, scenes or images which convey the psycho-aesthetic sense of being autonomous from human intervention.

[4.] The University of Virginia, *Japanese Haiku, a Topical Dictionary* is an online in-progress work based upon the *Nyûmon Saijiki* by the Museum of Haiku Literature in Tokyo. To find the reference, click the link "Full Entries," then scroll down to "*wataridori*" <http://etext.lib.virginia.edu/japanese/haiku/saijiki/full.html>.

[5.] Traditionally, the arrival of birds in autumn marks the season as a presence, much like specific seasonal varieties of blooming flowers, while the "negative" phenomenon of absenting birds does not occasion significance. This would seem a mark of kigo culture.

[6.] University of Virginia (*op. cit.*). Under "Full Entries" find "aki: Autumn," then the subsection, "The Heavens," and click the link "tsuki."

Endnotes

7. For those interested in a Japanese translation of "moonlit hills," some possibilities might be *tsuki oka ni, oka ni tsuki,* or *okatsuki.* In each case, the kigo is "*tsuki,*" moon.

8. University of Virginia (op. cit.). See Endnote 4.

9. See "Gendai Haiku Kyôkai" in "Works Cited."

10. Nebojsa Simin lives in Novi Sad and is editor-in-chief of the influential Serbian publication *Haiku Letter Magazine.*

11. Hoshinaga further comments: "[Notwithstanding,] *Kigo* are very useful and convenient for creating a sense of place (where) and time (when). We can say that a *kigo* is just one word—but this one word can speak volumes. . . . *kigo* [can be] more of a symbolic element. . . . I make *kigo* with my real experience, my sense of reality. . ." (Gilbert 34-35).

12. For a more detailed discussion of this point, please see the "Ônishi Yasuyo" Chapter.

13. For a detailed historical discussion of the nature/culture dicotomy in western civilization, see: White, Lynn. "The Historical Roots of Our Ecologic Crisis." *The Ecocriticism Reader.* Ed. Cheryl Glotfelty and Harold Fromm. Georgia UP, 1996. 3-14.

14. The text within parenthesis represents my added comment; this method seemed preferable to taxing the reader with footnotes. The original linear text was also separated into paragraphs. I wish to gratefully acknowledge the Kumamoto poets Kanemitsu Takeyoshi and Itô Yûki for help with the translation.

Works Cited

Bull, James. *American Haiku*. (1963). Quoted in Van den Heuvel, Cor. *The Haiku Anthology, 3rd ed*. New York: Norton, 1999.
Campbell, Joseph. (1988). *Inner Reaches of Outer Space: Metaphor as Myth and as Religion*. New York: Harper Collins.
Gendai Haiku Kyôkai [Gendai Haiku Association]. (2004). *Gendai haiku saijiki muki*. [Modern Haiku 'No Season' Season-word Glossary]. Tokyo: Modern Haiku Society.
Giddens, Leslie. (June 2003). "between silent moonlit hills something waiting to be named." *Blithe Spirit, 13.2*.
Gilbert, Richard. (Autumn 2004). "The Miraculous Power of Language: A Conversation with the Poet Hoshinaga Fumio." *Modern Haiku Journal, 35.3*. pp. 27-45.
Kacian, Jim. (1997). "the river the river makes of the moon." *daiichikai mainichi ikutai shyousakuhinshi* [First Mainichi Anthology of Winning Selected Haiku]. Tokyo: Mainichi Shimbun.
Simin, Nebojsa. (1999). "after the bombing ruins of a bridge linked by the fog." *Knots: The Anthology of Southeastern European Haiku Poetry*. Ed. and trans. Dimitar Anakiev and Jim Kacian. Slovenia: Prijatelj Press.
Snyder, Gary. *A Place in Space*. (1995). New York: Counterpoint. pp. 163-172.
Takiguchi, Susumu. (2004). "WHC News: On the Launching of the WHCworldkigo Project." *World Haiku Review* 4 (2004). 12 November 2005.<http://www.worldhaikureview.org/4-1/whcnews-worldkigo.htm>.
Tsubouchi, Nenten. *(1995)*. *An Introduction to Haiku* [*Haiku Nyûmon*]. Tokyo: Sekai Shisôsha. 50-54.
———. *Haiku Humor* [*haiku no yu-moa*]. (1994). Tokyo: Kodansha.
University of Virginia Library. *Japanese Haiku, a Topical Dictionary*. 12 November 2005. <http://etext.lib.virginia.edu/japanese/haiku/saijiki/index.html>.

Section 2: Multicultural Issues

8. Ônishi Yasuyo—Gendai Senryû

ÔNISHI YASUYO—GENDAI SENRYÛ

INTRODUCTORY REMARKS

Ônishi Yasuyo is a leading contemporary figure in gendai senryû, winner of the acclaimed Nakaniida Haiku Prize, in 1996 (a prize given heretofore only to haiku poets). Our interview took place at the *Kakimori Bunko,* in Itami, Osaka Prefecture, August 5, 2007.

In the genre of senryû, an attitude toward the social is termed "horizontal," while an attitude directed toward personal "inwardness" is known as "vertical." The popular senryû, which uses joke, satire, humor, etc., is categorized as "horizontal" senryû—an aspect or approach to the genre promoted by Meji era senryû poet Sakai Kuraki (1869-1945), who posited senryû as the poetry of people; ergo, the senryû is the poetry of equality: the poetry of the "horizontal." A different attitude altogether is found in the composition of senryû as pure poetry—this method is known as "vertical" senryû. The approach or attitude of gendai senryû is "vertical."

Ônishi Yasuyo comments:

> I am far from prolific, so I cannot help but feel frustration with myself. In addition, my mind tends to take on a "vertical thinking style." What I can do is only enter into the depths of myself—however awkward this is. And yet, I desire to keep the 17-*on* verse named senryû burning in myself, as if keeping a small fire on a twist of paper by blowing with my own breath (qtd. in *Gendai joryû senryû kanshô jiten* [Gendai Women's Senryû Encyclopedia for Appreciation], 2006, p. 67).

Ônishi Yasuyo—Life and Works, in Brief

Personal History

ÔNISHI YASUYO (1949—, Hyogo Prefecture), was fostered by her grandfather, as her father died when she was an infant. Her grandfather passed away when she was eleven years of age. From that time, she often visited Engyôji Temple, learning *goeika* [Buddhist chants in 31-*on* waka style verse], chanting in the temple with town elders. This was her first experience of short-form poetry. At age 26, she met the leading gendai senryû poet, Tokizane Shinko (1929-2007), and began writing gendai senryû. Her works attracted strong attention not only among senryû poets but also haiku poets. Her works are clearly beyond the "boundary lines" of senryû and haiku. Ônishi often participates in haiku *and* senryû groups, communicating and collaborating with both schools of thought; as to formal literary associations, she acts completely as a freelance poet, excepting for her membership in International PEN Japan.

In 1987 she became the proprietress of the "snack bar" *Bunko ya* [Library shop]. Several years later, she became a lecturer at Kobe Yamate College. In 1993, she edited *Tanka, haiku, senryû, 101 nen* [101 Years of Tanka, Haiku, and Senryû] with poet and critic Yoshimoto Takaaki (1924—), tanka poet Saigusa Takayuki (1944—), and haiku poet Natsuishi Ban'ya (1955—). In 1996, she won the renowned haiku award, the *Nakaniida Haiku Prize*, although being a senryû poet. This event occasioned controversy—one of the judges of the prize explained, "We wished to confer this prize based upon the excellence of the poetry, rather than the genre." In this spirit Ônishi accepted the prize. She is presently a lecturer at Kwansei Gakuin University and the University of Hyogo, a lecturer at the NHK Kobe Culture Center, and serves as a judge of the *NHK Kansai Senryû Program*, the *Asahi Newspaper Evening Senryû Column*, the "Ecological Senryû Competition," the "Sake Senryû Competition," and others.

Introductory Remarks

PUBLICATIONS
SENRYÛ: *Chin ji* [The Sudden Fortunate Event as a Falling of Camellia Flowers], 1983; *Seikimatsu no komachi* [Komachi, Fin de Siècle],1989; *Koibito ni natte kudasaimasu ka* [Could You Become My Lover?], 1995, and others.CO-AUTHOR: *Gendai Haiku New Wave* [Gendai Haiku New Wave], 1993; *Gen no haiku* [Haiku of Gendai], 1993; *Gendai haiku no panorama* [Panorama of Gendai Haiku], 1994; *Josryû haiku shûsei* [The Collected Works of Woman Haiku Poets], 1999; *Gendai joryû senryû kanshô jiten* [Gendai Woman's Senryû Encyclopedia for Appreciation], 2006, and others. EDITOR: *Tanka, haiku, senryû, 101 nen* [101 Years of Tanka, Haiku, and Senryû], 1993, and others.

Please note that parenthetical information in the transcripts indicates clarification by the translators. Example haiku with original kanji and additional commentaries can also be viewed on the accompanying DVD-ROM, and at the Gendai Haiku Website.

Gendai Senryû 1: History and Significance

Ônishi Yasuyo (interview), August 5, 2007
Kakimori Museum-library (*Kakimori Bunko*), Itami, Hyogo

RG: Could you discuss in overview the 250-year history of senryû, from the era of Karai Senryû, up to the present era of gendai senryû?

OY: Yes—In fact, this year is recognized as the 250th anniversary of senryû. This year of 2007 marks the 250th anniversary since the birth of the genre. As can be seen from this dating, senryû arose in the same era as haiku—though compared with the history of tanka, as you know, this history is short, as tanka is approximately 1000 years older than senryû. Even so, in my opinion, senryû certainly has a long enough history to justify its classification as a literary genre.

Nonetheless, it seems that few contemporary authors of senryû have an adequate awareness of genre history. One of the merits of senryû is that *it is the literature closest to us.* So, it has certain qualities, for instance: "easily enjoyed" and "involving of interest"—these "interesting" (*omoshiroi*) qualities are challenging and delicate issues to deal with . . .

Today, the senryû genre is generally regarded as "non-serious art," "mere word-play," "a poor sort of joking," or the art of the "bad pun." When and why has such a sad misunderstanding of senryû arisen? In order to solve these questions, it is worth studying the history of senryû from its origin, the era of "Karai Senryû, the First."

In 1757, "Senryû the First," Karai Senryû (1718-1790) as he is also known, became a *maekuzuke* judge (maekuzuke are the middle stanzas of haikai), and within ten years gained great fame. However, the term "senryû," given to this literary genre, first became popular only in the Meiji era (after 1868). What then were those terms used for this literature before the Meiji era? There were many—for example, *maekuzuke, senryû-ten* ('*ten*' means point-score) as Karai Senryû had himself scored the ku. As '*ten*' also implies "selection," the name *senryû-ten* was born. There were other terms, such as *manku-awase* (poetic verse from the "10,000 verses" competition), and others.

When I started to study, I did not have an adequate knowledge of senryû history, and perhaps at this point I am not yet a good scholar. However, during the process of my research, which has involved interviews and discussions with renowned senryû poets and scholars, and also quite a bit of reading—I began to comprehend deeper aspects of dimension. It is my strong sense that the literature of senryû is neither well known nor well understood, in comparison to haiku or tanka. As I mentioned, senryû is generally considered as delimited by a style of wit—yet there is another abiding aspect of senryû.

As this genre and its compositional intention is studied in more detail, one realizes that *this is an extraordinary literature*. Truly, the vehicle of senryû is an excellent way to express human pathos and the naked and true nature of *what a human being is*. In order to express such things, senryû may in fact be an ideal literary form. When I think of the powerful aspects of senryû, and consider the long history of senryû, I become painfully aware that the excellent qualities of senryû literature are still relatively unexamined.

Today, within Japan, senryû is known by such epithets as "'salaryman' senryû" (celebrated as a satire of society, or as a "working person's" self-satire). However, senryû is not limited to such stylism. The modern movement began with The New Senryû Movement in the Meiji era, and has evolved steadily. *Today,* senryû has attained the style of a unique art: gendai senryû. Although I have an acute sense that the achievements of senryû are neglected, I retain the hope that gendai senryû will one day become more known to society (in Japan), and around the world.

A frequently discussed issue concerns the difference between haiku and senryû. This is fairly difficult to explain. An a recent conference, I articulated the issue in this way: "One difference between haiku and senryû depends upon the author's name (whether a particular author has chosen to be known as either a haiku or senryû poet), and 'reader latitude.'" For example, when a poem is presented as senryû, and a reader appreciates the work, exclaiming "(I didn't realize) such a senryû exists!" this sort of response is indicative of (a limit in) reader latitude. And, as well, one must consider the latitude of poets as creators: "(yes is it possible,) this may in fact be expressed as senryû!" When these "latitudes" of readers and creators meet and are in agreement, we then define: "this is haiku" and, "that is senryû." However, when general ideas of these genres are used to define differences between haiku and senryû, the result is that there arises a divergence between poets as creators, and public understanding. So, I hope that these gaps in understanding become smaller.

And—how to express this issue in further detail—senryû poets tended not to publish their own books of poetry. This situation was quite different from that of the haiku world. In fact, until recently, even renowned senryû poets who composed senryû over dozens of years often never published their work. It has only been in the last decade or so that the publication of a poet's own collection of senryû has come to be regarded in a positive light.

Even among truly great senryû poets, most passed away without publishing any of their own work during their lifetimes. This situation has been one of the main causes for the divergence of senryû between poet and public, as mentioned. So the recent atmosphere of encouragement regarding the publication of senryû works is a sign of good progress, and the number of published senryû poets is now on the rise.

History and Significance

Nevertheless, most recent publications of senryû have been limited to contributions occurring within local social groups (local communities or literary associations) More bookstore shelf-display is needed—this is very simple thing, yet it's not happened: it is a rather absurd situation. Even today, it is a very rare to see a book of senryû displayed on a bookstore shelf. So I hope that bookstore displays of this poetry become more evident in order to connect with readers.

Gendai Senryû 2: Parsing Gendai Senryû and Haiku

Ônishi Yasuyo (interview), August 5, 2007
Kakimori Museum-library (*Kakimori Bunko*), Itami, Hyogo

RG: It seems that in the contemporary era, the border between senryû and haiku has become unclear. To take one example, one American editor regarded two haiku of Hoshinaga Fumio as senryû, rather than haiku. Could you discuss how you see the differences between these two genres?

OY: Reading the comment you just mentioned, concerning the poems of Hoshinaga—his poems are haiku because he wrote them as haiku, in my opinion (it was his authorial intention). And in a similar manner, my poems are frequently read as haiku. In certain situations—for example, if I were in front of such a reader, I would be able to state to them that I composed my poem as senryû. But following the publication of the work I must yield to the freedom of reader-interpretation.

So, numerous people have said to me, "Really? You are a *senryû* poet? I thought you were a haiku poet!" But, as I mentioned before, it is a difficult issue (defining the genre border). If the definition of the border between haiku and senryû were clear—as with the nonce: "haiku is a poetics of nature, senryû is a poetics of human nature and social events"—this simple notion of decades ago—there would be no difficulty. But today haiku grazes the realm of senryû, and senryû grazes the realm of haiku.

For example, some have said to me, "Your poems use such-and-such *kigo*. So, your poems *are* haiku, aren't they?" But as you know, the senryû genre does not contain the concept of *kigo*. Even so, I do not write summer poems in winter. So for instance, when Christmas comes I write poems on Christmas. Although I write (with some relation to season) defining the language in my poems, as some do declare: "this is *kigo*"—this is hard for me to take, as a senryû poet. I do not write according to such concepts in any way, whatsoever. So I think it obvious that *kigo* terms are not only—what to say—certain words, terms embodied in our language—these have not been determined to exist only as *kigo*, serving only for haiku, to my way of thinking. This (issue concerning *kigo*) is one of the definitional problems and likewise, the situation in which the following statement occurs: "Really? Is this poetry *senryû*? I thought it was haiku!"—this situation was partly created by the senryû poets themselves, in the sense that historically they did not publish their works or critical essays in the public forum. So, the issue is complex—.

To answer your question more directly, when a senryû poet writes a poem as senryû, and a haiku poet writes a poem as haiku, in terms of genre, I allow the author to inform me, according to their own creative stance. The haiku poet Hashi Kanseki (1903-1992) has said that, "As the two genres have the same form, they will arrive as a similar poetics as a result of the pursuits of excellent creative-poetic works on the part of poets working in both of these genres. Therefore, finding the two genres to be largely similar is an acceptable stance." I am in agreement with this opinion.

As a result (of similitude), there have been some strong moves made from the haiku "camp," to restrict senryû. So,—haiku—ah!—my apologies—such small and neatly arranged things—. Well, these days, from the perspective of haiku, there are some who would try to insist on the limitation or regulation of senryû, arguing that, "Senryû should be only this." And there have been statements made such as, "Senryû does not possess *kire* (cutting) and this (*kire*-lacking) style is the essence of senryû"; and, there have been other, similar, conceptual limits posed. Although there are those critics who would insist on such conceptual limitations as definitional for senryû, they are incorrect.

With some research it is not hard to see that just as with haiku, *kire* in senryû has been esteemed from ancient times. So, I feel that in comparison to haiku, senryû has unfortunately not received an adequate level of study and treatment. It is fair to say that senryû remains a pitiable literature, in a sense.

Ônishi Yasuyo: Selected Gendai Senryû

hibashira no naka ni watashi no eki ga aru

within a pillar of fire
 my station

watakushi no hone to sakura ga mankai ni

my bones and cherry blossoms
                reach full bloom

waga shigo no shokubutsu zukan kitto ame

during my postmortem
an illustrated botany—
rain comes, no doubt

fukurokôji de korobu to umi ga miete kuru

from a blind alley
tumbling to a scene
of the sea

ushirokara mizu no oto shite fu ga kitari

from behind
comes the sound of water
comes news of death

doko made ga kugatsu no kaze to naru inochi

where a life starts and becomes
                september wind

ajisai yami kako ga dondon yasete yuku

hydrangea darkness—
the past gradually withers

sogekihei no futokoro fukaku sarusuberi[1]

in the deep bosom
of a sniper—
myrtle blossom

gôkyûno otoko o hiite shigan[2] *made*

  tugging a wailing man
just to the riverbank edge
    of this world

NOTES
[1] *sarusuberi* (crape myrtle blossom) blooms in summer. The kanji are, literally: "100 days of crimson." The pronunciation "*sarusuberi*" contains a reference to the tree: "saru" is 'monkey,' and "to slip" is '*suberu*.' The trunk of this tree is so slippery that even a monkey cannot climb it.

[2] *shigan* (riverbank) has the additional Buddhist connotation of 'crossing over'—whether it be of death, or enlightenment.

Section 2: Multicultural Issues

9. Cross-cultural Problematics

A Cross-cultural Problematics—
Misrepresentations of Zappai in English Translation

Publication. *Simply Haiku 3.1* ("The Distinct Brilliance of *Zappai*," Richard Gilbert and Shinjuku Rollingstone, Spring 2005); abridged and revised (with permission) February, 2008.

Introduction

This short paper seeks to clarify a problem persistent in North American haiku criticism, involving the borrowing of pre-existing Japanese literary terms and assigning them mistaken or reductive meanings, prior to an adequate examination of their significance in source-culture settings. A similar paper needs writing concerning the genre of senryû, gendai senryû in particular, as Ônishi Yasuyo points out in the previous Chapter. It is worth noting as well that senryû exists as a sub-category of *zappai* literature. This is discussed in depth in the *Kodansha Encyclopedia of Japan* entry, shown below in Appendix B.

Zappai, a literary genre pre-existing in Japanese literary culture, has recently been borrowed into English, and equated with "doggerel verse" and "pseudo-haiku." As there has been scant public mention of *zappai* or substantive discussion relating to potential problems concerning its use,[1] it is unclear how this term has found its way into the two important existing English-language haiku-genre definitions—these definitions are mainstays for teaching and researching haiku. As the *zappai* genre is an active contemporary literature, evolved directly out of the ancient haikai tradition, the use of *zappai* as a derogatory term determining a trash bin category of the English-language haiku genre seems alarmingly inappropriate. A closer look the literature of *zappai* as it exists in Japanese literary history and contemporary literary culture is warranted.

Several questions will be investigated. What constitutes *zappai*? Why is the current appellation of *zappai* in English considered culturally insensitive, in Japan? Are *zappai* poems really "pseudohaiku," or something else altogether? Is there authoritative evidence establishing the literary value of *zappai* in Japan? Is *zappai* a poetic genre which garners respect among contemporary Japanese literary circles? Examples of prevailing expert opinion, poetic examples, and sources which may offer clues to *zappai* in its Japanese cultural context will be given. A number of books have been written on the subject in Japanese, and this paper presents an overview of preliminary findings.

Zappai usage: HSA definitions of haiku

In the Haiku Society of America (HSA) definitions of haiku and senryû, *zappai* is equated to "pseudohaiku" and "doggerel verse." The HSA states that:

> Many so-called "haiku" in English are really senryû. Others, such as "Spam-ku" and "headline haiku" seem like recent additions to an old Japanese category, *zappai*, miscellaneous amusements in doggerel verse (usually written in 5-7-5) with little or no literary value. Some call the products of these recent fads "pseudohaiku" to make clear that they are not haiku at all.[2]

As the HSA mentions in its "preliminary notes" to the definitions: "we hope the results of our efforts are faithful to the spirit of these words' Japanese origins . . ." If there is veracity to this statement, the HSA does need to remove the term from the definition. It is worth also pointing out that senryû is treated as an inferior genre here.

Defining *zappai*

The following commentaries are quoted from two *zappai* and haikai experts. A definition of *zappai* is given in the Chapter, "What Transcends Haiku Masterpieces" [*shûku wo koeru mono*] from the book *Is Japan a Haiku Country?* (*Nihon wa haiku no kuni ka*, Kadokawa Shoten, 1996), Katô Ikuya[3] has composed the following paragraph, with reference to another expert, Katsutada Suzuki:[4]

> *Zappai* means: other haikai schools with a wide variety of uncategorized styles; it does not mean pseudo-haikai [un- or non-formal haikai]. Suzuki Katsutada defined *zappai* this way: "*Zappai* can be defined as haikai in which human feelings are composed in *hiraku* form, which cannot be incorporated into existing haikai." It is quite displeasing that *zappai* has been looked down upon in relation to ordinary haikai, and mixed up with *maekudzuke* (in haikai-renga: completing a 7-7 verse with a 5-7-5 verse), senryû, or *kokkeiku* (a humorous stanza, usually 5-7-5 or 7-7 verse).

It can be seen that Ikuya writes "pseudo-haikai;" not: haiku/hokku. In the above determination, *zappai* has its primary historical origin in and relationship to the body-stanzas of haikai-renga, and not hokku (the first stanza, which developed into haiku). As we assembled this article, Shinjuku Rollingstone, who co-translated the Japanese examples commented: "The above definition is a bit abstract. Suzuki Katsutada states that *zappai* cannot be incorporated into haikai. The reasons seem fairly obvious, when considering the contemporary *zappai* genre: the use of local dialect, local compositional rules, and a variety of other possible local characteristics would probably be some of the main reasons." Some well-known and esteemed examples of *zappai* are *Awaji-zappai*, *Tosa-kyôku*, *Higo-kyôku* and *Satsuma-kyôku*. Non-Japanese people may not realize that the leading word in each of the above terms is a place name: Awajishima, Tosa, Higo, and Satsuma. Each of these locales has a highly prized form of "uncategorizable" haikai, due to vocabulary, dialect and local varieties of intonation—but also local rules of composition, which may involve social interaction— that is, the manner in which *zappai* (or *kyôku*—a *zappai* variant) schools operate. A person from Tokyo (who speaks the dialect of *hyôjyun-go*) may likely have a difficult time understanding *higo-kyôku*, a Kumamoto Prefecture (*Higo*) *zappai* form, without instruction from a native—as it is written in the local dialect and its rhythms expressed in unique regional style.

Zappai is generally considered a form of linked poetry, and there are many different rules for composition. For instance in *higo-kyôku*, the *higo-kyôku* master will write the first 5-*on* of a 5-7-5 stanza (this stanza may be over or under 5-*on*: *ji-amari* or *jitarazu*), and then poets in the group will add 7-5-*on* to complete the poem (this compositional style is known as *kasadzuke*). Unlike haikai, the part added by the poet (known as *tsukeku*) is always 7-5-*on*. (So, *higo-kyôku* is always 5-7-5-*on*; with the exception of the first metric line, as noted above.) There are other features found in *Awaji-zappai*. In one form of *Awaji-zappai*, the *zappai* master gives only the first sound (-*on*) of each metric line of 5-7-5-*on* (this compositional method is known as *oriku*, a technique of haikai).

EXAMPLES OF CONTEMPORARY *ZAPPAI*

Just below are some examples of *Awaji-zappai,* collected in *The Logic of Early Modern Fixed-form Poetry*, by Tsukushi Bansei (*Kindai teikei no ronri*, Yû Shorin, 2004). Unfortunately, the multiple resonances of regional flavor, rhythm, cultural and comic nuance are fairly untranslatable; there is often more than meets the eye in the translations here. The author Tsukushi offers his considered opinion of the literary merit of *zappai*, in comparison with the haiku genre, as a serious literature:

> Thus, unlike ["horizontal"] senryû, *zappai* is not only composed of humorous stanzas. Probably at this point, readers understand that *zappai* has a unique expression, techniques and approaches, and that some *zappai* are equal in measure to haiku (p. 42).

Examples of Contemporary Zappai

nekoronde rengebatake ni kumo wo oi
       Dandan

lie down over the lotus field chase clouds

nonbirito kesa no ame kiku sansuifu
       Misatoken?
       (uncertain pronounciation)

leisurely
listening to the morning rain
of the water man

Some examples of award-winning Kumamoto Prefecture *higo-kyôku*, from the 2003 annual contest sponsored by RKK Television:[5]

kikoen furi moutokkuri wa araiyoru

pretending deafness already washing the sake bottle
          Mitarai Kiyoshi

makkurayami hamatte wakaru mizutamari

sheer darkness falling and finding the rainpuddle
         Nakagawa Ryûseki

 The work done by the HSA to create improved definitions for the haiku genre is a laudable attempt to continue its fine accomplishments in promoting haiku in North America and around the world; but there are no generalized literary labels in Japanese literature for a variety of poetry that is "garbage." Shiki Masaoka famously used "*tsukinami haiku*" to mean formulaic, or hackneyed; and Hasegawa Kai recently introduced the term "*garakuta* ('junk') haiku" to describe a formulaic haiku sensibility possessing objective realism as a fundament (sadly, a majority of published haiku in English fit into this category). In any case, if there is a wish to create a "garbage" or "pseudo" haiku category in English-language haiku culture, why not stick to English? Where is the need to borrow a pre-existing term from the Japanese? There is a further issue—whether it is necessary to formally define such a category. As George Carlin might say, doesn't the word "trash" itself successfully cover the concept?

AN INSTANCE OF "HAIKAI TASTE"—
5-7-5 POETRY IN POPULAR CULTURE

Katô Ikuya partly defines *zappai* as "haikai schools" possessing "a wide variety of uncategorized styles." Taking his definition in its broad sense, we might say that 5-7-5 poetry which exhibits "haikai taste" and does not otherwise fall into the category of haiku or senryû could be considered *zappai*—not as a throwaway category but simply as an unclassifiable genre of 5-7-5 Japanese poetry with "haikai taste." Many poems fit this broad definition. As an example, the famous director, producer, actor, writer, comedian, and perennial television guest host, Kitano "Beat" Takeshi (recently appointed to a professorship at the Tokyo National University of Fine Arts and Music, *Tokyo geijyutsu daigaku*), composed a 5-7-5 poem which has become popularly known throughout Japan:

aka shingô minna de watareba kowaku-nai

at the red light
crossing all-together—
fearless!

This poem is based on *kôtsû anzen hyôgo*, "traffic safety mottos," which are written by kindergarten and elementary-school children everywhere (that is, everyone) as part of their Japanese language-learning. For instance, one of the most well-known mottos is:

An Instance of "Haikai Taste"

te wo agete ôdanhodô o watarô yo

Let's put out a hand: cross at the pedestrian crosswalk!

Even four and five-year olds know this one. Such a motto would not be classified as poetic, though it is 5-7-5, and participates in the unique flavor of 5-7-5 metrics, rooted in Japanese language and culture.[6] There are thousands of such sayings. Takeshi's play upon not only the genre of the traffic motto, but the intent (traffic safety), contains the quality of haikai taste. Nonetheless, it is not senryû, as it is a poem based on a coinage of the "traffic safety motto" genre. This may be classified as *zappai*, according to the broad definition. While Takeshi's coinage may not be high art, it is culturally significant, ironic, and playful—in fact, the poem points out the problematic phenomenon of mass psychology, as a form of social critique. Takeshi's *zappai* is justly memorable, as it resonates with prevailing cultural issues and its meaning is multilayered—is it actually high art after all? This issue must be left to the reader.

APPENDIX A: Definition of "Doggerel"[7]

DOGGEREL describes verse considered of little literary value. The word is derogatory, from Middle English. Doggerel might have any or all of the following failings:

- trite, clichéd, or overly sentimental
- forced or imprecise rhymes
- faulty meter
- misordering of words to force correct meter

Almost by definition examples of doggerel are not preserved, since if they have any redeeming value they are not considered doggerel. Some poets however make a virtue of writing what appears to be doggerel but is actually clever and entertaining despite its apparent technical faults.

APPENDIX B: The Kodansha Encyclopedia of Japan

Composed by Japanese scholars, this massive multi-volume encyclopedia is arguably among the best sources of Japanese cultural lore available in the English language. The following paragraphs are direct quotation:

> "*Zappai and Senryû*" entry (vol. 8, p. 368)
>
> ***Zappai*** is a general term covering a number of forms of comic poetry that evolved from haikai (see *renga* and *haikai*) verse during the Edo period (1600-1868). It established itself as an independent poetic genre directed toward popular taste during the Genroku era (1688-1704), when haikai drifted away from its original identity as a comic verse form and took on a more serious character. Most *zappai* [metrical] forms are based on the 5-7-5 syllabic structure of the *hokku* (see *haiku*). <u>Senryû is one of the best-known types of *zappai* and expresses the feelings and insights of people in everyday situations.</u> [my emphasis]

Appendices

TYPES OF ZAPPAI—Some *zappai* forms such as *maekuzuke* and *kasazuke* follow the principles of linked verse, in which the poet adds a capping verse *(tsukeku)* to a previously given verse *(maeku)*. Zappai also includes independent unlinked forms which developed from the *hokku,* such as *kiriku* and *oriku. Senryû* was a relatively late unlinked form which developed from the *tsukeku* portion of *maekuzuke* verses.

Maekuzuke was a traditional form of literary amusement in which a given short verse of 14 syllables was capped by a long verse of 17 syllables to arrive at the 31-syllable length of the traditional *tanka* form; alternately, a long verse could be capped by a short one. *Maekuzuke* represents the original font of Japanese linked verse, and even after it was superseded by the longer and more sophisticated linked verse forms of renga and *haikai,* it survived both as a comic entertainment and a practice form by which poets could study and improve their linking technique. In the early Genroku era *maekuzuke* achieved great popularity among the urban population, and *maekuzuke* competitions in which *tsukeku* on a given *maeku* were selected and graded by professional poetry masters drew large numbers of participants. Winning verses were printed and distributed, and prizes were awarded.

Unlike *haikai* poetry, in which the *maeku* and the *tsukeku* were considered equally important, *maekuzuke* composition emphasized the interest of the *tsukeku* alone. For this reason, the 14-syllable short verse was fixed as the *maeku,* and its content became simple to the point of being perfunctory. Ultimately it lost all poetic meaning and served merely to introduce the theme of the 17-syllable long verse, which simultaneously gained great freedom in both content and expression. With the surge in popularity of *maekuzuke* in the Genroku era [1688-1733], many professional poetry masters began to follow the public trend of viewing *maekuzuke* composition as an end in itself rather than as a mere practice technique, and some devoted themselves exclusively to the judging of *maekuzuke.* Among the most notable of these masters were Tachiba Fukaku (1662—1733), Shûgetsu (fl early 18th century), and Karai Senryû (1718—90).

In *kasazuke,* the major linked-verse form of *zappai,* a 5-syllable *maeku* is capped by a 12-syllable *tsukeku.* The completed poem is thus 17 syllables long, like a *hokku,* although unlike a *hokku* it does not require a season word. This break from the conventional number of syllables in each verse gave rise to numerous other metrical variations.

Kinku and *oriku,* both of which were nonlinked forms, also did away with the principle of establishing a seasonal theme. This feature greatly simplified verse composition and won favor with amateur poets daunted by the complexities of using season words. Unlike the linked-verse forms, *kiriku* and *oriku* were meant to be composed and appreciated as complete poems, rather than as parts of a continuing series. In *kiriku,* as in *kasazuke,* a verse of 12 syllables was added to a given verse of 5 syllables to create a complete poem of 17 syllables. Although originally less attention may have been paid to linking technique in *kiriku* than in *kasazuke,* the two forms were sufficiently similar to be considered later as a single type, commonly referred to as *kammurizuke*.

Oriku was an acrostic form in which either 2 given syllables were used respectively as the starting syllables for 2 lines of 7 syllables each, or 3 given syllables were used to start 3 lines of a verse in a 5-7-5 syllable pattern. While there were precedents for this type of poetic amusement in the earlier *waka* tradition, it reached the height of its popularity in the mid-18th century, especially in the Osaka area.

SENRYÛ—As the *tsukeku* portions of *maekuzuke* verses came to be read and appreciated by themselves, they were called *kyôku* to distinguish them from *hokku,* with which they shared the same 17-syllable structure. The style of *tsukeku* selected and published by the *maekuzuke* judge Karai Senryû swept the entire nation starting in the Meiwa era (1764—72), and came to be known as Senryû-style *kyôku*. *Senryû* is a modern abbreviation of this term.

Starting with *Mutamagawa* (1750), a number of collections of superior *tsukeku* from *maekuzuke* competitions had been published without their *maeku*. These collections were widely read in the city of Edo (now Tokyo), and led to the publication in 1763 of the first *Yanagidaru,* a collection of *tsukeku* selected by the immensely popular standards of Karai Senryû. Favorably received by Edo readers, it was followed by 22 more *Yanagidaru* collections issued by Senryû himself and, after his death, by 144 more issued by his successors. The early editions showed Senryû's marked preference for a style similar to that of contemporary haikai poetry, but in treating the verses as independent entities and completely ignoring their origin as *tsukeku* they went a step beyond *Mutamagawa*. The popularity of the Yanagidans series led to an increased emphasis on the independence of the *tsukeku* in Senryû's *maekuzuke* competitions, and in his last years the competitions abandoned the *maeku* entirely and were limited to 17-syllable *kyôku*. At the same time, the light, witty, realistic sketches of everyday life in the *haikai* vein that had been predominant in the early *Yanagidaru* collections were gradually replaced by verses with an emphasis on humor, often quite bawdy, and novelty. This tendency was intensified by the practice of using set topics *(kudai)* for verse composition in place of the *maeku,* and ultimately led to both the production of large numbers of nearly identical verses and a tendency to overindulge in obscenity and stilted wordplay in an effort to achieve new comic effects. After the Meiji Restoration of 1868, however, a reform movement worked to curb excesses in *senryû* and revive it . . .

[The 20th century, contemporary, and gendai senryû movements, are not addressed in the above.]

Endnotes

[1.] In the *Modern Haiku* journal was advanced a hierarchic schema of haiku, with *zappai* at the bottom (cf. Gurga 2000, pp. 62-63).

[2.] Haiku Society of America, Inc. "Report of the Definitions Committee" adopted at the Annual Meeting of the Society, New York City, 18 September 2004. Full text available online: http://www.hsa-haiku.org/HSA_Definitions_2004.html

[3.] Katô Ikuya (1929-2003) graduated from Waseda University. A renowned poet and critic, recipient of the Japanese literature Haiku Grand-Prix, and the Tomizawa Kakio Prize. In 1999 the Katô Ikuya Award for Poetry was established in his honor. The Japanese text quoted in this article is available here:

http://www.jfast1.net/-takazawa/dfrontpage/fudemakase/syuukuwokoeru.html

[4] Katsutada Suzuki the author of several books, including *Senryû zappai Edo shomin no sekai* [Senryû and Zappai: The World of Popular Edo-period Literature], Miki Shobo, 1996; also, *Shinpen nihon koten bungaku zenshu: kibyôshi, senryû, kyôka* [The Complete Works of Japanese Classic Literature 79, New Edition: Popular fiction, Senryû and Kyôka], Shogakkan, 1999.

[5] Available in Japanese: http://www.rkk.co.jp/piratto/higokyouku.html

[6] Cf. Gilbert and Yoneoka, "From 5-7-5 to 8-8-8: An Investigation of Japanese Haiku Metrics and Implications for English Haiku," *Language Issues: Journal of the Foreign Language Education Center. Prefectural University of Kumamoto, Kumamoto, Japan*, 2000. Online at: http:// research.iyume.com

[7] Source: http://en.wikipedia.org/wiki/Doggerel

REFERENCES

Blyth, R. H. (1949). *Senryû*. Tokyo: Hokuseido.
Katô, Ikuya. (1996). *Nihon wa haiku no kuni ka* [Is Japan a Haiku Country?]. Kadokawa Shoten.
Kodansha Encyclopedia of Japan. (1983, 1st ed). vol 8, Shiraishi Teizô (author of entry) Tokyo: Kodansha. p. 368.
Miyata, Masanobu. (1972). *Zappaishi no kenkyû*.
Okada, Hajime, ed. (1976-79). *Yanagidaro zenshû*. Tokyo: Sanseidô.
Suzuki, Masatada et al, eds. (1971). *Kibyôshi Senryû, Kyôka*, vol 46 of *Nikon koten bongaku zenshû*. Tokyo: Shôgakukan.

Section 2: Multicultural Issues

10. Yagi Mikajo

YAGI MIKAJO

INTRODUCTORY REMARKS

Yagi Mikajo is a legend. Not only is she one of the last living students to have studied directly under the New Rising Haiku poets Saitô Sanki and and Hirahata Seitô, she is also a cultural treasure. Her brilliance as a poet of gendai haiku is without equal—her radical voice, daring and cutting humor, and unpretentious poetic stance are fearless. Through more than five decades she has been not only a leader, but has served also as a guide to a new poetics. Mikajo is one of a handful of pioneering women of the postwar gendai movement who not only championed women's issues (in what had been something of a cultural vacuum), but also pioneered gendai haiku itself. She is one of the first woman poets to have kept her family name, after marriage. Drawing on her experiences as a woman, she presented new dimensions of contemporary haiku. In addition, through her career-success as an ophthalmologist directing her own clinic, she became a patron of the arts. In honor of her numerous civic achievements, including the vision, founding and construction of the Yosano Akiko Museum, Sakai City, she was awarded The 1984 Osaka 21st Century Association Celebration Shield.

We met Mikajo (as she is familiarly known) in her family home, on August 4, 2007, through the generosity of her son, Shiwa Kyôtarô (a.k.a. Professor Shimoyama Akira, Ph.D., Professor of Economics, Osaka University of Commerce; the second son of Yagi Mikajo), who acted as host for our meeting. Now in her later years, Mikajo is affected by Alzheimer's disease. Though ebullient and energetic, her ability to verbally articulate recollections has diminished. Due to this situation, the interview transcript is followed here by a series of translations from her recently published book of collected works (*Yagi Mikajo zen kushû* [The Collected Works of Yagi Mikajo], November, 2006, 515 pages). The enclosed DVD-ROM contains a photo series of the life and accomplishments of Mikajo.

YAGI MIKAJO—LIFE AND WORKS, IN BRIEF

PERSONAL HISTORY

YAGI MIKAJO (1924—, born as Yagi Michiko, Sakai City, Osaka Prefecture), graduated from Sakai Women's High School (the same institution from which tanka poet Yosano Akiko, 1878-1942, also graduated), and entered Osaka Women's Medical College (now Kansai Medical University). She received her MD Degree from Osaka City University, becoming the first female ophthalmologist in the history of Japan. Following the war, she was first taught haiku in the *shasei* style by Suzuka Noburo (1887-1971), then by the previously arrested New Rising Haiku poets, Hirahata Seitô and Saitô Sanki, as well as others. She was given the *haigô* (haiku pen-name) "Mikajo"—in emulation of the kanji found in "Yosano Akiko," by Seitô and Sanki. Her haiku style is known as *zen'ei* (avant-garde) haiku. She engaged in haiku activities not only with the senior poets of the New Rising Haiku movement, but also with the younger postwar haiku poets, such as Kaneko Tohta (1919—), Suzuki Murio (1919-2004), Akao Tôshi (1925-1981), and others. In 1964, she became the leader of her own journal-group *Hana* [Flower].

As well as a leading postwar haiku poet, she was active as a feminist, and as a commemorator of Yosano Akiko, who had also lived in Sakai City. In 1982, she founded "The Choral Group Association of Yosano Akiko" [*Yosano Akiko o utau kai*], becoming the group's director. From the following year, the "Akiko Recital" became an important annual event. In 1986, the first female prime minister of

Norway, Gro Harlem Brundtland (1939 -), became interested in Yosano Akiko, as the Japanese representative had previously quoted from her poetry at the UN Conference on Women, 1985. Mikajo, in an international spirit of friendship, became a founding patron of the "Yosano Akiko Bilingual (Japanese/Norwegian) Poetry Monument-stone," placed at Sakai Women's Junior College, and later traveled to Norway to present an official photograph of the monument to the Cabinet. She also presented her own haiku *tanzaku* (a formal presentation and mounting of haiku poems in calligraphic hand) to the Minister of Education, and Prince and Princess of Norway. In 1992, Mikajo founded the "Yosano Akiko Bilingual Poetry Monument-stone" at the Council of Gender Equality, in Oslo. In the same year, she became a founding patron of the Yosano Akiko Museum, which opened in Sakai City, Osaka Prefecture, in the year 2000.

PUBLICATIONS
HAIKU: *Benitak*e [The Scarlet Mushroom], 1956; *Akai chizu* [Red Map], 1963; *Rakuyôki* [The Season of Falling Leaves], 1974; *Sekichû no fû* [The Poetics of (Ancient Greek and Egyptian) Columns], 1985; *Shigo* [Personal Conversation], 2002; *Yagi Migajo zen kushû* [The Collected Works of Yagi Mikajo], November, 2006, and others.

Tasting the Era

Yagi Mikajo (interview), August 4, 2007
Sakai city, Osaka Prefecture,
(with special thanks to Shiwa Kyôtarô)

Interview participants.
YM: Yagi Mikajo, RG: Richard Gilbert, IY: Itô Yûki, SK: Shiwa Kyôtarô.

RG: I wonder? Do you have a favorite haiku, or a favorite haiku poet?

YM: Haiku poets? My favorite haiku poets are Saitô Sanki and Hirahata Seitô.

RG: Why is that?

YM: Well.. The journal of Yamaguchi Seishi (1901-1994), *Tenrô* (Wolf of Heaven/Sirius) began publication (in 1948), didn't it? Some years before that time, the pioneer "avant-garde" haiku poets . . . for instance . . . Hashimoto Takako (1899-1963), Hirahata Seitô, and Saitô Sanki had already founded their own groups.

SK: So it was among their haiku that the "avant-garde" quality expressed in the New Rising Haiku movement — "avant-garde" haiku, first appeared?

YM: That 'New Rising Haiku' was splendid for us! In our era, the traditional haiku had flourished, hadn't it? So, the New Rising Haiku itself was unusual. From a contemporary viewpoint, Yamaguchi Seishi's haiku is rather out of date! (laughs). But at the time, it appeared to be something fresh—but (jumping ahead), Sanki's haiku was uniquely interesting.

IY: Among Sanki's haiku works, which haiku are some of your favorites?

YM: His early haiku works are especially interesting.

IY: Ah, I thought this might be true. The "water cushion" haiku—

YM: water cushion—chomp!

IY: it's a chilly ocean

(Both quoting succeeding phrases from the original: "*mizumakura* (water cushion) *gabari* (chomp!) *to samui umi ga aru* (it's a chilly ocean)." This revolutionary haiku became Sanki's epitaph. Sanki died on April Fool's Day—now celebrated as "Saitô Sanki Day (*Sanki no Ki*)"):

> water cushion
> chomp!
> it's a chilly ocean

YM: In considering his haiku career, the era of the "water cushion" ku is the most interesting, isn't it?

IY: I imagine that from these two haiku poets (Sanki and Seitô), you learned many things—

YM: Yes—well—Sanki-sensei appeared as a droll and cheerful person, but he was in fact dark and melancholic. Seitô-sensei appeared as a kind of 'country bumpkin,' but he was actually quite upright (principled, urbane). It was interesting that the two together became as one mature person (laughs). In addition, in terms of character, Hashimoto Takako-sensei's overt quality was that of—*fu fu fu*—This might have been the most interesting time-period for haiku.

("*fu fu fu*" might be a likened to a slightly delicate-feminine style of laughter; see "Tsubouchi Nenten," p. 158, for further details. In the postwar era, Hashimoto Takako, as a haiku poet, was celebrated as a beautiful, well-born widow. It is possible that Mikajo is here referring to her popular image.)

IY: In such an atmosphere, you developed as "Mikajo-sensei" a celebrated haiku poet—And your *haigô* (haiku penname) Mikajo is—

YM: "Mikajo" is from the kanji of Yosano Akiko. It is a kind of anagram.

IY: Your *haigô* was given to you by Seitô-sensei?

YM: . . . hmm, Seitô-sensei—

IY: Or, both Seitô and Sanki?

YM: Yes—from both, mixing it up—and with plenty of jokes! ". . . *fu fu fu*!" (laughs)

Haiku, Commentaries and Anecdotes

• From the "Afterword" of *Benitake* [The Scarlet Mushroom] (1956; reprinted in *Yagi Mikajo zen kushû* [Collected Haiku of Yagi Mikajo] Tokyo: Shûsekisha, 2006, p. 43):

This book of poetry includes my haiku works from 1945 to 1955, the period which represents the era of my adolescence. Although my adolescence was distorted by World War II and the turbulence following its aftermath, somehow or other, in everyday life, the path I followed was ostensibly that of a typical woman, ostensibly a typical life. Having managed thus far, I have compiled the haiku of that period within this present volume. Pondering the fact that I continued to breathe, even though poor in health, I cannot but offer my gratitude, and acknowledge my great obligation to my teachers, senior comrades, friends, family, and others. In outward appearance, the scarlet mushroom [*amanita muscaria*] is alluring, yet it exhibits a toxic quality with regard to humankind and other creatures—I have found this intriguing, and for this reason have taken the image symbolically, in titling this volume, while adding a touch of color. This reflects my style of conscious resistance.

January 1956
Yagi Mikajo

• Comment by Kaneko Tohta (1919—). Included within the pamphlet insert, in *Yagi Mikajo zen kushû* ([Collected Haiku of Yagi Mikajo], Tokyo, Shûsekisha, 2006, pp. 1-2):

THE SPIRIT OF VENTUROUS EXPERIMENT
by Kaneko Tohta

I recall that my first encounter with Yagi Mikajo was sometime in 1956, during the time of the publication of her first book, *Benitake* [Scarlet Mushroom]. The publication celebration party was held in Osaka, and I attended the party, as I lived in Kobe at the time. My impression of Yagi Mikajo was very strong, and I recall the event quite clearly in memory. At the time, the topic of conversation was focused on (two) haiku containing the title of her book:

akaki take raisan shite wa keru onna

worshiping it, the scarlet mushroom
    kicks it, a woman

benitake no mae ni waga kushi suberi otsu

in front of the scarlet mushroom
    my comb slips off

The subtle wording, especially, in the first example, the use of *akaki take* [for scarlet mushroom], rather than *benitake* [indicating language nuance], suggests the presence of a partner to a man [a woman]; in our discussion of this expression, someone mentioned: "this wording is cleverly insidious." [Implying also "foxy" in all senses. *Dokubenitake*, another scarlet mushroom of Japan (*Russula emetica*), has a feminine form.] The discussion ended I recall with someone saying something like, "this haiku is about jealousy." In any case, the sort of woman who slips off a comb in front of a man, presents a considerable "challenge" to her partner. [The expression "my comb slips off" implies assertive sexuality. In Japanese culture at the time, a "decent" woman was expected to be passive.] We all laughed in admiration. Our group was a band of haiku poets filled with an energy to write haiku of "the human," not *kachôfûei*. [Traditional composition based upon "official" kigo, etc.]

So, the publication of the haiku book *Benitake* was warmly welcomed with real excitement and a sense of freshness. Mikajo had responded to the aims of our group through her body. Smiling, yet in a definitive manner she greeted us.

Strongly passionate—with piercing sharpness—she revealed a sensibility which encompassed the profound depths of human being. I realized that I was witnessing the emergence of a singular woman haiku poet who had the power to become a leader of the postwar haiku movement.

Her second book of haiku, *Akai chizu* [The Red Map] includes her haiku on Nagasaki. I lived there for a time, due to my business, so I had the chance to meet and talk with her, and realized my expectations were becoming confirmed. In fact, the book contains several of her haiku masterpieces, which caused some later controversy:

mankai no mori no inbu no era kokyû

full bloom
in the forest's genitals
respiration of gills

marason no ashi senkei ni taki no shito ka

a marathon runner's legs
fanning to and fro
apostles of a—waterfall

kichô no kiki no ki • damu tsukuru tetsu bô no ki

yellow-butterfly's-danger's-yellow-danger : dam-
   constructing-iron-helmet's-yellow

And the same experimental sense is also found in her later work,

> *mukade hyappiki senkotsu no gi wa sumishi kana*
>
> a hundred black centipedes—
> the ritual of washing bones
> accomplished . . .

Bold, adventurous, sexual, experimental. These are some of the qualities of Mikajo's work. Without concern for consequences, following her passion, creating haiku of the human, Mikajo is a haiku poet born in the vortex of the postwar haiku movement, and assuredly remains today a powerfully influential creator.

• Comment by Uda Kiyoko (1935—). Included within the pamphlet insert, in *Yagi Mikajo zen kushû* ([Collected haiku of Yagi Mikajo], Tokyo, Shûsekisha, 2006, pp. 3-4).

YAGI MIKAJO AND THE TRACE OF TIME
by Uda Kiyoko (excerpt)

In the late 50's and early 60's, I learned of and first laid eyes on haiku works possessing tremendous impact, such as those by Kaneko Tohta, Hori Ashio (1916-1993), Hayashida Kineo (1925-1998), Shimazu Akira (1918-2000) and so on. Among them was Yagi Mikajo [Uda quotes two haiku above, and adds]:

> *sanran no kame no namida ga toketa asa*
>
> laying eggs
> a sea turtle's tears melt
> a morning

.... From that time, almost a half century has passed, and the situation of the haiku world has changed. Nowadays, without any especially deep consideration, some reviewers and commentators from younger generations will comment, "avant-garde haiku was a failure."

However, I do not know of any other period than that of the postwar era when haiku poets wrote with such a strong consciousness in clarifying and discussing their own aims, directly addressing issues of self and society with an acute awareness—this was the so-called "avant-garde haiku" movement. Even in my eyes, a mere spectator's immature eyes, the senior haiku poets' outbursts of their passion toward haiku expression was intensely sharp and powerful. Even now, that time remains burned in my memory. It is absolutely unforgettable.

I have some copies of the haiku journals which Yagi Mikajo founded: *Fukurô* [Owl], *Yatôha* [Night Thieves' School], *Nawa* [Rope], and so on. These were all printed on old mimeograph machines, and the paper quality was poor as well. Nevertheless, every page of these journals is filled with the substantial power and passion of the young haiku poets of that era, who today have become foundational in haiku history. Yagi Mikajo's haiku works represent the traces of a woman who became a pivotal innovator in this era of haiku history.

• From Yagi Mikajo's Comment on *One Hundred Haiku of Saitô Sanki* (1990; reprinted and included within the pamphlet insert, in *Yagi Mikajo zen kushû* ([Collected Haiku of Yagi Mikajo], Tokyo, Shûsekisha, 2006, pp. 4-5).

COMMENT ON *ONE HUNDRED HAIKU OF SAITÔ SANKI*
by Yagi Mikajo (excerpt)

Around 1947 or 1948, in the time-period just after the war ended, there were uncountable numbers of starving people, and the black-markets fed and flourished on the destruction of the ruined country. At the time, I attended a lecture on psychiatry by Hirahata Seitô (1905-1997), who had returned from the battlefield of China in 1946. From 1947, while I was an intern, I went daily to his psychiatry laboratory, and became friendly with Saitô Sanki, who regularly visited there, about twice a week. Prior to Sanki's participation in Hirahata Seitô's haiku group in the medical college, Hirahata Seitô had invited Hashimoto Takako (1899-1963) to be a haiku teacher for the students. Therefore, when we held a haiku party-gathering (*kukai*), many haiku poets attended: Hashimoto Takako, Horiuchi Kaoru (1903-1996), Hirahata Seitô, Saitô Sanki, Fujita Katsutoshi (head of the pharmacy branch of the university), Okajima Kiyoko (psychiatry department assistant), and six or seven other female students. As well, Hashi Kageo (1910-1985) occasionally joined the haiku parties. In fact, these haiku party-gatherings became the core of the postwar haiku journal-group *Tenrô* [Wolf of Heaven].

A little bit later, the *Nara Kukai* (a Nara haiku-party-gathering) was founded. At the time, Saitô Sanki and other haiku poets were consumed with an ardent passion to break the silence they had held during the wartime era. As a result, the atmosphere of the haiku party was quite fantastic. [. . .]

NOTES

[1.] Hirahata Seitô, Saitô Sanki, Horiuchi Kaoru, and Hashi Kageo were all members of the New Rising Haiku journal-group, *Kyôdai Haiku*. During wartime, these four haiku poets were arrested by the Secret Police of Imperial-fascist government of Japan, due to their liberal-progressive thought, and for additional reasons (*Cf.* Itô Yûki. *New Rising Haiku: The Evolution of Modern Japanese Haiku and the Haiku Persecution Incident*, Red Moon Press, 2007; available online, <http://tinyurl.com/yrka65>).

NOTES

2. Hashimoto Takako is a notable woman haiku poet, and a disciple of both Shigita Hisajo (1890-1946) and Yamaguchi Seishi (1901-1994). She is known as one of the "Four T" female haiku poets, the group which is the counterpart to the notable "Four S" male haiku poets.

3. In 1948, the haiku poets, Hirahata Seitô, Saitô Sanki, Horiuchi Kaoru, Hashi Kageo, and Hashimoto Takako, and other notable haiku poets founded the journal-group *Tenrô* [Wolf of Heaven] with Yamaguchi Seishi, and this group became one of the most influential groups of the postwar haiku, and the gendai haiku movement. In the same year, Saitô Sanki founded his own haiku journal-group, *Gekirô* [Violent Waves]. Yagi Mikajo participated in this journal-group, rather than the *Tenrô* group, and in 1951, she founded her own journal-group, *Fukurô* [Owl].

• From, "A Commentary on *Yagi Mikajo zen kushû*" ([Collected Haiku of Yagi Mikajo], Tokyo, Chûsekisha, 2006): "Yagi Mikajo as female 'avant-garde' haiku poet" [*Joryû "zen'ei" haijin to shite no Yagi Mikajo*] by Shiwa Kyôtarô (1954—) [a.k.a. Professor Shimoyama Akira, Ph.D., Osaka University of Commerce].

YAGI MIKAJO AS A FEMALE "AVANT-GARDE" HAIKU POET
by Shiwa Kyôtarô (excerpt)

[. . .] Indeed, the generation of Yagi Mikajo was born in the Taishô era (1912-1926); this is the generation which experienced three main historical periods: Taishô, Shôwa (1926-1989), and Heisei (1989-). Many people consider the greatest turning point of this generation to be "the gap between the pre-war and postwar eras." However, if instead one considers modern history from the viewpoint of a change in social perception of events and a societal shift in values, then the promotion of the advancement of women, in an actual sense, may be definitive. In this regard, when looking at the pre- versus post-1960's era, a complete break or shift occurred in society—a point of paradigmatic change. . . .

> *mata no ma no ubugoe megi no yami e nobi*
>
> between thighs
> the birth cry stretches into
> budding tree darkness

Yagi Mikajo had a baby just like this. In 1954, when this event occurred, it was an era when many ponds, lakes, and rice fields still remained scattered throughout Sakai city; a time when many street stalls set up in front of our neighborhood houses during festival days. Within such a scene, Yagi Mikajo seemed to feel "darkness." It was the "darkness" that was expressed in the novel *Kappa* [a water sprite, in Japanese folklore], written by Akutagawa Ryûnosuke (1892-1927), and similar to the "darkness" that Shakespeare addressed in *Macbeth*.

> When I was a child, fishermen would come to our house from Sakai harbor, as they wandered through the streets selling sardines, chanting, "Wouldn't you like to try '*tete kamu iwashi*' [sardines so fresh they'll bite your fingers]?

In this way, Yagi Mikajo recalls the past—. That fishermen's sea has disappeared. Today, such a sea does not exist in Sakai city. Although the mythical and elegant place name [for Sakai city], "Hagoromo" [from the Noh plays of Zeami: "heavenly feathered dress"] remains, and people once boasted of "the absolutely whitest seashore in the East," the coastline of Sakai city is now decorated by polluted sediment and foul breezes. The sea, which nature had purified through hundreds of millions, billions of years. The sea, from which our ancestors had fished "*tete kamu iwashi*" through hundreds, thousands of years. The sea was "cut" between Yagi Mikajo's and my own generation—this is the gendai [contemporary] situation. The actualities of the era cannot help but include darkness.

Through the baptism of the New Rising Haiku, Yagi Mikajo managed to express the "gendai" era in her haiku works, within the current of our contemporary time—in which everything was "cut" apart. In 1957, she published her book of haiku, *Benitake*. At that time, in the early 1960's, her title of, "The Flag-bearer of Women's Avant-garde Haiku," appeared in many haiku magazines. When we read her writings of that period, it is possible to clearly discern her inclination toward the philosophies of Jean-Paul Sartre and Simone de Beauvoir. As a result, her various writings were attempts to express "existence [*Existenz*]" in "extreme/boundary conditions [*Grenzsituation*]," inclusive of her haiku works. She also wrote numerous challenging essays, in a sense aiming for conceptions possibly beyond her ability to articulate [in prosaic fashion]; it could be said that her essential character was not that of a philosophical thinker. On the contrary, her definition of "avant-garde" was essentially ambiguous.

Within the darkness: there is no "here"; the real aim of Yagi Mikajo has been to find those vectors or dimensions of existence which touch upon this theme. In any case, after the publication of *Benitake*, she began writing essays and criticism for the major haiku magazines, such as *Haiku*, *Haiku Kenkyû* [*Haiku Study*], *Haiku to Essay* [*Haiku and Essays*], and many haiku group-journals blossomed out of *Kaitei* [Ocean Distance; led by Kaneko Tohta], her own journal-group, *Hana* [Flower], and so on.

Section 2: Multicultural Issues

11. Stalking the Wild Onji

Stalking the Wild Onji:
The Search for Current Linguistic terms
Used in Japanese Poetry Circles

Publication: *Language Issues: Journal of the Foreign Language Education Center 5.1*, Prefectural University of Kumamoto (Kumamoto: 1999); *Frogpond: Journal of the Haiku Society of America, XXII: Supplement* (1999); revised for this volume, 2008.

Introduction

Many challenges confront poets and educators in the burgeoning international haiku and tanka poetry movements who, researching Japanese forms of poetic composition in English translation, wish to better understand these genres and skillfully emulate them. Differences between the two languages and inadequate presentations of these differences have created confusion, misusage of terms, and in some quarters a reductionistic sensibility regarding formal aspects of Japanese poetry. *Onji*, the Japanese term commonly used in the West to count up and define Japanese "syllables," has had a contentious history in North America, having served as one of several loci of controversy regarding how the haiku, particularly, is best emulated in English. This paper investigates the historic usage of onji as a linguistic term in Japan and presents an argument for its removal from usage. Linguistic terms that are in widespread use within contemporary Japanese haiku circles are described, defined, and suggested as replacements. A brief overview of the evolution of the Japanese writing system and issues relating to the modern Language Reform Movement provides a historical context for the terms and concepts discussed.

SYNCHRONIC FORAYS

Finding the Forest

In the course of exploring differences between haiku written in English and Japanese, inevitably the question of which syllables to count has come up, and indeed what to call them; whether in Japanese they are called *jion*, or as I had been taught to call them, *onji* (i.e., "In fact, Japanese poets do not count "syllables" at all. Rather, they count onji." Higginson, 1985, p. 100).

My anecdotal research into the usage of Japanese poetic terms began when, some ten years ago in several of my university classes I experimentally wrote lines of hiragana on the board and asked the students to count the onji (speaking in Japanese). In every case, the students had no response at all to my request, there were only blank stares. I was especially surprised that Japanese Literature students had the same reaction as general-education students; I began to wonder if the term itself was problematic. Later, I asked several professors who attended a university haiku circle to explain "onji." None of those I queried recognized the term. This seemed surprising and mysterious. How could contemporary haiku writers, engaging with the haiku tradition, as well as Japanese Literature students, be unfamiliar with this word, considered in North America to be the only term used by Japanese poets to count up "syllables"?[1]

Quizzing Kojô-sensei, a scholar of Old English stylistics and a haiku poet, I asked, "What is this word onji and how is it used?" He likewise did not recognize the term. I found the situation rather odd, as Kojô-sensei had spent many years as a dedicated haiku writer and aficionado. What words do poets and readers of haiku in Japan commonly use to describe and count haiku kana or "syllables"? What is the meaning of onji? Why is this word unknown in Japanese poetic circles? Is the English use of the term onji related to another word altogether in Japanese? And, how does the

English use of the word "syllable" relate to the Japanese language? These are some of the questions I set out to answer in my search for the apparently elusive onji.

FROM 5-7-5 TO 8-8-8: HAIKU METRICS AND ISSUES OF EMULATION

As to the question of whether haiku in English is, should be, has always been, was ever, or can be, defined as a genre through syllable-counting—the brief answer is, "No." Quoted below are two paragraphs from the "Conclusion" section of the long paper, "From 5-7-5 to 8-8-8: Haiku Metrics and Issues of Emulation—New Paradigms for Japanese and English Haiku Form" (co-authored with Professor Judy Yoneoka, Kumamoto Gakuen University). Through the course of the research, it was exhaustively determined that haiku "syllable counting" in English (e.g., 5-syllables/7-syllables/5-syllables) is an inherently non-viable emulatory technique or definition for haiku in English (or any non-moraic language). Syllable-counting cannot be offered as definitional of the genre in English (though it may appear superficially as a sweet solution). As regards haiku form, syllable-counting is unsupportable linguistically, and worse, restricts poetic creativity in English. Notwithstanding, the research revealed that *metrical emulation* was possible, and had already been serendipitously applied within the English-language haiku form for some decades by dedicated poets publishing in prominent haiku journals (for more information on metrical emulation, please see the full paper):

> To our knowledge, a demonstration and application of Japanese haiku metrics has not heretofore been presented in English. It may perhaps be only through a metrical analysis that formal and structural similarities between the English and Japanese forms become evident and compatible. Because Japanese morae are so unlike English syllables, any formal rule for versification that remains at the lowest metrically-hierarchical level is bound to be misleading, reductive, and restrictive in its treatment of haiku form, whichever cultural

form you are looking at. A metrical approach seems an obvious boon for Japanese haiku study on the part of Westerners; it may seem a less palatable approach as a means of English free-verse poetry analysis. In fact, within the science of English versification, "free verse" is defined as "non-metrical verse." What the versification studies are really saying is that free verse is not regularly metrical when compared to the regulated metrical verse forms, that is, the historic cannon of English poetics. There is a world of difference between "non-metrical" and "not regularly metrical." "Non-metrical" in its bald sense, is a linguistic oxymoron. All language has meter. Free-verse poetry is not regularly metrical only at the level of the syllable—the basis of traditional verse analysis. We have found that English haiku, perhaps due to its brevity, combined with aesthetic and semantic verities, is amenable to a straightforward metrical treatment, but only at a metrical level hierarchically higher than where any single syllable might be placed.

It is at this higher-order metrical level that formal emulation becomes a reasonable prospect. For those persons who demand a singular equation between Japanese morae and [an exact counting up of] English syllables, an [analogically musical] metrical approach as we suggest will never be acceptable; just as, for those who demand that an English haiku must equal 5-7-5 syllables, a "fuzzy logic" form whose mean is approximately 11-12 syllables [the statistical verity for contemporary haiku in English] will not meet with approval. One must keep in mind that the higher-order metrical approach in English does not create identities between syllables and metrical pulses. It is a musically analogical approach that finds the typically varied readings of English haiku to have one of several similar temporal structures and metrical patterns (and these patterns are yet to be fully explicated). One can make the same statement about the Japanese haiku, though readings in Japanese are, taken as a whole, less varied than English readings. The pattern is flexible, and is cognate with the musical measure and musical time signatures (Gilbert and Yoneoka, *Language Issues: Journal of the Foreign Language Education Center, vol. 1*, Prefectural University of Kumamoto, March 2000).

Back to Onji: Conduct of the Research

Research has been conducted on several fronts. Primary textual research was conducted with the help of Prof. Kojô; additional internet-based research and Meiji-era translation was conducted at the Prefectural University of Kumamoto, with Ryoji Matsuno, Professor of Information Science; a third research group composed of Japanese Linguistics and Phonology post-graduate research students, directed by Kai Tomoko, also at the Prefectural University of Kumamoto, aided in confirming current academic linguistic usage of terms. In addition to anecdotal evidence, the following resources have served as primary sources:

- *Dai Nihon Kokugo Jiten.* Mannen & Matsui. (Eds.). [Japanese Language Dictionary].
- *Fukui University Linguistics WWW Site* [Japanese]
- *An Introduction to Japanese Linguistics.* Tsujimura.
- *The Japan Encyclopedia.* Campbell et al.
- *Kenkyusha's Japanese-English Dictionary.* 4th ed.
- *Koujien.* Shinmura. (Ed.). [Encyclopedic Dictionary of the Japanese Language].
- *Nihongo Hyakuka Daijiten.* [An Encyclopedia of the Japanese Language].
- *Nihon Kokugo Daijiten.* 20 vols. [The Encyclopedic Dictionary of the Japanese Language].
- *Nihongo Kyoiku Jiten.* Kindati, Hayasi & Sibata. (Eds.). [Japanese Language Education Dictionary].
- *Shogakukan Jiten.* [The *Shogakukan* Dictionary].

The results, aided by later confirmations, provide evidence that *onji* is no longer an appropriately communicative term. Additionally, it is my belief that the two 'counters,' *-on* and *-ji*, used for counting Japanese kana or the Japanese "syllables" in haiku and tanka, have been artificially fused or confused with the term *onji* (or sometimes *jion*) as used in English.

Some time ago the poet, publisher and translator, Jane Reichhold, (see Kawamura & Reichhold, 1998; 1999), wrote to me about the controversies that had first occurred in the 1970s surrounding the English use of the term *onji*, and methods for counting *-on* in haiku and tanka. Here is an excerpt from our dialogue:

> Did you know that *haiku wars* were waged in the 70s over this issue of *onji* and "syllable" counting? Friendships were permanently destroyed. Haiku groups split up. New ones formed. Persons were reviled. There was much sneering, jeering, and rejection. It was terrible. The problem remains and is just now entering the tanka scene. From Japan, one group is pushing that all our tanka be written in 5-7-5-7-7 but 5-7-5-7-7 *what?* How can we count our syllables and equate them with this unknown factor which the Japanese count and hold in such high esteem? (J. Reichhold, July 11, 1998. Personal communication.)

It is ironic that there were such bitter arguments over a Japanese word—and the "syllable" counting battles it typified—which had exited the Japanese linguistic vocabulary years before the "haiku wars."

Counting in Japanese, and Some Differences Between English and Japanese "Syllables"

Japanese counting systems use 'counters,' which are special counting terms for things. There are many different counters, or counting terms, for all sorts of things in Japanese, including phonetic characters, alphabetical symbols, spoken sounds, and sound-units in poetry.[2] Onji is an obsolete linguistic term used to define "phonic characters," that is, characters (*ji*) which have sound (*on*), but not meaning. In modern times, this word has been supplanted by the term hyouon moji (similarly): characters (*moji*) which are representative (*hyô*) of sound (*on*), or simply "sound representative characters." Onji and *hyouon moji* are terms of categorical definition; neither term has ever been used to count up "syllables" in Japanese poetry.

Japanese generally uses two different counting terms for counting "syllables." One counter is *-on*. The other is *-ji*. They are two separate words. *On* means "sound," and *-ji* means "character." One can count up the 17 "syllables" in the typical haiku using either term:

1. *go-ji shichi-ji go-ji*
literally, "five characters, seven characters, five characters." Similarly one can count:

2. *go-on shichi-on go-on*
which has a meaning similar to #1 above: "five sounds, seven sounds, five sounds."

If the number of "syllables" are referred to in a poem, we can ask, "How many *-on?*" or "How many *-ji?*" These questions ought to be easily understood in Japan, when referring to poetry. For counting the total number of "syllables" in a poem, two terms are generally used. The first, and more strictly correct is *-on*, as in: "There are 17-*on* in that haiku." Also, *moji* is informally used. *Moji* is not generally used as a counter, but its meaning is virtually identical to *-ji*: a letter or character, that is, any written character. So it can be said, "That haiku has 17-*moji*." *Ji* is not commonly used to count totals of "syllables" in poems. So, the most communicative terms used in contemporary Japan to count "syllables" in poetry are *-on* or *–ji*, and sometimes *moji*, for totals.

"Syllables" has been enclosed within quotation marks, because with only few exceptions due to dialect, there is virtually no perception of English-style syllabification of words on the part of adult Japanese speakers. Natsuko Tsujimura mentions that, "Specifically, English speakers divide words into syllables while Japanese speakers divide words into *morae*. Due to this difference, a native speaker of English divides 'London' into two syllables, while a native speaker of Japanese considers the word as consisting of four *morae*. [lo/n/do/n] . . . *Mora* is considered as a timing unit, especially within the larger context of words" (Tsujima 1996, pp. 64-66).

Basically, this means that, perceptually-speaking, Japanese speech is composed of small, timed units of sound, rather than syllables. *Mora* (plural, *morae*) is the term that both Japanese and English linguists often use to identify the 'time-unit sounds' of speech, which when put together, compose words in spoken Japanese.[3] With regard to Japanese poetry, the terms *-on* and *-ji* identify these same time-unit sounds. It is this time-sense division of sounds, rather than syllabification, which accounts for how words are parsed by Japanese speakers.

One term that can be used for the English-style syllabification of Japanese is *on-setsu*. It is both a name and a counter. *On-setsu* has several conflicting definitions, and there is some controversy right now in Japan about its appropriate use. Here, following one of the two main definitions advanced by Hattori (1961; *cf.* Campbell et al, 1993, p. 670), *on-setsu* will be used to indicate English-style syllabification of Japanese, and additionally, the perception of *on-setsu* in non-moraic languages.

If one gives Japanese students the task of separating English words into syllables, and then asks them to describe what they are doing, they explain: "These are English *on-setsu*." *On-setsu*, then, is indicative of the closest available Japanese concept to the English-speaker's perception of "syllable." However, there are compelling differences between syllables and *on-setsu*, as applied to Japanese. For a start, there are no *on-setsu* in Japanese which are longer than two combined -*on*. Japanese *on-setsu* are always either one or two *mora* in length. Therefore, it can be said that spoken Japanese is a language composed of either long or short *on-setsu*, the long *on-setsu* being more or less exactly twice as long as the short *on-setsu*. When English-speakers hear the word *nihon*, they will perceive the word syllabically as "*ni/hon*." Are these two English syllables reasonably similar to what is meant by the two *on-setsu*: "*ni/hon*" in Japanese? Actually, not—because *on-setsu* remain rooted in Japanese language perception, and so carry a precise time-sense that is fundamental to the language. English syllables are not only vastly more variable in length, but further, are paradigmatically disjunctive to moraic timing in Japanese.[4] Thus, the term "syllable" is conceptually counter-intuitive to the way in which native-speakers of Japanese perceive and cognize their language.

Though the use of the term "syllable" may seem expedient and practical in its application to Japanese poetry from an English-language standpoint, the main concern here is to promote clear bilingual, cross-cultural communication. When using the word "syllable" in referring to the individual sound-units which we may naively perceive and count up in haiku or tanka, it is not being correct, certainly, in terms of Japanese usage or sensibility, and we further run the risk of distancing ourselves from cogent factors that are innately a part of those original poetic works serving as a basis for translation, or study in English. It seems more elegant, as well as accurate, to use the terms *-on* or *-ji*, and avoid the use of the term "syllable," if possible, when counting up the separate sounds (*hyouon*) in Japanese poetry.

From this point, terms typically used in Japan will be used to distinguish between English-style syllabification and individual sounds, as follows: *on-setsu* to indicate English-style syllabification, and *-on* to indicate the separable sounds (*hyouon*), or time-units of speech (*mora*), which are what we want to count up in Japanese poetry.

There are two Japanese phonetic alphabets in contemporary use, i.e. the kana alphabets. *Kana* can refer to an individual alphabetical character, or group of characters. The kana alphabets have often been described as syllabic alphabets, but we can consider each kana character as one -*on*. Each kana character is, then, representative of a separable, timed, sound-element of language.[5]

Here is an example of the difference between *on-setsu* and -*on* counting: *nihon* (*ni/hon*) has two *on-setsu*. Notice that a single sound (-*on*) can sometimes function as an *on-setsu*, as in the case of *ni* in *ni/hon*. With "*nihon*," we count the three -*on* as: *ni/ho/n*. Some further examples which illustrate problems that can arise when counting -*on* in *romaji*, the Roman letter alphabet, are detailed below:

Enpitsu (pencil) is made up of four kana: *e/n/pi/tsu*, so there is a total of 4-*on*. In *romaji*, we might mistakenly count *enpitsu* as *en/pi/tsu*. Parsing *enpitsu* this way separates the word into three *on-setsu*. To get an accurate count of *hyouon moji* in Japanese poetry when we are using *romaji*, it is necessary to count the sounds just as they would be represented by the kana alphabets. Here are a few other examples: *eigo* (English) has three -*on*: *e/i/go*. But two *on-setsu*: *ei/go*. *Nihongo* (Japanese language) has four -*on*: *ni/ho/n/go*. And three *on-setsu*: *ni/hon/go*. *Koukousei* (High School student) has 6-*on*: *ko/u/ko/u/se/i*. And three *on-setsu*: *kou/kou/sei*. A word like this may be written in *romaji* as *kokosei* in some variants, with the -*u* kana left out, making it more difficult to accurately count the total -*on*. Usually, an omicron over the '*o*' will indicate the presence of the additional -*u* kana. *Kekkon* (marriage) has a doubled consonant, which indicates the presence of the small "*tsu (t)*" kana, a "stop" or pause in speech of one *mora*. *Kekkon* has 4-*on*: *ke/(t)/ko/n*. And two *on-setsu*: *ke(t)/kon*." Remember, each -*on* or -*ji* can always be represented by one (mono- or digraphic) kana character in Japanese.

Morae and Prosody

The term mora, and its plural, morae are English linguistic terms which are also found as Japanese loan-words. In typical Japanese spoken style, each -*on* takes approximately the same amount of time to speak. In fact, each kana, including digraphs like kyo, jyo, gyo, etc., takes about the same amount of time to speak. This time-sense or time-count is defined by the term mora, or we could say by kana or hyouon time-units.

Mora is a technical term, not generally known or used outside the field of linguistics. The more commonly known term is *haku*. Currently, mora(e) are undergoing intensive linguistic studies, which show connections between spoken and written Japanese that reveal underlying relationships not altogether unlike English prosody. Recent research shows that the perception of *moraic* length and timing on the part of native speakers is highly complex, being influenced by the accent, pitch shift, duration, and volume-level of words.[6] Consequently, it has become somewhat reductive, linguistically, to consider *morae* purely as measures of abstract time-units, a view which was widely held some 20 years ago. *Mora* research is mentioned, then, to call attention to *layers* of prosodic complexity in Japanese language and poetry that go far beyond -*on* counting alone, which if taken as a singular, defining formal feature of haiku, leads to reductive structural interpretations. In terms of written Japanese, the number of *mora* will always agree with the number of kana (with digraphs considered as single kana), and therefore the number of -*on*.

A "Lexical Glossary" of all the terms covered in this paper is found in the Appendix.

DIACHRONIC EXPEDITIONS

A Brief History of Kanji and Kana

Next presented is a brief history and overview of the Japanese language from an orthographic viewpoint. "It is generally believed that kanji came to Japan from China through Korea [between 300—400 CE]. No record of a written language exists in Japan before this time" (Mitamura & Mitamura, 1997, p. xi). Kanji themselves are much more ancient, "attributable to the scribes of the Yin Dynasty [1700—1050 BCE]" (p. xi). The oldest kanji descend from hieroglyphs or pictographs ("*shoukei moji*," op cit, p. xiv). Japanese kanji, as presently used (with some exceptions) are ideogrammatic, not phonetic. Each character represents a singular concept or idea rather than a singular sound. The group of characters from which kanji spring are called: *hyoui moji*, meaning, "characters (*moji*) which are representative (*hyou*) of meaning (*i*), not sound." An older term for *hyoui moji* is *iji*: meaning (*i*) + characters (*ji*).

In China, the meaning and sound of the kanji were originally directly related, but when kanji were imported into Japan, some interesting changes occurred. First, the original Chinese sounds which came along with the kanji were changed to accord with Japanese, which does not use pitch to ascribe meaning, as does Chinese. (This is called the ON reading of the kanji.) Then, pre-existing Japanese words which had the same meaning as the Chinese kanji were added to each kanji. (This is called the KUN reading of the kanji.) Over the centuries, the same kanji was reintroduced to Japan, sometimes repeatedly, from various regions of China, and from succeeding Dynasties. With each reintroduction to Japan, the same kanji took on yet another form of pronunciation.[7] Kanji were also created and further adapted in Japan, and rarely, a kanji from Japan went back to China.[8]

> The typical kanji now has two or three ON readings and two or three KUN readings, while some of the commoner kanji, such as "life" and "below" can have as many as ten fundamentally different readings . . . As a result of fundamental differences between the monosyllabic Chinese language and the polysyllabic, highly inflected Japanese language the Chinese writing system proved decidedly

unsuitable in the case of inflected items such as verbs. ... the potential for confusion was obviously considerable . . . (Henshall, 1988, p xiv).

"The number of kanji in actual use probably did not exceed 5,000 or 6,000 [before 1946]" (Campbell et al, p. 669). Eventually, novel 'problem solving' phonic characters (absent of intrinsic meaning) were evolved in stages to distinguish between alternate readings of the same kanji and determine verb inflections, among other uses.

Today, there are two phonic alphabets, hiragana and katakana, in general use. Japanese is written with a mixture of kanji and kana, mostly hiragana. There may be a sprinkling of katakana and a smattering of roman letters, usually for foreign names or places, and technical words (also plenty of advertising). Current linguists now consider contemporary Japanese to have three separate alphabets, plus the 1,945 *Jôyô kanji* approved for general use—unless you are a haiku poet, in which case you probably know many more kanji than the average person on the street. (*Jôyô kanji* instruction is not completed until the end of the 9th grade.) When a Japanese poem is read in romaji, we are looking at a special form of *hyouon moji,* called *tan-on moji*: a "single-phoneme character" alphabet. However, outside of a few historical social and literary experiments, romaji is not ordinarily used by the Japanese themselves in written discourse. Romaji is mostly used for the benefit of those who cannot read the kana alphabets.

The term *hyouon moji* is very useful in Japanese linguistics, because historically, various phonic characters were employed before the later development of the kana alphabets currently in use. The Manyôshû, 759 CE, the earliest collection of poetry, is written in Manyôgana, a script in which certain kanji were designated as 'sound-only' kanji (see Campbell et al, pp. 730-31). *Hyouon moji* can be used to describe all of these phonic characters, and *hyouon* can be used more generally to describe phonic representations, without the need to discuss characters, specifically.

Hiragana in its modern form is composed of 48 kana characters. "*Hira* means 'commonly used,' 'easy,' rounded' (Campbell et al, p. 731). Hiragana was developed from simplified kanji, and takes its name,

> because the [kana] are considered rounded and easy to write [when compared with the original kanji]. In its early [9th century Heian era] forms, hiragana was used by women [who were not permitted to learn the Chinese script], while the unsimplified kanji were used by men; for this reason, the earliest hiragana was also called *onnade*, "women's hand." By the end of the 9th century, *onnade* ceased to be a system limited to women and... [only] gained full acceptance when the imperial poetic anthology [*Kokinshu*, pub 905CE] was written in *onnade* (op cit).

"The *kata-* in *katakana* means 'partial, 'not whole, 'fragmentary' (op cit). This name stems from the fact that many *katakana* were taken from only a part of the original kanji. In its earliest use, "*katakana* was a mnemonic device for pronouncing Buddhist texts written in Chinese" (op cit). By the mid-10th century, poetic anthologies had been composed in *katakana*.

THE RISE AND FALL OF ONJI

The year of the Meiji Restoration, 1868, marked the beginning of the modern Japanese language reform movement.

> Although much of the development of modern Japanese proceeded spontaneously, the role of planned development was considerable.... It was necessary to select a single variety of Japanese... to increase literacy, [and] create an extensive modern vocabulary" (Campbell et al, p. 669).

As well, grammatical and stylistic usages began to be codified, [and Japanese began] to be liberated from its dependence on classical Chinese. [It was felt by a number of eminent scholars that] the only way to modernize the language—and the minds of the people that spoke it—was in affiliation with the languages by means of which the knowledge of the developed West [could be] introduced (*op cit*).

It seems likely that the entrance of *onji* into the Western lexicon was a result of the publication of Nishi Amane's landmark text, the *Hyakugaku Renkan*, in 1870 (see Campbell et al, p. 1098), soon after his four-year sojourn in Europe. Amane equated the pre-existing Japanese term *onji* orthographically with "letters." In this first Western-style encyclopedia, "patterned after the works of Auguste Comte . . . Amane introduced the full spectrum of Western arts and sciences to Japan" (op cit). The encyclopedia contains hundreds of Western terms, which are correlated with Japanese terms or concepts (and vice versa). Amane's translation is preserved in the *Nihon Kokugo Daijiten*, which annotates the *Hyakugaku Renkan* as the root-translation of *onji* to the English "letters" (*cf. Nihon Kokugo Daijiten*, 1988, Vol. 4, p. 159). The *Hyakugaku Renkan* was an important source of English-Japanese and later, Japanese-English translations (based upon Amane's correlations) throughout the Meiji era (1868-1912), during which time the Japanese vocabulary developed with phenomenal rapidity.

Meiji-era grammarians typically used *onji* to describe phonic characters, while its sister-term *iji* was used to describe ideogrammatic kanji characters. Prior to 1900, language reform groups were urging the government to take steps to modernize the Japanese language, but no major language reforms occurred. The changes that did result were serendipitous. Two varieties of Japanese emerged: the classical standard, based on pre-Meiji styles, used only in writing; and the colloquial standard, rooted in the spoken language and more or less identical to modern Japanese. Literacy was also rapidly improving through the implementation of compulsory education.

By the early 1900s Ueda Kazutoshi, also known as Ueda Mannen (1867-1937), a professor at Tokyo University (influenced by his studies with Basil Hall Chamberlain and "the first Japanese trained in Western linguistics..." Campbell et al, p. 670), had become a member of the National Language Research Committee. Ueda introduced Western linguistic research methods into Japan, trained researchers, and contributed greatly to national language reform policies. In a relatively early monograph *Kari-ji Meishyou-kou* [The Origination of Kana], (1904 or prior), he used the term *onji* exclusively. One of Ueda Mannen's crowning achievements was the *Dai Nihon Kokugo Jiten* [Japanese Language Dictionary], (1972, reprint), originally published in four volumes, 1914-1919. "Containing over 200,000 entries, it became the standard work for editors of later dictionaries . . . it is distinguished by its cautious treatment of etymologies and its policy of including only information of unquestioned accuracy" (Campbell et al, p. 266). Within, *onji* is cited, and a brief definition is included (p. 254). There is no reference to *hyouon* or *hyouon moji*. In fact, examining citations for hyou, we find no entry (see p. 1666). Evidently, neither *hyouon* nor *hyouon moji* had entered linguistic parlance prior to publication.

Hashimoto Shinkichi (1882-1945), a noted Japanese linguist and grammarian, graduated from Tokyo University in 1906 and served as assistant to Ueda Mannen from 1909 to 1927, when he succeeded Ueda as professor of Japanese at Tokyo University. We find in his *Kokugakugairon* [An Outline of Japanese Linguistics], (1967, reprint), originally published in 1932-33, a chapter titled *moji no shurui* [Types of Characters]. On page 104 is the statement: "Concerning onji, it is synonymous with *hyouon moji* and *onhyou moji*" (my translation). In the remainder of the chapter, *onji* is the term Hashimoto prefers; he uses it on two occasions.

This situation is reversed some ten years later in a paper written in 1943, titled *nihon no moji ni tsuite* [About Japanese Characters], (*cf. moji oyoubi kana ken no kenkyu* [Research into Kana and the Usage of Characters], 1976, reprint, pp. 226-36). The paper's subtitle, *moji no hyoui-se to hyouon-se*, means roughly, "The Ideogrammatic and Phonic Nature of Characters." On page 226 is found: "Concerning *hyouon moji*, it is synonymous with *onji*." Hashimoto uses *hyouon moji* throughout the paper (I count eight times), and no longer uses *onji*. So, though it is unclear when exactly the term *hyouon moji* entered the linguistic lexicon, it seems apparent that it was becoming more popularly used by grammarians by the 1930s, and likely was becoming or had become the preferred term just prior to the post-war period. At this time, the field of linguistics was developing quite rapidly, and a large number of language reforms were being implemented. Significantly, Hashimoto, in concert with a group of linguistic scholars, was responsible for the *Supplement to the New Grammar* (*Shin bunten bekki*), the official school reference grammars established by the Ministry of Education, as late as 1939. Hashimoto's grammatical ideas were widely distributed and remain influential to the present.

Further references to *onji* in Hashimoto's papers on Japanese phonology written in the 1930s and 1940s have not been located. It is likely that *onji* was removed from educational grammars during or following the 1930s reforms, being supplanted with *hyouon moji*. As to the exact date of the disappearance of *onji*, and a significant referential notation regarding its disappearance, none has been found to this date. Okajima Teruhiro, Professor of Japanese Language and Linguistics at Fukui University, who has done extensive research on the Language Reform Movement and the works of Hashimoto Shinkichi, searched for particular references and reported that there were indeed very few references to *onji* whatsoever. Okajima suggests:

> As the field of Japanese linguistics developed, there arose confusions in the usage of *onji* with another term, "*on-se kigô*," a term used to denote the special characters used for

phonetic representation. It is likely that the more accurate term, *hyouon moji*, was chosen to replace *onji* in order to avoid confusions caused by variant usages of *onji*" (Personal communication, July 30, 1998, my translation).

Onji is no longer included as a reference in many current Japanese dictionaries. For instance, there is no reference in the *Nihongo Hyakuka Daijiten* (Kindati, Hayashi and Sibata, 1988), an encyclopedic linguistics dictionary, where in the same dictionay *hyouon moji* receives a lengthy treatment (p. 307). An electronic translation dictionary, the Canon IDX-9500, containing nearly 400,000 Japanese word-entries and over 250,000 English word-entries, finds *hyouon moji,* only, when a search is performed using "*hyoun*" as a keyword. Keying in "phonogram" in English, the dictionary translates the term as *hyouon moji*, only. Searching with the keyword "onji" results in zero hits. Onji is not contained in the database.

The above facts must give one pause. There are references in some academic dictionaries, for instance, the massive 20 volume *Nihon Kokugo Daijiten*, (1988), as previously mentioned. In the *Koujien*, (Shimura, Ed., 1998), perhaps the best and largest of the single-volume unabridged dictionaries in Japan, we find a citation for *onji* (p. 419), which simply says, "please see *hyouon moji*." It is only under this citation for *hyouon moji* (p. 2275), that a definition is given. There is also a single reference found in the largest of Kenkyusha's Japanese-English translation dictionaries, (1978), where *onji* is translated by the word "phonogram," with a reference to "see: *hyouon*."

How "onji" likely came to the Haiku Society of America

Clearly, *onji* is not recognized in contemporary Japanese poetic circles. In contrast, the term *hyouon moji* is fairly well-recognized as a defining term, in both linguistic, and, as we have found, literary environments. Onji was first brought to the United States haiku audience via a letter published in the Haiku Society of America's *Frogpond Journal of Haiku* (1978), written by Tadashi Kondo, in response to the Haiku Society of America, under the direction of Harold G. Henderson, having previously adopted the term "jion." Kondo wrote that "Jion is a specialized term from linguistics relating to the pronunciation of a Sino-Japanese character. Onji means 'phonetic symbol' (or 'sound symbol,' and seems to be the term desired. . . . [however] while the concept of onji has often been translated into English as 'syllable,' it would be more accurate to say that the onji is a 'mora.' . . " (op cit). Following the *Frogpond Journal* publication, onji became an important part of the English language haiku-study vocabulary. Hopefully, current research will suffice to change this usage, which still remains active throughout the West. Kondo recently commented:

> I knew Professor Henderson through letters exchanged three or four times before his death in 1974. I did not meet him in person, since his death came the day after I arrived in this country. I know he was a fine linguist, and would never make such a trifling mistake. My personal speculation is that the mistake, of having jion instead of onji, could have simply been a typo. It could have been done either by Professor Henderson himself or by the printer. This type of mistake could have happened easily; as most people do not pay much attention to these words, the mistake might have passed by many peoples' eyes. [Nevertheless] in the early 70s . . . Haiku poets who would come to the HSA monthly meetings at the Japan Society were using jion, as in: "haiku is written in 5-7-5 jion," which is absolutely wrong. . . . When I found this mistake, my simple reaction to it was to flip the word order, from jion to onji, because that seemed the most reasonable correction . . . ([When you] look up onji in older dictionaries, you may find explanations given, instead of a simple direction to see hyouon moji or onpyou moji.) . . . I found the problem and decided to write a letter to correct the misunderstanding. So the issue is basically technical and I was not concerned about its popular usage. It is another issue. (T. Kondo, April 3, 1999. Personal communication.)

The well-known haiku poet James Kirkup, a frequent resident of Japan, has commented that "few [Japanese] have ever heard the word onji" (*Frogpond Journal*, 1995); we assume he is referring in particular to the Japanese short-form poetry community. Due to the obscurity of onji, some rather ironic cross-cultural miscommunications have been occurring with greater frequency at one of the most active areas of international exchange—internet haiku and tanka websites. In a typical scenario, an aspiring non-Japanese haiku poet wishes to discuss how to count -*on* in haiku, and uses the term *onji* in an e-mail to a newsgroup. Japanese respondents, who are rarely fluent in English, do not recognize the term, and assume it is a mysterious English word. A potentially edifying cross-cultural dialogue is thus thrown into confusion; the topic under discussion, -*on* counting, is never effectively evolved. Terms such as -*on*, -*ji,* or -*moji*, while they might not always be applied with technical precision, would be communicative. One can also imagine that the use of communicative terms, combined with a more refined understanding of Japanese language issues on the part of haiku poets who are otherwise unfamiliar with Japanese, would create an atmosphere more conducive to a multicultural exchange of poetic ideas. Communication problems, as in the example above, only serve to maintain historical patterns of isolation and insularity between the Japanese, North American, and increasingly, international haiku and tanka cultures which use English as a medium of exchange.[9]

The Persistence of Onji

It is now possible to summarize some probable reasons for the persistence of *onji* in the English-language poetic lexicon:

1. A number of influential translators and Japanese authors used the term, following the Meiji restoration (1868),

through the 1930s. Later translators, seeking translation sources, may have continued to follow English translations by previous translators.

2. *Onji* continues to be indexed in the best available Japanese-English translation dictionary as well as in some of the academic and collegiate Japanese dictionaries. This is a primary source of information for those living outside Japan. Although in all the cases we found, *hyouon* is referred to as an operative term, *onji* is implied by description as archaic only in the *Nihon Kokugo Daijiten*. Kenkyusha's translation dictionaries, good as they may be, are no substitute for an unabridged Japanese-language dictionary, which does provide enough information to discern an archaic attribution, if one researches the indicated references.

3. Under the influence of Western linguistic methods and the pressing need for language reform, the Japanese language has undergone rapid change in the 20th century, especially in the use of grammatical terms. The Japanese pay a great deal of attention to their language: Japanese language history, grammar, and phonology are taught in public schools, and knowledge of such terminology is often required for college entrance exams. Any changes made by Ministry of Education linguistic research groups tend to be rapidly implemented in future textbook changes. Given this atmosphere of change, it is possible for a term to quickly exit the Japanese lexicon, say in a period of 20 or so years from the date of textbook removal. Obviously, World War II also had an enormous impact in creating a 'break' from some aspects of pre-war linguistic usage: outmoded aspects of pre-war language dropped from usage with extreme rapidity. This scenario implies that a Japanese word could enter the English language while shortly thereafter disappearing from the Japanese lexicon.

4. A 'culture-gap' can occur through purely written communication with Japanese correspondents. In correspondence with Japanese writers in which I was soliciting information about *onji*, informants never mentioned their personal experience. If they were questioned about an unfamiliar word, a dictionary was consulted. Not finding the word in abridged dictionaries, informants tended to seek out a dictionary such as the *Nihon Kokugo Daijiten*, whose *onji* information was then quoted. However, the archaic nature of the term, which takes additional research to verify, was not mentioned. Generally, informants tended not to offer personal opinions or their lack of acquaintance with *onji* in personal communications, unless they were teachers of Japanese linguistics and phonology, had access to numerous sources, and perhaps therefore considered themselves informed enough to comment. Due to differing cultural styles of communication, English informants, on receiving communications from correspondents, may have been lead to believe that *onji* was a viable term of discourse.

5. There is little readily available research into contemporary Japanese terms utilized in Japanese linguistic phonology in English translation. Japanese Linguistics texts often apply English linguistic terms and categories to the Japanese language. Much of the linguistic commentary on Japanese poetry (in English) has taken a Western-oriented approach to the language, as is the case with the term "syllable." This has been true even within Japan, though the situation is changing. In addition, the disappearance of *onji* is not of particular significance within Japanese phonological studies.

6. The Japanese use of 'counting' terms has caused misunderstandings in English. The specific counting terms and concepts utilized in Japanese poetic circles have not been broadly introduced.

7. Few Western poets or translators with an interest in Japanese poetry have lived and worked in Japan, gained Japanese language ability, joined haiku circles, and inquired about linguistic terms. Short visits and overseas inquiries may not have elicited the necessary cultural information.

8. Research into *onji* twenty to thirty years ago might have yielded different results. If Japanese grammarians had been consulted, researchers may have found that some scholars had knowledge of the term, having been educated during a time when *onji* was still in usage.

NOTES

[1.] I first became interested in this subject nearly twenty years ago, while attending the Naropa University, in Boulder, Colorado. I encountered the traditional haiku masters through the auspices of Patricia Donegan (Donegan & Ishibashi, 1998), and became involved with various American haiku circles over succeeding years. This paper focuses on linguistic issues related with the most popular traditional Japanese poetic forms, both within and outside of Japan: haiku and tanka. Nonetheless, one can likewise apply this discussion to other forms of Japanese poetry, where counting *hyouon moji* comes into play.

[2.] Some examples of 'counters,' also known as 'numerators' or 'numeral classifiers': round slender objects take *-hon*; flat objects take *mai*; (postal) letters take *-su*; footgear take *-soku*; vehicles take *-dai*; animals take *-hiki*, etc. (cf. Inamoto, 1993, pp. 69-73.)

[3.] Apparently, mora, defined by the American Heritage Dictionary, 1992, as "(Latin) The minimal unit of metrical time in quantitative verse, equal to the short syllable," has entered Japanese linguistic circles as a loan-word. I have found this term used frequently within Japanese as well as English linguistics contexts and have also noted its use as a 'counter' in Japanese.

[4.] Hence the controversy, from the Japanese side, regarding the use of the term *on-setsu*, when applied to non-moraic languages like English.

5. Incidentally, this includes the digraphs, or 'double-characters,' such as *kyo, jyo, gyo*, etc. These combined characters too are each counted as one -*on* (or one -*ji*), and they take about the same amount of time to speak as *ko, ji, go*, etc. For simplicity's sake, and the benefit of a readership possibly unfamiliar with the kana alphabets, the digraphic kana are being included here under the appellation "single kana characters," though they are actually composed of two kana characters, which produce a single "combined" character.

6. "Previous researchers insisted that only the duration of vowels affects the perception of the number of morae. . . . however it is clear that not only the duration of the vowel sequence but also the accentual change has an important influence on the perception of Japanese subjects" (Omuro, Baba, Miyazono, Usagawa and Egawa, 1996, p. 6). ". . . Various kinds of information (pitch, rhythm, duration, lexical information) contribute in segmentation of three or more consecutive vowels" (Kakehi and Hirose, 1997, p 1, abstract).

7. For example, the kanji *i*, as in *iku* (to go), takes the sound *gyou* in *gyouretsu* ("procession," introduced to Japan, 5th-6th century CE), takes *kou* in *koushin* ("march, parade," introduced, 7th-9th century CE), and *an* in *anka* ("foot warmer," introduced, 10th-13th century CE). (cf. Mitamura & Mitamura, p. xiii).

8. "In a handful of cases new characters were created in Japan using Chinese elements, such as 'dry field' and 'frame,' and some of these have since been borrowed for use in Chinese (such as 'work.') These 'made in Japan' characters usually—but not necessarily—have KUN readings only" (Henshall, p xiv).

9. It is only in the last few years that contemporary tanka and haiku poets have begun to be published with some frequency in English translation. Very little is known about contemporary Japanese haiku and tanka culture in North America, and vice versa. Translations from English haiku and tanka into Japanese are still relatively rare.

APPENDIX: Lexical Glossary (Thematically Arranged)

Moji—Any written character. Moji describes all of the characters that are used in Japanese, which can include both kanji and kana. Moji is also sometimes used informally to count totals of *-on* or *-ji* in poems. We can also say that, "this haiku has 17 moji."

Hyoui—"Representative of ideas." Ideogrammatic representation.

Hyoui moji—"Characters (moji) which are representative (*hyou*) of meaning (*i*)." Kanji are *hyoui moji*. *Hyoui moji* are ideogrammatic. A number of *hyoui moji* are directly traceable to hieroglyphs or pictographs (*shoukei moji*).

Iji—An archaic term for *hyoui moji*. "Meaning (*i*) characters (*ji*)." No longer in use.

Hyouon—"Representative of sound." Phonic representation.

Hyouon moji—"Characters (moji) which are representative (*hyou*) of sound (*on*)." "Sound-representation characters." *Hyouon moji* include the hiragana and katakana alphabets. (Romaji is also a form of *houon moji*.) In modern Japanese, *hyouon moji* are individual phonic units, each of which is a separate alphabetical character (including digraphs) in the hiragana and katakana alphabets.

Onji—An archaic term for *hyouon moji*. "Sound (*on*) characters (*ji*)." No longer in use.

On-setsu—A term which has a variety of sometimes contradictory definitions in contemporary Japan; one of the definitions, given by Hattori, defines on-setsu as a term indicative of English-style syllabification as applied to Japanese, as well as English, among other languages (e.g. "English *on-setsu*"). The word *koukousei* has three *on-setsu*: kou/kou/sei, but six -on: ko/u/ko/u/se/i. *On-setsu* is the closest available term to the English "syllable." But this would be an improper method for parsing words in Japanese poetry (see "*ji*" and "*on*," below). Word-parsing by *on-setsu* is counterintuitive to the perception of Japanese native-speakers.

On—(lit. "sound")—A term used to count kana, or individual phonic units (*hyouon*) in poetry. It is this counter (or see "*-ji*," below), which we want to use when we are counting the *hyouon* in Japanese poetry, as in: "The first line of this haiku has 5-*on*." On is also used to express the total number of kana (or phonic units) in a poem, as in: "This tanka has 31-*on*." koukousei has 6-*on*: ko/u/ko/u/se/i. Properly, we can say that most haiku contain 17-*on*.

J<small>I</small>—(lit. "character")—Along with -*on*, another often-used counting term to count kana, or individual phonic units (*hyouon*) in poetry. We can use -*ji* when we count up the kana in Japanese poetry, as in: "The first line of this haiku has 5-*ji*." *Ji* is not generally used to express the total number of kana in a poem. The word: *koukousei* has 6-*ji*: ko/u/ko/u/se/i. As with -*on*, above, this is another appropriate method for counting kana in Japanese poetry.

K<small>ANA</small>—This term has several referents. It can refer to the hiragana or katakana alphabets, as in: "Write it only in kana; no kanji, please." It can refer to an individual alphabetical character, as in: "Which kana is that?" "It's *ko*." Most kana are single characters; however the group that uses -y glides, like *kyo, jyo*, etc., are made up of two combined characters. These are digraphic kana. In this article, for simplicity, digraphs are here included as "individual alphabetical characters." English-speakers will use the term informally, when speaking in English, as in: "I tried to write a poem in Japanese. I used 24 kana." Kana are *hyouon moji*.

K<small>ANJI</small>—Kanji are generally classed as ideograms, originally imported from China, with many later additions and alterations in Japan. Kanji are *hyoui moji*, with some exceptions.

R<small>OMAJI</small>—Romaji is a transcription alphabet which uses roman letters. Romaji is not a kana alphabet, nor is it a properly Japanese alphabet. It was primarily designed to aid those unable to read Japanese kana. The Roman alphabet is one variety of *hyouon moji*, known as *tan-on moji*, or single-phoneme characters, in Japanese linguistics. Many contemporary Japanese transliterations now use the modified Hepburn Romanization (see Campbell et al, pp. 665-68).

M<small>ORA</small>—A linguistic term used to identify the sense of "phonic (*hyouon*) time-units" or "time-lengths" in Japanese speech.

Appendix

Mora, and morae, its plural, are English linguistics terms and also Japanese loan-words. In written Japanese, the number of mora will always agree with the number of *-on* in a poem. The actual number of perceived mora may differ in spoken Japanese.

HAKU—A synonym of mora. Mora is the technical linguistic term, while *haku* is the more commonly known term, familiar to most Japanese people. Both are used to count phonic (*hyouon*) time-lengths in Japanese. *Haku* is also a 'counter.'

References

American Heritage Dictionary. (1992). New York: Houghton Mifflin.

Campbell et al., eds. (1993). *The Japan Encyclopedia*. Tokyo: Kodansha.

Donegan, P. and Ishibashi, Y. (1998). *Chiyo-ni: Woman Haiku Master*. Tokyo: Tuttle.

Hashimoto, S. (1976). *Nihon no Moji ni Tsuite* [About Japanese Characters] In *Moji Oyoubi Kana Ken no Kenkyu*. Tokyo: Iwanami Shoten. (Republication of original work published 1943). [Research into Kana and the Usage of Characters]. Accessed July 23, 1998, <http://www.d1.dion.ne.jp/tnozaki/NIHONNOMOJI.html>.

Hashimoto, S. (1967). *Moji no Shurui* [Types of Characters]. In *Kokugakugairon* [An Outline of Japanese Linguistics]. Tokyo: Iwanami Shoten. (Republication of original work, 2 vols., published 1932-1933). Accessed July 23, 1998, <http://kuzan.f-edu.fukui-u.ac.jp/hasi/hasi8.html>.

Hattori, S. (1961). "Prosodeme, Syllable Structure and Laryngeal Phonemes." *Linguistics in Japan*, 1980, vol. 2. 186-218. Shibata, T., Kitamura, H. and Kindaichi, H., eds. Tokyo: Taishukan.

Henshall, K. (1988). *A Guide to Remembering the Kanji Characters*. Tokyo: Tuttle.

Higginson, W. (1985). *The Haiku Handbook*. Tokyo: Kodansha.

Inamoto, N. (1993). *Colloquial Japanese*. Tokyo: Tuttle.
Kakehi, K., & Hirose, Y. (1997, September). "Mora Identification and the Use of Prosodic Cues." *Transcripts of the Technical Committee on Psychological and Physiological Acoustics*. H-97-68. [Japanese].
Kawamura, H. and Reichhold, J. (1998). *White Letter Poems: Fumi Saito*. Gualala, CA: AHA Books.
Kenkyusha's Japanese-English Dictionary. (1973). (4th ed). Tokyo: Kenkyusha.
Kindati, H., Hayasi, O. & Sibata, T., eds. (1988). *Nihongo Hyakuka Daijiten* [An Encyclopedia of the Japanese Language]. Tokyo: Taishukan Shoten.
Kirkup, J. (1995) [quoted by Sato, H.]. *Frogpond: Journal of the Haiku Society of America*, 18:1, 39.
Kondo, T. (1978). In support of onji rather than jion [Letter to the editor, dated January 29, 1976]. *Frogpond: Journal of the Haiku Society of America*, 1:4, 30-31.
Mannen, U. (1904 or prior). *Kari-ji Meishyou-kou* [The Origination of Kana]. Retrieved July 23, 1998, <http://kuzan-edu.fukui-u.ac.jp/ueda/KANA.html>.
Mannen, U. & Matsui., K. (Eds.). (1972) *Dai Nihon Kokugo Jiten* [Japanese Language Dictionary]. Tokyo: Fuzanbou.(Republication of original work, 4 vols, published 1915-1919; first single vol. ed., 1952).
Mitamura, J. and Mitamura, Y. (1997). *Let's Learn Kanji*. Tokyo: Kodansha.
Nihon Kokugo Daijiten. (1988). [The Encyclopedic Dictionary of the Japanese Language, 20 vols]. Tokyo: Shogakukan.
Omuro, K., Baba, R., Miyazono, H., Usagawa, T. & Egawa, Y. (1996, December). "The Perception of Morae in Long Vowels." *Proceedings of the Third Joint Meeting, Acoustical Society of Japan*. Honolulu, Hawaii.
Reichhold, J. (1999). AHA! POETRY Website. Accessed July 23, 1998, <www.ahapoetry.com>.
Shinmura, I. (Ed.). (1998). *Koujien* [Encyclopedic Dictionary of the Japanese Language, 5th ed]. Tokyo: Iwanami Shoten.
Tsujimura, N. (1996). *An Introduction to Japanese Linguistics*. Cambridge, MA: Blackwell.

Section 2: Multicultural Issues

12. Afterword

Afterword

This last decade has been a journey of discovery, involving meetings and discussions with "primary sources," living authors. One of the remarkable aspects of the poets represented here, and what is generally true in the contemporary gendai world, is that notable poets are often just as creative and articulate in the field of literary criticism as that of poetic composition. These two fields, separate intellectual worlds in the west, ride in tandem. This seems due to an ancient, abiding social structure, based on the *kukai* (translated as "haiku gathering-party"). The practice of haiku naturally requires introspection, yet the poem is routinely wedded to social occasion. It is rare to compose and publish haiku as a completely unassociated poet. The *kukai* is at the heart of haiku, quite as much as theory (*kire, katakoto, kotodama shinkô,* etc.). Haiku gatherings are energizing, festive, educational, and enjoyable.

In becoming a professional "haijin," a poet becomes a social leader. In concert with those attracted to the work and personage of the poet, a journal-group is formed (the journal bearing the name of the group is published on a regular basis). This cultural practice provides a strong contrast to the professional western poetics-journal. It is said there are about 1,000,000 people in Japan actively engaged in haiku practice (active within *kukai*); the number of haiku journals nationwide may be in the thousands. As a founder-leader of a haiku group and journal, part of the poet's job-description is critical evaluation, teaching and guidance. If a poet and their circle are not socially skillful and expansive in engagement, the group will not likely last. Success for a haijin (both ancient and contemporary) is not primarily about the text—even if texts do becomes *ars memoria*. The text is a social work, and would in normal conditions not appear without *kukai*: locality, local community, local engagement. It is for this reason that a DVD-ROM accompanies this book—the energy of gendai haiku can be personally experienced, via the video interviews. In Japan, pragmatic poetic engagement in both the haiku and senryû arts remains routinely social.

Along this journey there has occurred a second level of participation, the co-translation of interviews, texts and poems. From each poem issues of language, culture and context arise, so poetic translation is rarely a simple matter. This inherent complexity is also a joy (though unfortunately, many source texts were unable to be included due to time constraints, and I accept full responsibility for remaining errors). The translation process is a powerful means of entering and contemplating poems and critical materials. As Paul Muldoon recently mentioned, "I translate mostly to be able to understand a poem, translation being the closest form of reading we have."[1] Translation has been our *kukai*—a deeply rewarding and enriching experience of shared cultures and languages. As translation team-members (listed in the Dedication) have discussed: the experience of co-translation often provides unique avenues to the heart of poems and the nature of language itself as a vehicle of expression.

One aspect of *kire*—or disjunction—has to do with the reader-sense of how at the moment of entering a haiku there can be experienced an instantaneous cutting away of linear time and place, in terms of reality-sense. At the completion of the haiku there is, again, an abrupt return. In the English-language tradition, the *kireji* has been heretofore seen as the only significant element of juxtaposition, which has also been limited in function to juxtaposing realist-oriented, naturalistic imagery. The implications of Hasegawa's outlining of the centrality of *kire* ("cutting"), including *zengo no kire* ("before-and-after cutting"), and his

Afterword

emphasis on psychological nuance (*ma*; a "psycho-poetic interval of betweenness") in cutting technique offer an expansive, even revolutionary conception of haiku. Significantly, *kire* was a central aesthetic for Bashô, but was marginalized as the *shasei* approach evolved throughout the prewar era. Importantly, *kire* (as well as disjunction) is not only related to textual language but refers equally to *experiences of cutting*—the psycho-physical presence of the haiku abiding in reader consciousness.

At the time of writing "The Disjunctive Dragonfly," I had not yet come into contact with Hasegawa's works, or the term *kire,* coining instead "semantic kireji," and in the last few years have read his books with excitement. In describing the function and attributes of disjunction, I had wondered at the time whether this concept would seem inappropriate or even irrelevant within the context of gendai-haiku culture in Japan. Through this research I have found that not only had Hasegawa re-oriented (and re-awakened) the contemporary reader to the central importance of *kire* in haiku, he had also gone into great detail in discussing types of *kire* and the usage of *kire* techniques on the part of individual poets. Whether considering haiku from aspects of disjunction, or within the scope of *kire*, there exists a cross-cultural conversation: a sharing of poetry, and a new poetics, with points of connection beyond any one language or single culture.

How can the image (or image-schema) arrive which connotes more than naturalism or literalism, without leaving sensate images entirely behind? Through an examination of gendai haiku, avenues of cross-cultural linkage can be found—those means and modes through which fundamental haiku principles can be fused or blended with elements of modern poetry—including an expansive vocabulary (slang, dialect, idiolect), and irruption (as in Stein, cummings, Cage, language poetry, etc.). To what extent has the western haiku genre rejected other modern poetic genres in its quest for exclusive definition? Has the definition of the "modern haiku" in English tossed out too much of the baby with the bathwater? The two questions, "what is haiku?" and, "what can haiku be?" seem as relevant today as they were to the Beats in the 1950's.

Any excellent haiku is uniquely creative, existing in its national, regional cultural context and language. While gendai haiku are an inspiration in translation, techniques that are fitting within a Japanese context (certain concerns that crop up in a 400-year-old genre), may not be relevant within the international literary environment. A "gendai" development is not necessarily a matter of capturing a new tradition. Emulation as a singular approach seems both limited and inadequate—as each language, culture, and literary environment has its own uniqueness—its unique strengths and abilities. In this sense, one of the greatest differences between Japanese and occidental haiku is not that of language but of validity. In Japan, the haiku genre is central to the identity of Japanese literature, while the English haiku genre has yet to produce a well-known poet.

Concision, disjunction and imagery largely contribute to the effect of haiku, yet such elements on their own are not enough to convey poetic power. When a reader scans quickly without pause, much of the drama and vividness of the brief poem may be lost. What happens when the reader slows down, allowing this unique poetic form to come to life? In some measure there occur experiences of remembrance. Such may be said for any art one becomes absorbed in and passionate about; nonetheless, haiku are quite uncompromising in the way they cut into reality.

"Remembrance" is a multifaceted, holistic theme. It is a central concern of ecocriticism and feminism, as found in the haiku of Uda and Mikajo; in the ethno-aesthetic concerns of *katakoko* in Tsubouchi, and *kotodama shinkô* in Hoshinaga; and, seen in the inspiration of Ônishi, in relation to the "vertical" aspects of senryû—a concern as well of

Afterword

depth psychology and Heideggerian philosophy, to list a few themes presented in this book. It is also worth noting that the contemporary haiku genre in Japan is represented not only by its poems, but by a sophisticated, diverse community vibrant with insight and energy. The conversations and transcripts here presented barely scratch the surface. In contradistinction to a predominantly materialist cultural ethos lived at a certain insular velocity—the pressure and speed of industrial, urbanized life—gendai haiku poetry offers an intangible richness often missed, forgotten until the poem hits you; with Walt Disney *in absentia* and Huxley's brave new world open to contemplation. This has been a primary reason for my own continual return to the wellspring of gendai haiku. Literally: to remember.

> The doors of perception open slightly and the other time appears, the real one we were searching for without knowing it: the present, the presence (Paz, *ibid*).

Gendai haiku, and contemporary haiku in English offer innovative ways in which presence can be uniquely and powerfully articulated as anamnesis, reflecting the contemporaneity of our historical moment—Bashô's "immutable mutability." This work has sought to validate poets and poems across cultures, working from newly expanded conceptions of haiku form.

Note
[1] "Muldoon mulls over nature, candy bars." Interview by Becky Lang in *The Minnesota Daily*, November 29, 2007, University of Minnesota.

Afterword

Author Information

Richard Gilbert (1954—, Westport, CT), rebuilt his first car and motorcycle at age 17 listening to Frank Zappa, Bert Jansch, Morton Subotnick, Ravel, delta blues, and 50s-60s jazz. A Math/Computer-science major at Western Connecticut State University, automotive engine rebuilding and work in electronics funded a transfer to Naropa University, Boulder, Colorado, to study with Beat poets Allen Ginsberg, Gregory Corso, Peter Orlovsky, Gary Snyder and others. Richard became a Tibetan Buddhist meditator in 1981. In the following years he produced conceptual art and multi-disciplinary works as a poet, videographer, and guitarist. His BA thesis (Poetics and Expressive Arts, 1982), concerned Japanese classical haiku. After receiving an MA in Contemplative Psychotherapy (Naropa University, 1986), he worked as a licensed adult outpatient psychotherapist at the Boulder Community Mental Health Center, to 1991. A Ph.D. in Poetics and Depth Psychology from The Union Institute and University Doctoral Program, September 1990, prompted a move to Los Angeles, and a return to a career in the arts as an audio post-production engineer, and later a position at Denver Community Television as a show-runner.

In 1997 Richard moved to Japan and began publishing academic papers on haiku in 1999. In 2002, he became a tenured Associate Professor. He has published over 50 academic papers on haiku, learner autonomy, and multimedia educational software design, currently directs the haiku translation group, Kon Nichi Haiku (Kumamoto University), and is a judge of the Kumamoto International Kusamakura Haiku Competition. A partial result of funded research is the evolving Gendai Haiku website <www.gendaihaiku.com>, which contains video interviews with notable Japanese haiku poets and critics. In 2006, Richard engineered the shakuhachi and koto CD, *Silent Letters, Secret Pens*. A documentary film on gendai haiku is planned to begin production in 2008.

Afterword

Recent haiku

dedicated to the moon
I rise
without a decent alibi

a nun beats a drum;
fretful by the shrine
at nightfall

a drowning man
pulled into violet worlds
grasping hydrangea

Publication. *NOON: Journal of the Short Poem, vol. 1*, Philip Rowland, ed., Tokyo: 2004, pp. 25-27.

flown,
her grainy image resolves
from surveillance

blood orange:
the curving radius
of sunset

after the rush
the hollow sound
of the holy

three oceans
exported into orbit
in a small cocoon

Publication. *NOON: Journal of the Short Poem, vol. 6*, Philip Rowland, ed., (*forthcoming*), Tokyo: Summer, 2008.